D0594390

KALMIA

THE LAUREL BOOK II

KALMIA
THE LAUREL BOOK II

Richard A. Jaynes

TIMBER PRESS
Portland, Oregon

ISBN 0-88192-082-7
Printed in Singapore

Timber Press
9999 SW Wilshire
Portland, Oregon 97225

Library of Congress Cataloging-in-Publication Data

Jaynes, Richard A., 1935-
     Kalmia : the laurel book II / Richard A. Jaynes.
         p.   cm.
     Rev. ed. of: The laurel book. 1975.
     Bibliography: p.
     Includes index.
     ISBN 0-88192-082-7
     1. Kalmia--North America. 2. Mountain laurel--North America.
   3. Botany--North America.   I. Jaynes, Richard A., 1935-   Laurel
   book. II. Title.
   SB413.K3J38 1988
   635.9'3362--dc19   87-26731
                                                            CIP

CONTENTS

In memory of
EDMUND V. MEZITT
1915–1986
Plantsman, Breeder, Nurseryman

PREFACE

*The mountain laurel of the American states (*Kalmia latifolia) *is one of those plants which, if of recent introduction, would be eagerly sought after; but having been an inhabitant of our gardens for nearly a century and a half, it receives but little attention. (Alpha) —pen name for anonymous author — 1882)*

Mountain Laurel, the favorite garden Laurel, has been admired and cultivated since the discovery of America. It is the state flower of both Connecticut and Pennsylvania and is native to 23 states from Louisiana to Ohio and Vermont, east to the Atlantic. It is grown extensively in southeastern Canada and in the northwestern United States. All seven *Kalmia* species are indigenous to North America, and between the western and the southern coastal species, there are several kinds, each adapted to one or more of a wide range of climates. Despite this presence, from an experimentalist' point of view, *Kalmia* has been completely neglected.

Prior to 1961, when I began a breeding and genetic study of all the *Kalmia* species at the the Connecticut Agricultural Experiment Station, no one had successfully bred Laurel. Indeed, except for some good selection work by C. O. Dexter and successors in Massachusetts, hardly anyone had tried. The neglect of *Kalmia* is even more puzzling when one considers that the closely related Rhododendrons have been successfully hybridized in large numbers for more than 150 years. Why Laurel has been neglected is unknown. Perhaps it was feared the obstacles would be great and the rewards small.

But today renewed interest in all native American plants and in their garden value has led to a reawakening to the possibilities of the Kalmias. In this book I attempt to show that the obstacles to cultivation of the Laurels are not many and that the rewards are indeed great. So here is the record of Laurel's history, botany, taxonomy, genetics, culture, and propagation—a record which stresses the genetic variation and rich diversity among the plants in the Laurel genus. Lines of future research and development are sketched, and the cultivars (cultivated varieties) worthy of propagation are identified. Like all books of this nature, information on the "best cultivars" and pest control chemicals will become outdated, but I hope that this book will provide a basic reference of immediate and lasting value to the gardener, the student, the horticulturist, and the nurseryman.

The scientist side of me has fought some with the "dirt gardener" side as to what kinds of information to include. The resolution has been to write a book which supplies sufficient detail to be worthwhile to experienced plants-people but not (I hope) in a form that would overwhelm amateurs with jargon and superfluous information. This is not a novel designed to be read from cover to cover in one sitting, although I am flattered by those who claim to have done so with the first edition. I have always suspected, however, that they are cronic insomniacs looking for the ultimate cure!

Rediscover the long-neglected Laurels, a favorite and familiar American plant. But beware that you may experience frustration, for Mountain Laurel selections are difficult to root and slow growing; hence, named cultivars are just becoming available. Gardeners with the patience to work with woody plants, which often may take more than 5 years from seed to flower, will learn to enjoy the excitment and discovery that the waiting itself brings: every day and every season the plants change, and watching them grow, develop, and mature is its own reward. Add to this the challenge of developing improved cultural methods, and you have added another dimension to the breeding of new varieties. My first Mountain Laurel seedlings took nearly 8 years to flower. With the improved techniques described in this book, I now routinely obtain flowers in the fourth and fifth year, and occasionally in the third year.

After your first group of seedlings mature and flower, you will be trapped, and in your mind, if not in your garden, a procession of new flowering types will bloom. So you had better get started....

ACKNOWLEDGEMENTS

Study and experimentation are never done entirely independently, nor are they ever entirely self-motivated. While at the Connecticut Agricultural Experiment Station an atmosphere conducive to independent research was engendered by my department head and graduate school adviser, the late Donald F. Jones, and has been invaluable to me in my work. My interest in Laurel crystallized in 1960 and was nurtured under the stimulating guidance of Harry T. Stinson, Jr., successor to Dr. Jones. Other colleagues, former and present, to whom I am indebted include John F. Ahrens, Carl D. Clayberg, Peter R. Day, Dennis Dunbar, William L. George, Jr., Gary Heichel, Bruce Miner, Robert E. Moore, Thomas Rathier, George R. Stephens, and Gerald S. Walton. Several college students and technicians found the research a challenging endeavor. I am particularly indebted to Carol Barbesino, Nancy DePalma, Rita Sorensen Leonard, Mark Neuffer, and Richard Wetzler for their cheerful, valuable assistance. Many of the drawings are by Mrs. Leonard.

John E. Ebinger's contribution goes well beyond the two chapters he wrote, "Laurels in the Wild" and "Toxicity of Laurel Foliage." His tireless efforts in completing the taxonomic study of the genus are notable, and I am indebted to him for insights gained in our many lively debates and discussions on *Kalmia*. Keith E. Jensen's offer to write the chapter on micropropagation was timely and welcome. He has summarized the varied procedures of some dozen or so tissue culture labs in a balanced and informative way. ◄

My wife and children soon found that my interests in Laurel were not limited to the confines of the Experiment Station. They gave support and understanding as seedlings, grafts, and cuttings took over our greenhouse and grounds. Indeed, in 1984 after 25 years with the State, it became obvious that it was time to leave and start my own nursery to continue the breeding, growing, and selection of new forms of Mountain Laurel.

It is impossible to list all the gardeners, nurserymen, horticulturists, and botanists in this country and Europe who have contributed materials and ideas. However, at the risk of offending those not mentioned I cite Charles Addison, Bruce Briggs, Tom Dodd, Jr., the late John Eichelser, Ludwig Hoffman, Mike Johnson, Deborah McCown, Robert Tichnor, Clarence Towe, and Gerald Verkade. Their cooperation and enthusiasm have been an inspiration to me and indicated the wide spread interest in these plants. With pleasure I cite the three genera-tions of Mezitts (Peter, Edmund, and Wayne) of Weston Nurseries, Hopkinton, Massachusetts, who, in my many visits literally made avail-able any Laurel that caught my eye.

Richard A. Jaynes
Hamden, Connecticut
April, 1987

Chapter 1_____

FROM DIVERSITY COMES PERFECTION

The woods, plains, mountains and deserts of North America are an immense reservoir of exciting plant material waiting the hand of the plant breeder who has the vision and desire to explore the unknown . . . (G. Viehmeyer 1974).[1]

"Wouldn't you like to have been the geneticist who developed Laurel?" Donald F. Jones, famous for his work in genetics and the development of hybrid corn, once asked this question of a colleague. Here was the perfect shrub—flowering, evergreen, hardy. But if it were "perfect," there would be no need for the experimenter. As we shall see, it is neither uniform nor perfect. Mountain Laurel and its close relatives exhibit wide variation and give the grower opportunity for selection and manipulation.

A common misconception, even among those familiar with the plant, is that only a single good plant or clone exists of the unusual kinds of Mountain Laurel; that is to say, one red-bud, one deep pink, or one miniature. This book should dispel that oversimplified concept. The characteristics that make these forms unique are under the control of one or several genes and modified by other genes. The number of minor variants of any one form seems almost limitless and depends in large measure on the number of seedlings grown of various parent plants. While each seedling will be slightly different from every other one, it will be recognizable as a particular form as long as it carries the right determinant genes. The more seedlings that are raised to flowering age, the better our chance of selecting individuals which surpass existing clonal selections.

By sowing seed and growing Laurel seedlings, we are merely doing—in a convenient way—something that nature does on its own every year. Obviously, nature's way of sowing on bare mineral soil in a shaded or protected spot is a successful, if much slower, means to the same end. The special way we treat plants is designed to speed up the process and make it more efficient and selective.

An advantage of growing large populations of seedlings from

_____
[1]See Bibliography for literature cited.

selected parents is that we can improve other characteristics along with the one of particular interest. For example, red-budded Mountain Laurel tends to have fewer, smaller, and more twisted leaves than the pink or white selections, and it flowers a few days later. With additional breeding and selection, red-budded seedlings with dense foliage and broad flat leaves are being developed. I have named one 'Carol' with good habit and thick glossy leaves and Weston Nurseries also has a low growing, densely branched one they named 'Twenty'. In selecting for one trait, it is important that other good plant characteristics are not neglected or weakened. Now that several Mountain Laurels have already been named, more emphasis is being given to not just the flower color or just the growth habit but to the overall effectiveness of the plant on a year round basis, and even its quality over a period of years.

Our search for better Laurel has been filled with its own excitements, adventures, and rewards. To sample the natural variations of the *Kalmia*, we canvassed botanical gardens, nurserymen, and home gardeners asking about unusual and distinctive kinds. Slowly we began to accumulate selections and information on the limits of variation.

One of my first memorable encounters was with a man who managed a whole mountainside of Laurel which was open to the public during the nearby town's annual June Festival. I asked him if he had ever noticed any plants with unusual flowers or foliage. Of course he had, but solemnly assured me that in spite of these variations, all Mountain Laurel was really the same. Any differences, he said, were due to different exposures and varying amounts of minerals, such as copper and iron, in the soil. Fortunately, for me this interesting theory turned out to be false.

The idea that Mountain Laurel had immutable characteristics was not confined to the Connecticut country squire and his mountain-side of Laurel. I still have a 1961 letter from a reputable then state botanist known for his work on the native flora stating that ". . . *Kalmia latifolia* is one of the least variable shrubs." Even the professionsals sometimes overlook the obvious.

Having worked with woody plants before, I anticipated the need for patience in propagating and breeding the plants. I did not anticipate that in several cases the real test would be in actually obtaining the material in the first place. Some people, perhaps with good reason, are highly reluctant to share the unusual plant they have. For example, learning of a unique Mountain Laurel clone in 1963, I wrote for a few scions. The ensuing correspondence makes quite a file, and it was not until I had exchanged—over a decade!—numerous letters about the plant with three different persons, that cuttings were finally obtained. Most amazingly, I was dealing with a "public" garden. Happily, such stories are the exception and not the rule.

The quest for live, native plants of the Miniature and Willow-leaved Mountain Laurel has been, without doubt, the longest lasting saga. In May of 1962, the late Professor J. T. Baldwin, Jr. of William and Mary College, wrote to me that Henry M. Wright, Highlands, North Carolina, had collected some interesting native plants including at least one unusual *Kalmia* variant. He also added that there was no point in writing Mr. Wright for he would not reply and, indeed, if I visited he might not be willing to show me the plants.

Sure enough, Mr. Wright did not reply to letters. I thought it might just be the inertia of a good southerner not anxious to respond to a "Damned Yankee." I considered sending a copy of my birth certificate that places my origins on the bayous of the Mississippi in Louisiana. Only later did I learn Mr. Wright was a carpenter of New England origins. Like a good, rock-ribbed New Englander he enjoyed his privacy.

I would almost forget about the recluse Mr. Wright and then reference to him and his plants would turn up again. In 1969 Professor Fay Hyland at the University of North Carolina, Raleigh, described in a letter two unusual Mountain Laurel plants that Mr. Wright had collected in the wild. Indeed, someone from the University had even obtained live material, but like a true botanist the cuttings had been pressed between paper, dried, and put in the herbarium collection.

In the early 1970's horticulturist, graduate student, and teacher, Russell Southall, also at Raleigh, did taxonomic research on *Kalmia*. He did his best to get live material from Mr. Wright, but to no avail.

In the first edition of this book, I made reference to my difficulties in obtaining these two unusual Mountain Laurel forms growing in the southern Appalachians. That is all amateur botanist, Clarence Towe of Walhalla, South Carolina, had to read in 1976 and he was on the trail. He made contact with Mr. Wright's niece and inveigled an invitation to the garden through her. By 1979, and thanks to Clarence Towe, I finally had cuttings of the Miniature and Willow-leaved plants that Henry Wright had collected in the wild perhaps 50 years earlier. (Clarence Towe's description of the late Mr. Wright and his garden of unusual native plants is well documented in an article in the *Journal American Rhododendron Society* in 1985—see bibliography.)

Failure to obtain a plant is not the only frustration facing the plant breeder. Sometimes the people cooperate and the plants don't. Ralph Smith found a sectored Mountain Laurel in New York, but the first few scions he sent me failed to take upon grafting. When I requested more material for another try two years later, it was too late. The plant had died. This was a hard-earned lesson on the need to propagate immediately any unusual, potentially valuable plants to ensure their preservation.

Plain luck also plays its part in acquiring unusual plants. Robert Bird of the Bristol Nursery in Bristol, Connecticut, tells this amusing story about a fabulous Broad-banded Laurel of theirs. In the fall they did some landscaping for a woman in town. When the Laurel plantings began to flower the following June, she called them to complain that the flowers on one of the plants were abnormal. A nurseryman was sent to examine the plant. Within minutes of his arrival he obligingly replaced it with a "normal" one. The abnormal, broad-banded one, among the most attractive ever found up to that time, is now proudly displayed in front of the Bristol Nursery. It is also in the parentage of the new cultivars: 'Bullseye', 'Hearts Desire', and 'Kaleidoscope'.

In addition to seeking unusual Laurels, I searched for representative seeds or seedlings of the different species from numerous locations within their native ranges. On one trip to Peaked Hill Pond, near Thornton, New Hampshire, I arrived late in the day and camped, in the loosest sense of the word, in nearby White Mountain National Forest. It was one of the worst nights I've ever spent: I had only a sleeping bag, no tent, and no netting; and the tiny no-see'ems greeted me in swarms. To sleep with my head in the bag meant suffocation; to sleep with my head out meant torture. So shortly after 3 A.M., I gave up and went for a walk in the moon-light. At dawn I drove to Thornton and started the 2½ mile (4 km) trek from the road into the Laurel stand. By sunup I reached it, collected a few small plants, seeds, flowers, and cuttings, and by 7:30 was back at the local restaurant for breakfast.

The sun was well up by 9 when I got back to the Laurels to take pictures. It was truly an idyllic setting with beaver pond, laurel in bloom, a Sugar Bush nearby, wildflowers beneath the trees, and bird songs. This was worth one night with no-see'ems.

To my disappointment a few years later I learned that this northern strain of Mountain Laurel—which I assumed would be very hardy—was, in fact, very weak. Compared with every other source tested, it did poorly in either sun or shade. The only explanation is that the Laurel at Peaked Hill Pond is an isolated population and may have suffered from inbreeding depression.

To collect Laurel specimens along Connecticut state highways and on state lands, I obtained a special permit from the state capital. But, because of the state law which forbids collecting Laurel and the public stigma attached to it, I felt self-conscious digging up plants along the roads in full view of passersby. But I stuck to it and one summer I searched for the pinkest and the whitest Laurel in the state. My assistant, in response to my guilt feelings, had developed the ability to dig and load a 3 ft (1 m) plant in less than a minute. As we approached a previously spotted plant, he would hop out of the truck as we rolled to a stop, shovel in hand. By the time I could turn the truck around, he would be waiting to put the plant aboard. The only plants I remember not surviving this snatching technique were those that came out of deep shade and ones which were not pruned heavily on transplanting.

As a known Laurel "fanatic," news of striking and remarkable plants sometimes comes to me out of the blue. For example, I learned of the native stand of Mountain Laurel which includes 'Goodrich' and other banded laurels through Henry Fuller of the Rock Garden Society. He had not seen the plants himself, but he had heard that there were some purple-flowered Mountain Laurel near Willimantic, Connecticut. Fuller was skeptical, because he said the report had come from an economics professor and not a biologist. I wrote the professor's friend who had first-hand knowledge of the Laurel, fully expecting to find it was nothing more than a native stand of Sheep Laurel. But to my surprise the letter to John Goodrich was answered immediately, and his answer contained colored slides of the unusual, banded flowers. On a visit to the native stand in June, I discovered at least 20 of the banded plants. The best was used in crosses, and the most heavily pigmented one was named 'Goodrich' as a tribute to the man who discovered it.

News of other Laurels has come to me from farther away. One day I received a letter from Marjorie and Hollis Rogers of Greensboro, North Carolina. They enclosed a slide of a completely unknown Mountain Laurel. Here was a new flower type of the genus, found in the wild more than 700 miles (1100 km) away. Through the Roger's wonderful cooperation, within weeks I had cuttings for grafts, pollen for crosses, and seeds for planting. The result is a newly named cultivar, 'Shooting Star,' and the start for breeding other new cultivars with this flower form.

Closer to home, Dan Cappel, a high school biology teacher from Wilton, Connecticut, discovered a plant that was still in bud on Independance Day, July 4, about 2 weeks later than normal Mountain Laurel. Further observation revealed that in most years the flowers never open, but remain in bud for a few weeks as if trying to open and then collapse. The plant appears to be completely sterile, no good pollen and no seed production. As often happens, when a unique plant is found, another similar one turns up. Henry Wright collected such a plant years ago and in 1980 Clarence Towe "rediscovered" it in Henry's garden and sent me cuttings. Clarence's name for it, 'Tightwad', is appropriate for the flowers just refuse to open up.

Other selections are out there in the wild to be discovered or developed. No one has found a good double flowered or hose-in-hose Mountain Laurel but Clarence Towe found a plant in which 25% of the flowers have a double corolla where anthers are converted to petals. His plant could be the start of a new breeding line. At the least, it tells us that double flowers are possible with *Kalmia*.

These recent discoveries of new Laurel variants convince me that there are many other variations to be found, and, as each distinct form is discovered, breeding possibilities will increase.

I noted in 1975 that it would take a crystal ball to predict how these selections of Mountain Laurel would be propagated in the future. As a plant breeder on the public payroll at the time, I was concerned that I might be producing museum pieces of limited value because of difficulties in propagation. Well, the haze on the ball is clearing. Micropropagation, also called tissue culture, of Mountain Laurel in laboratories has come into its own in the last decade. Numerous commercial nurseries are commiting themselves to growing named selections. These plants are being readily sold and the increasing market in turn is spurring on the growing and naming of even more fancy selections.

Traditional means of propagation will not disappear. Some of the desirable forms will come true-to-type from seed, and it is from seed of selected parents that new generations of even better cultivars will come. Easy-to-root selections will be cutting propagated. Grafting, though labor intensive, will fill the need for immediate multiplication of one-of-a-kind plants and where only small numbers of plants are required.

To gain some insight into the leverage and advantages of tissue culture propagation, let me give you an illustration comparing the traditional rooting of stem cuttings with tissue culture propagation of Mountain Laurel. In June, 1965, I selected a pink-flowered plant from a commercial nursery to use in crosses. By 1971 we had learned and demonstrated that cuttings of this plant rooted well and limited quantities of cuttings were made available to Connecticut nurserymen. By 1974 two nurseries were impressed enough with their success in growing this plant that it was named 'Pink Surprise'. However, it was not until 5 years later, 1979, that one of the nurseries had enough material of a sufficient size to begin selling plants. (The other nursery never did get into commercial production.) So, 14 years after a flowering plant was selected one nursery was in production on a limited scale.

Compare that to the situation in the spring of 1981 when I mailed three to four cuttings each of four unnamed, promising selections to a tissue culture laboratory. By fall the selections had been isolated in culture and shoots were beginning to be produced. I had to decide if they could be distributed and, if so, were they going to be released under number or named. With some concern because of minimal testing, they were named: 'Carousel', 'Elf', 'Freckles', and 'Sarah', and thousands of small plants of these new cultivars were sold commercially within 2 years of putting them into tissue culture. The four cultivars have done well to date.

This abililty to get a new plant into the market place seven times faster than before is astounding, exciting, and revolutionizes the whole business of plant breeding, selection, and release.

Because of tissue culture successes, the prime problem of the nurseryman is no longer how to get plants of a fancy cultivar started, but how to best grow a good looking plant fast and economically. Progress continues and, though nobody said it would be easy, growers are succeeding.

Some indication of the appreciation that people have for the native Mountain Laurel is indicated by the number of communities that have incorporated Laurel in their name. I thank Richard Miller for identifying the following 19 localities. Most, but certainly not all, are within the range of Mountain Laurel:

Laurel, Delaware	Laurelville, Ohio
Laurel, Florida	Laurelton, Pennsylvania
Laurel, Indiana	Laurelville, Ohio
Laurel, Iowa	Laurel Springs, New Jersey
Laurel, Maryland	Laurel Hill, North Carolina
Laurel, Mississippi	Laurel Fork, Virginia
Laurel, Montana	Laurel Garden, Pennsylvania
Laurel, Nebraska	Laurel Creek, Kentucky
Laurel, New York	Laurel Springs, North Carolina
Laurel, Washington	Laurel Bloomery, Tennessee

Perhaps most unique is Laurel Bloomery, Tennessee, surely a small, rustic, charming and quiet town.

The origin of the genus name *Kalmia* is discussed in the next chapter. The common name, Laurel, is derived from the resemblance of the foliage of American Mountain Laurel to the Laurel of antiquity, *Laurus nobilis,* or Sweet Bay. The branches of this Laurel, from the Mediterranean area and celebrated in poetry, symbolize victory or accomplishment. The "bay" leaves are used as a condiment. Many other plants have Laurel as at least part of their common name as the following incomplete list indicates:

Alexandrian L.—*Calophyllum inophyllum, Danae racemosa*
Australian L.—*Pittosporum tobira*
Black L.—*Gordonia lasianthus*
California L.—*Umbellularia californica*
Cherry L.—*Prunus caroliniana, P. laurocerasus*
Chinese L.—*Antidesma bunius*
Drooping L.—*Leucothoe fontanesiana*
English L.—*Prunus laureocerasus*
Great L.—*Rhododendron maximum*
Ground L.—*Epigaea repens*
Himalaya L.—*Aucuba*
Indian L.—*Calophyllum inophyllum, Ficus retusa*
Japanese L.—*Aucuba japonica*
Laurel—*Cordia alliodora, Ficus benjamina, Lauris, L. nobilis* of
    antiquity
Laurel-leaved Greenbrier—*Smilax laurifolia*
Laurel Oak—*Quercus laurifolia*
Laurel Willow—*Salix pentandra*
Portugal L.—*Prunus lusitanica*
Purple L.—*Rhododendron catawbiense*
Red-twig L.—*Leucothoe recurva*
Sierra L.—*Leucothoe davisiae*
Spurge L.—*Daphne laureola*
Tasmanian L.—*Anopterus glandulosus*

> Tropic L.—*Ficus benjamina*
> Variegated L.—*Codiaeum*
> Weeping L.—*Ficus benjamina*

Kalmia Away from the Native Range

Information on the growing of Mountain Laurel or other Kalmias outside of the United States is sketchy and sometimes contradictory. The situation in Great Britain is a notable example. Several of the earliest color selections of Mountain Laurel and Sheep Laurel were not available in the U.S. but could only be obtained from Great Britain (Figure 1-1). Indeed, 'Splendens' and 'Clementine Churchill', two of the first named Mountain Laurel cultivars, are of British origin. Furthermore, Mountain Laurel was once used as a pot plant in England and seedlings produced there were imported in large numbers by nurseries in eastern United States. Despite this history, Mountain Laurel is a bit finicky in the British landscape and often not a heavy bloomer. The commonly invoked reasons for this less than stellar performance are the cool maritime climate and the often overcast skies. I also suspect that something less than ideal soil drainage and aeration are equally important. Unfortunately for us Kalmiaphils, Rhododendrons and Azaleas are often more tolerant of tight soils than Mountain Laurel.

The Bog Laurels do quite well in Scotland. Mountain Laurel is also grown to a limited extent in Belgium, Czechoslovakia, France, Germany, and Netherlands.

In the northwestern United States and southwestern Canada there are mixed reviews on how well Mountain Laurel does (Figure 1–2). Again the more maritime climate, as with the British Isles, may have a negative influence, although the summer growing season is usually quite sunny in the Northwest. Certainly the plants can be grown well there, but less than ideal soil drainage may also be a common problem.

Gardeners in Japan have successfully grown Mountain Laurel for many years, including more recently selections with pink, red-budded and banded flowers (Figure 1-3). Named cultivars from micropropagation laboratories are now becoming available in Japan, as well as New Zealand and Australia. J.P. Rumbal, with the large New Zealand nursery firm of Duncan and Davies, says that *Kalmia latifolia* is highly regarded as an ornamental there. In the New Plymouth district it grows well in acidic, free draining, volcanic loam soils where rainfall is 50–60 in (1.25–1.5 m). Soils are light and summer shade is essential; mulching with humus material is beneficial. Mountain Laurel does not do well in the warmer, dryer areas with heavier clay soils. The situation in Australia is somewhat similar in that plants do best in Tasmania and the moister areas of southern Victoria (Figure 1-4). Summer heat and parching winds are limiting factors in much of Australia.

Figure 1-1. Mountain Laurel 'Clementine Churchill' in a garden in England. (Harper)

Figure 1-2. Vigorous, well grown Mountain Laurel at the Oregon State University Test Garden, Willamette, Oregon: 'Ostbo Red' *left* and 'Silver Dollar' *center.* (Ticknor)

Figure 1-3. Color selections of Mountain Laurel growing well in a nursery in Japan. (Suzuki)

Figure 1-4. A handsome Mountain Laurel at the Royal Botanic Garden, Melbourne, Australia, with Rhododendron in the background. (Macoboy)

The potential or success of Kalmias in South America is a matter of speculation. The plants should grow well in some of the temperate climate areas such as parts of Argentina. By the next edition of this book there should be more substantial information on the successes and failures of Mountain Laurel and other *Kalmia* outside of the United States. Surely there will be some disappointements, but equally true there will be some surprises at how well they perform in locations distant to their native habitat.

This book should encourage others to pursue further improvements in the breeding, selection, propagation, and culture of Laurel. A better understanding of the genetics of the species and the inheritance of specific traits will lead to cultivars only dreamed of today—perhaps to some not yet imagined.

Chapter 2 _____

LAURELS IN THE WILD

Professor John E. Ebinger,
Eastern Illinois University Botany Department,
Charleston, Illinois 61920

> *Among the dwarfer evergreens there are few that rank higher in merit than the Kalmias. There are altogether seven species known, but of these only three appear to be in cultivation, all of which are valuable as garden shrubs. The genus is purely an American one, extending from arctic regions in the north as far as Cuba in the south. The tallest growing . . . is commonly known as Mountain Laurel, and is one of the chief favorites among the many plants suggested for the national flower of the United States. (Bean 1897)*

The Laurels, a small group of interesting and beautiful shrubs, are still relatively unknown, even though some of them were used by the early colonists and the Indians before them. Botanists recognize seven species of Laurel and group them in the genus *Kalmia*. All are native to North America. These plants, which have adorned yards and gardens in the eastern United States since colonial times, deserve rediscovery, for improved horticultural forms have gone virtually unnoticed and unused. Mountain Laurel, *Kalmia latifolia,* is the best known species and is considered by many to be the most beautiful flowering shrub in North America. This explains why it is highly prized as an ornamental (Figures 2-1, 2-2, 2-3, 2-4).

References to Mountain Laurel are found in early colonial literature. Possibly the "Rose-trees" in Henry Hudson's log of his 1609 trip to Cape Cod were this species. Captain John Smith observed the occurrence of Laurel as an understory shrub in Virginia in 1624. By the early 1700s a few species of the genus had been described and illustrated in some of the botanical works of the colonies.

One of the first detailed accounts of Laurels is found in Peter Kalm's journal. This Swedish botanist, a student of Linnaeus, was sent to the New World in 1748 by the Swedish Academy of Science. His mission was to obtain seeds of plants hardy enough to thrive on Swedish soil and in particular to discover dye-plants, new food and fodder crops, and hardy Mulberry trees to develop a silk industry. During his 3 years in America his explorations extended through Pennsylvania, New

York, and New Jersey and into southern Canada. He ventured as far west as Niagara Falls and was the first man to describe the falls in English from first-hand observations. Although primarily a naturalist who made numerous observations of plants and animals, he also made many valuable observations of the colonists themselves. Thus his journal, written after his return to Europe, is an interesting account of life in colonial times: how the people lived, what they ate and drank, how they dressed, the native plants they used, and what they learned from the Indians. In this journal he describes in detail the poisonous properties of the "Laurel Trees." He also discusses the characteristics, economic importance, habitat requirements, and general distribution of Mountain Laurel and Sheep Laurel, *Kalmia angustifolia*.

Figure 2-1. Mountain Laurel, *Kalmia latifolia*, is the state flower of Connecticut and Pennsylvania and one of our most beautiful native plants. (Jaynes)

Figure 2-2. An older plant of Mountain Laurel on the edge of a woods and pond with a graceful and artistic form. (Jaynes)

Figure 2-3. Native Mountain Laurel at the Laurel Preserve of the Nipmuck State Park, Union, Connecticut. (Redfield)

Figure 2-4. Natural variation in flower color of native Mountain Laurel plants growing side by side. (Harper)

Upon his return to Europe, Kalm gave his collection of about 380 species of plants to Carolus Linnaeus, the Swedish naturalist and taxonomist. It was from this material that Linnaeus published a dissertaion in which he proposed the generic name *Kalmia* to honor the collector. In this publication both Mountain Laurel, *K. latifolia,* and Sheep Laurel, *K. angustifolia,* were named and distinguished from other related genera and species. Linnaeus included both in his *Species Plantarum* (1753), making the names official. Of the 700 species of North American plants described by Linnaeus in the *Species Plantarum,* Kalm was mentioned as the collector of many, with at least 60 new species founded upon specimens he collected.

The use of Laurels as ornamentals in colonial gardens was well established when Peter Kalm was in America; in fact, some species were already being used as ornamentals in Europe. Twelve years before his visit, living specimens of both Mountain Laurel and Sheep Laurel had been sent to Peter Collinson, a London merchant, by American naturalist John Bartram. Other reports in 1740 tell of Mountain Laurel flowering in England. A third species, the Eastern Bog Laurel, *K. polifolia,* made its way to England by 1767. As a result of these beginnings numerous European horticultural forms have been developed, some of which have found their way back to America.

The genus *Kalmia* is regarded as a relatively primitive member (in an evolutionary sense) of the heath family, Ericaceae. This family occurs mainly throughout most of the temperate zone with some species found in the mountains of the tropics and others in subarctic regions. It includes a great variety of plants, most of them shrubs and subshrubs, some herbs, others fairly tall trees, and a few trailing vines. The family contains about 3500 species; the largest genera are the true Heaths (*Erica*), the Rhododendrons and Azaleas (*Rhododendron*), the Wintergreens (*Gaultheria*), and the Blueberries and Cranberries (*Vaccinium*).

Economically the family is important primarily for its many ornamental species; among them the most popular are the Azaleas and Rhododendrons. The evergreen Mountain Laurel and Rhododendron species are popular greens in the floral industry especially at Christmas, and of course Blueberries and Cranberries are an ever popular source of food.

BOTANICAL CHARACTERISTICS OF LAUREL

The Laurels are a purely North American genus occurring from Alaska south to the mountains of California and Utah, east through Canada to the Atlantic Ocean and south through the eastern United States to Florida and Cuba. All of the species are low to medium-sized shrubs or rarely small trees, usually with leathery, evergreen, entire margined, mostly short-petioled leaves (Figure 2-5) that are alternate,

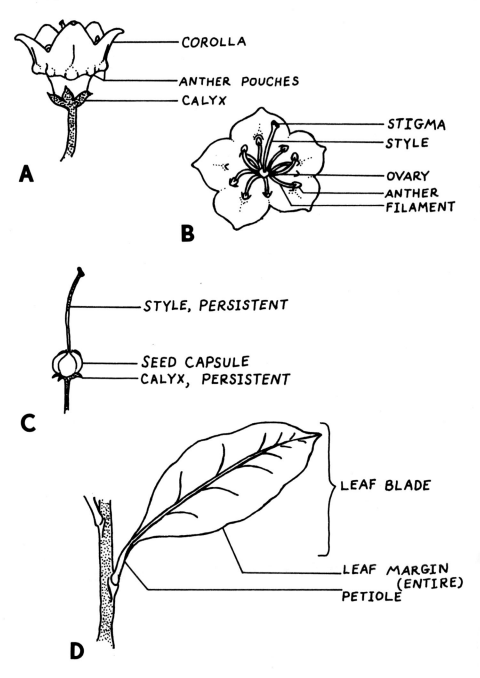

Figure 2-5. Laurel flower, capsule, and leaf diagrams: (A) flower in profile, (B) face view, (C) developed seed capsule before splitting to release seeds, (D) leaf attached to stem. (Sorensen-Leonard)

opposite, or whorled. In some species the flowers are solitary in the axils of the leaves, while in others they are in terminal or axillary clusters. The flowers are relatively large, varying from ¼–1 in (6–25 mm) in width. The calyx is five-parted and is usually persistent in fruit. The shallow, five-lobed petals are fused into a saucer-shaped corolla with a short narrow tube. Each has 10 small pouches holding the anthers. The 10 stamens have slender filaments, and anthers that open by apical slits. The five-celled ovary is superior, while the fruit consists of a globose capsule holding numerous small seeds.

The most distinctive feature of the genus *Kalmia* is the pollen-discharge mechanism. Near the middle of the corolla are 10 pouches forming small lobes on each ridge of the fower bud (Figure 2-5, A and B). Just before the bud opens, the elongating filaments push the anthers upward into these pouches. As the corolla opens, the elastic filaments bend backward under tension, and the anthers are held in the pouches and carried down and outward. When the flower is disturbed by a large insect, one or more of the anthers is released. When this occurs, the tension of the elastic filament is strong enough to throw the pollen 3–6 in (7.5–15 cm) from the flower. Many early botanists thought this mechanism insured self-pollination, because the pollen was thrown toward the stigmas of the flower. American botanist and horticulturalist, Dr. William J. Beal, was probably the first person to report that cross-pollination was necessary for pollination in the Laurel species and was the first to describe the way in which cross-pollination occurred. He observed that a bumblebee seaching around the base of the flower would release the stamens with his proboscis, thereby projecting the pollen onto the underside of his body. This pollen was then rubbed onto the stigmas of subsequently visited flowers.

The flowers of Laurel do not readily attract insects, although they are necessary for pollination. In fact, casual observations might lead to the conclusion that no insect pollination occurs. Furthermore, little nectar is secreted at the base of the corolla tube, and none can be found in many flowers, apparently accounting for the comparatively small number of insect visitors. But closer observation now reveals that insects are indeed necessary fo pollination in Laurels. This can be verified by preventing insects access to the flower clusters. In flowers thus isolated, none of the stamens are released from the pouches and no seed is produced. Also, most species of Laurel are self-incompatible, producing almost no seeds when self-pollination does occur. On the rare occasion when self-pollination does occur, the seedlings show inbreeding depression and are small and slow growing. In fact, measured by height growth, the vigor of outcrossed seedlings is usually twice that of inbred seedlings.

Compared with other insect-pollinated plants, few species of insects have been observed pollinating Laurel. In one study, a population of Sheep Laurel in an abandoned Maine pasture was observed for 3 weeks to determine the agents of pollination. Fourteen species of insects were identified with the ability to spring the stamens while foraging for nectar. Of these, the bumblebee, *Bombus ternarius,* and the mining bee, *Andrena vicina,* were the most common visitors. Other insects observed visiting the flowers occasionally included smaller bees of the superfamily Apoides, three butterflies, one hawkmoth, and one beetle. During the study no honeybees, *Apis* sp., were observed even though an apiary was located only a third of a mile (0.5 km) away. Present information suggests that under normal conditions honeybees rarely visit the Laurels.

Bumblebees are by far the most important pollination agent, because these large insects easily spring the stamens while foraging for nectar. As they alight on the flowers, their ventral parts touch the projecting stigma. But in most instances the stamens are not released when the bee lands but are sprung by the insect's legs (which get caught under the filaments) or by the insect's proboscis as it searches for the nectar. The proboscis is inserted near the base of the flower between the filaments and the corolla tube, and, in a single circular motion, probes completely around the base of the ovary. This liberates all the stamens, projecting the pollen onto the underside of the insect. After being sprung, the stamens remain erect and in contact with the style for 2–3 hours; then the filaments bend backward and the anthers rest on the corolla.

In most flowering plants, the pollen grains are produced in tetrads (groups of four) as a result of meiosis, and these four cells develop into separate and distinct pollen grains. In the genus *Kalmia,* as well as in many other members of the family Ericaceae, however, these four cells remain united at maturity and are released from the anther as a single unit. These four-celled, compound pollen grains are released as a fine powder in some species of *Kalmia* and in others as a sticky net formed by the presence of fine, noncellular, tacky threads which hold the tetrads together. These threads are derived either from small quantities of protoplasm excluded from the tetrads during development or from the breakdown of elements in the tetrad's outer wall. They have been observed in Mountain Laurel, Sandhill Laurel, and the little known *Kalmia ericoides,* which grows only in Cuba. The function of these threads is not known, but they may facilitate pollination in the relatively large upright flowers found in these species.

THE FOSSIL RECORD

Four extinct species of *Kalmia* have been described, but their fossil remains are extremely fragmentary. As a result it is difficult to form definite conclusions concerning their relationship to present-day members of the genus. Three fossil species are known only from leaf impressions, and, except for size, shape, and probable coriaceous (leathery) texture, there is little reason to consider them members of this genus. They vary in age from Upper Cretaceous to Miocene and were found in various locations throughout North America. The fourth species, *Kalmia saxonica,* from the Lower Miocene period of Europe, may represent a member of this genus or of a closely related genus of the Ericaceae. The remains of this species consist of pieces of leaf cuticle with some upper epidermis attached. The structure and arrangement of the cells and the type of glandular hair bases are similar to that found in present-day Laurel.

One present-day species is suspected to have existed from scant fossil evidence. Fossils of the Eastern Bog Laurel, *K. polifolia,* were first reported from interglacial deposits at Point Grey near Vancouver, British Columbia. The leaf impressions are the same shape and size as those of living Bog Laurel. This species was later reported from Pleistocene lake deposits of the upper Connecticut River valley in northern New Hampshire. These fossils are postglacial in age and appear to be representative of the flora that migrated northward in the wake of the retreating Wisconsin ice sheet. The other fossils in the same deposits indicate a habitat and climate similar to that presently prevailing in the area. Positive identification of these leaf impressions as Bog Laurel is impossible because of the similarity of the leaves of many Ericaceae.

THE SPECIES OF LAUREL

The genus *Kalmia* consists of seven species. For the most part they are quite distinctive, and no problem is encountered in identifying them. A description of each of these species follows with their general range, habitat, and economic importance. Descriptions are also included of the varieties and forms that are sometimes encountered in the wild. See the last page of this chapter for a botanical key to the species.

Western Laurel, *Kalmia microphylla*

This short alpine plant is sparsely branched, grows up to 2 ft (60 cm) tall, and has slightly two-edged branchlets. The leaves are opposite, leathery, flat, evergreen, ovate to oval, short-petioled, and ¼–1½ in (6–35 mm) long. The midrib of the leaf lacks glandular hairs, and the leaf margins are not revolute. The inflorescence is a few-flowered terminal raceme (simple arrangement of stalked flowers on an elongated stem); the flowers on slender stalks grow to 1 in (25 mm) long. Flowering occurs in late spring or early summer. The individual flowers are rose-purple to pink, and ¼–¾ *in (6–19 mm) across. The fruit is a globose capsule; the seeds have short projections on each end.*

The Western Laurel is the only species of the genus found west of the Rocky Mountains. It extends from central California north to Alaska and east to the extreme northwest corner of Manitoba (Figure 2–6). This low-growing alpine shrub rarely exceeds 6 in (15 cm) in height, but in bogs at lower elevations it may reach a height of 2 ft (60 cm). The species contains two varieties, the Western Alpine Laurel, *K. microphylla* var. *microphylla,* and the Western Swamp Laurel, *K. microphylla* var. *occidentalis.*

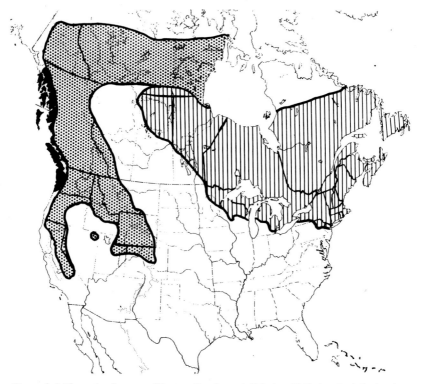

Figure 2-6. The natural range of Eastern Bog Laurel, *Kalmia polifolia* (vertical shading); Western Alpine Laurel, *K. microphylla* var. *microphylla* (dotted area); and Western Swamp Laurel, *K. microphylla* var. *occidentalis* (black area). (Ebinger)

The two varieties are distinct in habit and general appearance. The Western Alpine Laurel rarely exceeds 6 in (15 cm) in height and has small oval leaves usually less than ½ in (12 mm) long. Its flowers are relatively small. The Western Swamp Laurel, in contrast, is a larger plant growing up to 2 ft (60 cm) tall with lanceolate leaves ½–1½ in (12–38 mm) long and slightly larger flowers.

WESTERN ALPINE LAUREL, var. *microphylla* Commonly called the Alpine Laurel or the Small-leaved Kalmia, this species is found in alpine meadows, bogs, and other open, wet areas where it usually forms dense mats. It is distributed throughout the mountainous regions of western North America from central California, Nevada, Utah, and Colorado, north through the Rocky Mountains to the Yukon and the Northwest Territories (Figure 2-6). There are some reports of its occurrence north of the Arctic Circle.

Plant and leaf size in Western Alpine Laurel are controlled to some extent by the environment. In the typical alpine plant the leaves are extemely small, usually less than ½ in (12 mm) long; the entire plant may be less than 3 in (7.5 cm) tall (Figure 2-7). At lower elevations the leaves average about ¾ in (19 mm) in length and the plants 6 in (15 cm) in height. Larger individuals are rarely found.

Figure 2-7. Western Alpine Laurel, *Kalmia microphylla* var. *microphylla,* from the Cascade Mountains of Oregon. Total plant height with flowers of this high-altitude form is about 2 in (5 cm). (Jaynes)

WESTERN SWAMP LAUREL, var. *occidentalis* Sometimes called the Western Bog Laurel, this variety is found in marshes, bogs, and wet open areas at low elevations in the coastal regions and on the islands of southern Alaska, British Columbia, Washington, and northwestern Oregon.

Eastern Bog Laurel, *Kalmia polifolia*

Common names for this species include Bog Laurel, Swamp Laurel, Pale Laurel, and Gold Withy. This low, sparsely branched, straggling shrub grows less than 3 ft (90 cm) tall with leathery, linear to oblong, evergreen, opposite, short-petioled leaves that are ½–1½ in (12–38 mm) long (Figure 2-8). The midrib of the leaf is covered with small, purple, glandular hairs, while the leaf margins are usually revolute (rolled under). The inflorescence is a few-flowered terminal raceme with the flowers on slender stalks about 1 in (2.5 cm) long. Flowering occurs early in the growing season. The individual flowers are

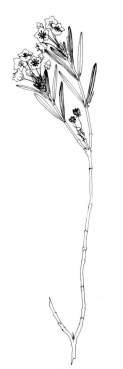

Figure 2-8. Eastern Bog Laurel, *Kalmia polifolia*. Plants from the southern part of the range, such as this one from Connecticut, typically have a lanky growth habit. Northern plants are more compact. (Sorensen-Leonard)

usually rose-purple and ½–¾ in (12–19 mm) across. The fruit is a globose cap-sule, and the small seeds have projections on each end.

The Eastern Bog Laurel is found in swamps and other wet places, usually forming a border around ponds and lakes. In bogs, its roots form dense mats that extend out over the water. Also found at higher elevations in the mountains of northeastern United States and Canada, this species is the most widely distributed member of the genus (Figure 2-6). It ranges from northeastern Alberta, across Canada to the east coast, and south into the United States. In the Great Lakes region this species extends as far south as northern Illinois and on the east coast as far south as central New Jersey. Its entire range is, however, hard to determine with certainty. The two reports of its occurrence in the Arctic Circle now appear to have been based on specimens of the Western Laurel, *K. microphylla*. The species is naturalized in Scotland.

The Eastern Bog Laurel and the Western Laurel are similar and are often considered together as one highly variable species. Recent genetic studies now confirm, however, that they should be considered separate species. The chromosome numbers are different and the hybrids are sterile. When considered as separate species, the plant and leaf size are used to make the distinction (Figures 2-7, 2-8). (The Eastern Bog Laurel is larger by at least a foot (30 cm); its leaves are ½–1½ in (12–38 mm) long, and the leaf margins are strongly revolute. Western Laurel, in con-trast, is most often a mere 6 in (15 cm) tall, and its leaves are less than ½ in (12 mm) long and have nonrevolute margins. Usually these characteristics are enough to distinguish the two species.) The most reliable characteristic, however, that separates the Eastern Bog Laurel from the Western is the presence of purple glandular hairs on the leaf midrib of the former. Another easy way is to compare the seeds. Those of the Eastern Bog Laurel are about twice as long as those of the Western.

A white-flowered form, *leucantha,* of the Eastern Bog Laurel has been found growing along with the typical rose-purple flowered form in a bog in Newfoundland.

Mountain Laurel, *Kalmia latifolia*

Other common names include Broad-leaved Laurel, Calico-bush, Spoonwood, Ivy, Mountain Ivy, Big-leaved Ivy, Laurel-leaves, and Calmoun. The leaves of this many-branched shrub are alternate, flat, leathery, elliptic, dark green above, light green to reddish below, petioled, 2–5 in (5–12 cm) long and less than 2 in (5 cm) wide. The inflorescence consists of a terminal compound corymb (convex flower cluster with the outer flowers opening first) with glandular and mostly sticky stalks and numerous flowers. Flowering is usually in late spring or early summer after new shoot growth has begun. The calyx is green to reddish and usually has stalked glandular hairs, while the corolla, up to 1 in (2.5 cm) across, is usually light pink with purple spots around each anther pocket. The fruit is a depressed globose capsule with numerous light brown seeds with short projections on each end.

Mountain Laurel commonly forms dense thickets in rocky and sandy forests throughout most of its range, particularly where there are openings in the canopy. It is also found in pastures and open fields and often forms thickets at the edges of roads. This species is restricted to the eastern United States and occurs from southern Maine, west through southern New York to central Ohio, south to southern Mississippi, Alabama, and Georgia, and northwestern Florida (Figure 2-9). There are some reports of Mountain Laurel being native to Canada, but there is no conclusive, supporting evidence. Possibly these reports were based on cultivated plants or on large-leaved specimens of the more northern Sheep Laurel, *K. angustifolia.*

Mountain Laurel is usually a tall, spreading shrub that throughout most of its range rarely exceeds a height of 12 ft (3.7 m). Yet in the fertile Blue Ridge valleys and in the Allegheny Mountains members of this species may attain the size of a small tree (Figures 2-10, 2-11). In 1877 American botanist Asa Gray observed a number of large individuals growing at the bottom of a dell, in back of Caesar's Head, on the extreme western border of South Carolina. One of the trunks, at a point 1 ft (30 cm) above ground, measured 4 ft 1¼ in (1.25 m) in circumference. The largest specimen listed by the American Forestry Association has a similar trunk diameter and is located at Oconee County, South Carolina. This specimen measured at a point 4½ ft (1.4 m) above ground is 15 in (38 cm) in diameter. It has a spread of 26 ft (8 m) and is

Figure 2-9. The natural range of Mountain Laurel, *K. latifolia,* is indicated by the shaded area. Plants from the southern and northern extremes of the range are adapted to entirely different climatic conditions. They appear the same but southern Mountain Laurel does not adapt to the Northeast. (Ebinger)

Figure 2-10. A giant Mountain Laurel growing with Rhododendron in the Chattahoochee National Forest, Georgia, near the border of North Carolina and Tennessee. The base of the plant is more than 4 ft (1.2 m) in diameter. About 2½ ft (75 cm) up, it branches into three major stems, two of them living. The largest stem is over 17 in (43 cm) in diameter, 4½ ft (1.4 m) from the ground. Size can be judged by the 1-ft (30 cm) ruler and hard hat. (Durkas)

Figure 2-11. Stem of another exceptionally large Mountain Laurel in the mountains of northern Georgia. Such old plants are commonly found on islands in a stream or on raised land surrounded by wet areas and thus protected from fire. (Jaynes)

28 ft (8.5 m) tall.

Like most members of the family Ericaceae, Mountain Laurel is dependent on a mycorrhizal fungus associated with its roots. This symbiotic relationship insures adequate absorption of water and minerals by the plant, particularly in acid soils. Some members of the family are so dependent on this association that they have lost the ability to make their own food. This condition is well known in the nongreen Indian Pipe, *Monotropa uniflora,* and a number of its relatives.

Economically, the Mountain Laurel is the most important member of the genus *Kalmia.* The species is sold as an ornamental, particularly in the eastern but also the northwestern United States. The foliage is also used for floral displays and Christmas decorations, continuing a tradition started in colonial times. Suggestions were made early in 1913 that the species should be protected against indiscriminate collecting. In 1924, 1,000 tons of Mountain Laurel foliage was estimated as the amount used annually in New York City alone. The estimate for the United States exceeded 10,000 tons. No figures are presently available for decorative use of Mountain Laurel, nor do we know if significant amounts are still used to produce a yellow dye.

The wood of Mountain Laurel was occasionally used to make small items such as pipes where it was a substitute for brier. Peter Kalm mentioned in his journal that this strong wood was fashioned into weaver's shuttles, pulleys, and trowels. American Indians used the wood for small dishes and spoons, which probably accounts for the common name Spoonwood. Today the wood is rarely used except for tool handles and novelties (Figure 2-12). The wood weighs 48 pounds per cubic foot which is about the same as Apple wood and a bit lighter than Hickory.

Figure 2-12. The fine grained wood of Mountain Laurel is still valuable in the hands of skilled craftsmen. Shown are two candlestick holders turned recently by Andre Jacques of Connecticut. (Jaynes)

Mountain Laurel, as an understory shrub, effectively prevents water runoff and soil erosion. Studies in the southern Appalachian Mountains have shown that excessive cutting of dense laurel stands greatly increased the amount of water runoff. Since dense thickets of Mountain Laurel also prevent the natural regeneration of timber trees, the thickets must be cleared to encourage natural regeneration or to plant desirable tree species. Clumps and thickets of Mountain Laurel are, of course, a haven for wildlife providing year round cover and protection for large and small animals alike.

Because of the many variations in flower color, leaf shape and size, plant size, and pubescence, several variants and forms of Mountain Laurel have been named. A number of these are within the normal range of variation of the population, even if at the extremes, and should be treated as cultivars.[2] At least five, however, are true genetic variants that are distinguished by one or several linked characters from the

[2]Cultivar, a contraction of "cultivated varieties," is the generally accepted term to designate single plant selections of horticultural merit that receive fancy names (e.g., 'Pink Surprise') and are vegetatively propagated. The term variety may be used the same way, but variety is used here only in the botanical sense, as a subdivision of a species.

normal populations and are designated botanical forms:

WILLOW-LEAVED MOUNTAIN LAUREL, form *angustata* First reported in 1945 in Cape May County, New Jersey, this rare foliage form exhibits very narrow, willow-shaped leaves less than ½ in (12 mm) wide (Figure 2-13a). Another reference suggest that a plant of this form may have been discovered as early as 1833.

MINIATURE MOUNTAIN LAUREL, form *myrtifolia* Also called Dwarf Mountain Laurel, this form has been under cultivation since 1840 and is occasionally found in small gardens. It is in all respects a Miniature Mountain Laurel, compact, slow-growing, and rarely exceeding a height of 3 ft (90 cm) (Figure 2-13b). The leaves are generally smaller than those of typical Mountain Laurel, averaging ½–1½ in (12–38 mm) long and about ½ in (12 mm) wide. Flower size and the length of the stem internodes are one-third to one-half those of normal Laurel.

A

B

C

Figure 2-13. Three foliage forms of Mountain Laurel. (A) 'Willowcrest', a willow-leafed or *angustata* form, having flowing, strap-shaped, attractive leaves. (B) The miniature or *myrtifolia* form, which by appropriate crosses can be obtained true-to-type from seed. (C) A compact seedling, hedge laurel or *obtusata* form, with near-normal-sized leaves. All three photos taken from above and at the same magnification. (Jaynes)

HEDGE MOUNTAIN LAUREL, form *obtusata*   First found near Pomfret, Connecticut in 1903, this rare foliage form has oval leaves. The leaves are usually 1–2½ in (2.5–6.5 cm) long and up to 1½ in (3.8 cm) wide. Most specimens are slow growing and form compact plants (Figure 2-13c).

BANDED MOUNTAIN LAUREL, form *fuscata*   Also called the Crowned Mountain Laurel, this flower color form has been reported from many localities in the northeastern United States since 1868 or before. Its white to pink flowers have a heavily pigmented, usually continuous, brownish purple or cinnamon band on the inside of the corolla at the level of the anther pockets (Figure 2-14). This band breaks up into brownish dots toward the base and the margin of the corolla. Because it shows through the bud, the corolla often has a muddy appearance. Variation exists in the size, shape, and color of the band with an interrupted band having been observed in some individuals.

FEATHER PETAL MOUNTAIN LAUREL, form *polypetala*   Found on Mount Toby, near South Deerfield, Massachusetts, this form has also been found growing wild in North Carolina and has been known since 1871. The corolla is deeply divided into five narrow to broad petals (Figure 2-15, left). In some individuals the extremely narrow and thread-like petals are caused by a rolling of the petal margin. Normally the petals are broader, and a few specimens have been found with flowers like apple blossoms. Other variations are mere extensions of the polypetala type or may be distinct forms. One lacks petals altogether, Apetala, (Figure 2-16) and a cultivar in which the corolla is reduced in size and deeply lobed has been named 'Bettina' by T. R. Dudley of the National Arboretum.

Figure 2-14. A fairly typical expression of the banded Mountain Laurel, form *fuscata,* which is only rarely found in the wild. (Jaynes)

Figure 2-15. Feather petal
Mountain Laurel, form
polypetala, with each flower
usually having 5 petals.
(Jaynes)

Figure 2-16. The apetala
form of Mountain Laurel,
an extreme condition in
which the corolla, or
petals, are lacking entirely.
(Jaynes)

Sheep Laurel, Kalmia angustifolia

This many-branched shrub may grow 6 ft (2 m) tall and has reddish brown branchlets. The leaves in whorls of three are somewhat leathery, ever-green, flat, mostly oblong, and 1–2½ in (2.5–6.5 cm) long. The leaves and stems are slightly hairy and have stalked glandular hairs on their surfaces. The flowers are borne in numerous small clusters from the axils of last year's leaves (Figure 2-17). The blooming period is generally June (earlier south and later north), about the same time as Mountain Laurel. The calyx is usually green with red tips or red throughout, while the corolla is less than ½ in (12 mm) across and reddish purple to pink. The fruit is composed of a depressed globose capsule with numerous small, yellowish seeds that have two short wings.

Figure 2-17. Sheep Laurel, *Kalmia angustifolia,* in a garden. This is the selection named 'Hammonasset', (Jaynes)

The Sheep Laurel is common in northeastern and eastern North America (Figure 2-18). John K. Small, an American botanist who studied the flora of the southeastern United States, classified it as two separate species in 1914 and more recently Southall and Hardin also treated Sheep Laurel as two species. Most botanists, however, consider the Sheep Laurel complex as being one species with two fairly distinct varieties. The genetic and morphological similarities make it more realistic to follow this latter view. Therefore, we treat this species as the Northern Sheep Laurel, *K. angustifolia* var. *angustifolia,* and the Southern Sheep Laurel, *K. angustifolia* var. *caroliniana.* The two varieties are similar in habit and general appearance but are easily distinguished by dif-ferences in leaf and calyx pubescence. In the Northern Sheep Laurel the calyx is densely glandular pubescent (small hairs), and the leaves are

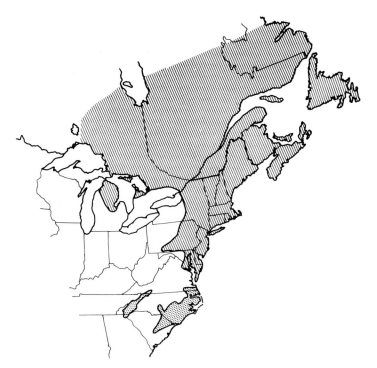

Figure 2-18. The natural range of Northern Sheep Laurel, *K. angustifolia* var. *angustifolia* (vertical shading), and Southern Sheep Laurel, *K. angustifolia* var. *caroliniana* (dotted area). With such a broad range and disjunct distribution considerable variation exists within the species. (Ebinger)

glabrous (hairless). The Southern Sheep Laurel has no glandular hairs on the calyx, and the leaves are densely pubescent beneath with a mat of extremely short hairs.

NORTHERN SHEEP LAUREL, var. *angustifolia*   Common names for this variety include Lambkill, Sheepkill, Wicky, Narrow-leaved Kalmia, Dwarf Laurel, and Pig Laurel. It occurs in bogs, swamps, and other wet places, forming dense thickets around ponds and lakes, and in open woods, as a weed in pastures, and in the moist openings of pine savannas. It is distributed from the northeastern part of the Michigan peninsula and the eastern half of Ontario, east through Quebec, the Maritime provinces, and Newfoundland; north to the Attawapiskat River (Kenora District) in Ontario, and to Goose Bay and Cartwright in Labrador; and south in the eastern United States through New England and eastern New York, eastern Pennsylvania and Maryland, to the coast in New Jersey and Delaware, and the southeastern tip of Virginia.

Most of the subspecific categories proposed for the Northern Sheep Laurel are for variations and extremes in flower color, variation in size and habit, and variation in leaf shape and color (Figure 2-19). In general, the differences in flower color represent natural variation within populations and should be treated as cultivars. The variation in

Figure 2-19. A particularly attractive Sheep Laurel photographed in Newfoundland. (Redfield)

leaf shape and color, and, in part, variation in plant height, should be treated the same way. Low growing plants are generally selections of more northern or high-altitude sources, or the result of inbreeding depression.

A white flowered form, *candida,* of the Northern Sheep Laurel was first reported from Newfoundland in 1915 and has now been observed in a few other locations in Canada and the northeastern United States (Figure 2-20). The presence of pigment in Sheep Laurel is controlled by a single dominant gene, and the true-breeding recessive is white-flowered. These white-flowered individuals also have green stems, unlike the normal wild types which have reddish stems.

SOUTHERN SHEEP LAUREL, var. *caroliniana*   This variety is common in North Carolina and occurs in open woods and shrubby bogs in the mountains, in sandy woods, pocosins (marsh or swamp), savannas, and bogs on the coastal plain (Figure 2-18).

Sporadic occurrence has been reported on the coastal plains of South Carolina and southern Virginia and in a few locations in the mountains of eastern Tennessee and two mountain bogs in the Blue Ridge of northeastern Georgia.

A white-flowered form of the Southern Sheep Laurel also exists. It is similar genetically to the white-flowered form of the Northern Sheep Laurel in that the true-breeding recessive is white-flowered. The only known plants of this form came from Garden in the Woods, Framingham, Massachusetts. No wild individuals have been observed, and the origin of the nursery material is unknown.

Figure 2-20. The white flowered Sheep Laurel, form *candida,* grown from seed collected at Madison, Connecticut. (Jaynes)

White Wicky, *Kalmia cuneata*

One of the rarest shrubs in North America, this many-branched, erect shrub may become 5 ft (1.5 m) tall. The leaves are alternate, deciduous, thin and flat, petioled, oblanceolate (lance-shaped but broadest near the apex) and 1–2½ in (2.5–6.5 cm) long. Stalked glandular hairs are scattered over most parts of the plant. The flowers are borne in clusters of three to ten in the upper axils of the

Figure 2-21. White wicky, *Kalmia cuneata,* an endangered species. (Jaynes)

previous year's growth. Flowering is in early spring before new foliage and shoots expand. The corolla is ½–¾ in (12–19 mm) across and creamy white with a red band within. The fruit is a depressed globose capsule on a recurved stalk. The light brown seeds are small.

White Wicky is a distinctive species (Figure 2-21). It could only be confused with the Sheep Laurel, since their general habitat and leaf size are similar. White Wicky, however, is the only deciduous member of the genus. It is found only in wet thickets and shrub bogs (the pocosin ecotone) in eight counties of southeastern North Carolina and adjacent South Carolina (Figure 2-22). These sites are marshy upland areas of the coastal plain between two ecological zones.

Figure 2-22. The natural range of White Wicky, *K. cuneata* (dotted area) and Sandhill Laurel, *K. hirsuta* (vertical shading). Despite limited geographic distribution, there exists within each species considerable variation for plant form and flower color. (Ebinger)

Sandhill Laurel, *Kalmia hirsuta*

Sometimes called Calico-bush, this species is a low, lightly branched shrub less than 2 ft (60 cm) tall with alternate, commonly short-petioled, elliptic to ovate leaves less than ½ in (12 mm) long with margins only slightly revolute. The leaves and stems are covered with short, densely packed hairs as well as scattered, long coarse hairs and stalked glandular hairs. The flowers are usually solitary in the axils of the leaves of new growth (Figure 2-23). The blooming period is extended, often from early summer until fall. The calyx is green, leaf-like, and tardily deciduous in fruit. The corolla is about ½ in (12 mm) across and light pink with red markings around the anther pockets and a red ring near its base. The fruit is a subglobose capsule covered with glandular hairs and containing numerous light brown seeds.

The Sandhill Laurel has a relatively limited distribution, occurring along the coastal plain in the southeastern United States (Figure 2-22). It has been observed from extreme southern Alabama and northern Florida and north through Georgia to the southeastern tip of South Carolina. Usually found in low, sandy pine savannas, sandhills, dunes

Figure 2-23. Sandhill Laurel, *Kalmia hirsuta*, with leaves about ½ in (1.3 cm) long. (Jaynes)

and flat relatively open pine woods, this low-growing plant forms clumps among the understory. It does extremely well in sunny areas and is found in pine woods openings resulting from logging or burning.

Horticultural variants of Sandhill Laurel have not been described in the literature, but Tom Dodd of Semmes, Alabama, observed a colony of Sandhill Laurel with hose-in-hose (double-cupped) flowers while on a field trip in southeastern Georgia. This trait would be of great ornamental value in cultivated Laurels. Sandhill Laurels with a banded or fuscata type flower have also been observed.

Cuban Laurel, *Kalmia ericoides*

Sparsely branched, this erect to spreading shrub sometimes reaches a height of 3 ft (1 m). The leaves are alternate, persistent, thick, leathery, subsessile (virtually no petiole), linear, about ½ in (12 mm) long with strongly revolute margins. Most of the plant is covered with short, densely packed hairs, scattered long coarse hairs, and well-developed stalked glandular hairs. The flowers are solitary in the axils of the leaves near the ends of the branches, forming tight terminal clusters. The calyx is green, leaf-like, and tardily deciduous in fruit. The corolla is about ½ in (12 mm) across and light pink with red markings around the anther pockets and a red ring near the base. *The fruit is a subglobose capsule covered with glandular hairs and containing numerous reddish brown seeds.*

The Cuban Laurel is endemic to the savannas and pine barrens of western Cuba. Though it has a very limited distribution, the variation that exists in leaf pubescence and in the compactness of the inflorescence led to the division of this species into three species by some botanists, while others have considered it a single highly variable species. It now appears that the compactness of the inflorescence is not a completely reliable characteristic. The variation in leaf pubescence, however, is relatively stable; two varieties do probably exist in this complex.

The Cuban Laurel appears to be most closely related to the Sandhill Laurel of the southeastern United States. Both have relatively small leaves (about ½ in (12 mm) long), covered with long coarse hairs and stalked glandular hairs. Their flowers are borne singly in the axils of the leaves, and the calyx is leafy and tardily deciduous in fruit. The two are easily separated, however, since the leaves of the Cuban Laurel are thick and leathery with strongly revolute margins, while in the Sandhill Laurel the leaves are thin and lack a strongly revolute margin. Also, the flowers are scattered along the stem in the Sandhill Laurel while those of the Cuban Laurel are found toward the end of the stem, giving the appearance of a terminal cluster.

BOTANICAL KEY TO SPECIES OF LAUREL

a. Leaves opposite
  b. Midrib of leaves lacking stalked glands; seeds less than 1/16 in (1.5 mm) long
          Western Laurel, *K. microphylla*
  b. Midrib of leaves with stalked glands; seeds more than 1/16 in (1.5 mm) long
          Eastern Bog Laurel, *K. polifolia*
a. Leaves alternate or in whorls
  c. Leaves mostly more than ¾ in (20 mm) broad; inflorescence terminal, much branched
          Mountain Laurel, *K. latifolia*
  c. Leaves mostly less than ¾ in (20 mm) broad; flowers solitary or in racemes in the axils of the leaves
    d. Leaves more than ⅝ in (15 mm) long; flowers in racemes
      e. Leaves in whorls of three, evergreen
          Sheep Laurel, *K. angustifolia*
      e. Leaves alternate, deciduous
          White Wicky, *K. cuneata*
    d. Leaves less than ⅝ in (15 mm) long; flowers usually solitary

in the axils of the leaves
- f. Leaves broad, flat, margins only slightly rolled under
  Sandhill Laurel, *K. hirsuta*
- f. Leaves narrow, margins strongly rolled under
  Cuban Laurel, *K. ericoides*

Chapter 3 _____

SELECTIONS WORTHY OF
PROPAGATION—CULTIVAR LIST

To the horticulturist, color is an important criterion in the breeding of plants, in description and identification of cultivars, and in selection of plants for landscaping. Ironically, cultivar description (frequently accomplished by horticulturists) may be more demanding in some respects than the formal description of species (usually done by professional botanists). The differentiation of cultivars can call for specification of color differences more subtle than those between species. This puts a premium on precision, but hybridizers and growers often have scant experience with color systems, color matching, and color names. Moreover, the welter of color systems and names confronting the horticulturist is even more baffling than the profusion of common names for plants. Catch 22, indeed! (Huse and Kelly 1984)

   As tempting as it might be to draw up a list of the "best" Mountain Laurel cultivars, I won't. Most of the cultivars have been in propagation for less than 10 years and no one, including myself, has enough experience in growing them in the nursery as well as the landscape to fairly evaluate and compare more than a few. In the following cultivar descriptions I have tried to include noteworthy observations, favorable and unfavorable, of my own and others. Hence the reader will note that 'Goodrich' is of questionable merit for plant growth and vigor, whereas selections such as 'Bullseye' and 'Nathan Hale' have done well, especially in containers.
   If there is a bit more information on my own releases, this is not really intentional but merely the result of having more information available. It is my intention to keep this list up-to-date. Corrections, additions, and comments in general are welcomed. (R. A. Jaynes, Broken Arrow Nursery, 13 Broken Arrow Rd., Hamden, Connecticut 06518)
   The color photographs should be helpful in distinguishing the selections. (Copies of 35mm slides are available at a nominal fee from the author: see above note for address.) Perhaps in the next published list color descriptions from one of the standard color charts can be used as well as standard color names from the Universal Color Language (Inter-Society Color Council—National Bureau of Standards) (see

quote above). The next five years will see some of these cultivars become very popular with growers and homeowners, others will fade away, and new ones will be introduced.

CULTIVARS

The *International Code of Nomenclature for Cultivated Plants* (Brickell 1980) provides the rules for naming cultivated varieties (cultivars) of plants, and the Council of the International Society of Horticultural Science designates International Registration Authorities. I have been the designated National Authority since 1977 and more recently the International Registration Authority for *Kalmia*. What this fancy title really means is that I have agreed to try to keep track and coordinate the naming of new cultivars. One of the first steps was to publish in 1983 in the *Bulletin of the American Association of Botanical Gardens and Arboreta* a checklist of all cultivated laurels then known. No checklist or register of cultivated names had previously been published for the genus.

The first horticultural varieties of *Kalmia latifolia* were described in the 1800's and, with few exceptions, most cultivated *Kalmia* are of this species. The selection and propagation of *K. latifolia* has been sporadic until recently. The breeding of *K. latifolia* in the last 30 years, combined with the recently acquired ability to clonally propagate selections in sterile (tissue) culture, has resulted in the release of several new cultivars. There were 26 valid cultivars recognized in the 1983 list. More than a dozen were named in the next 3 years and several more are sure to be added soon.

The purpose of the list is to inform, reduce confusion, and encourage stability of nomenclature within the group. Botanical nomenclature is from Ebinger, 1974 (see Chapter 2).

Format:
1. Regardless of rank, all names (botanical varieties, botanical forms and cultivars are listed in alphabetical order under each species.
2. The earliest published reference for a name and description of a plant in cultivation is placed within parentheses.
3. Descriptive information from published as well as unpublished sources is included.
4. a) CULTIVAR NAMES are initially shown in capital letters. The usual convention of single quotes around cultivar names is then followed.
   b) Invalid names are shown in small, lightface type.
   c) *Botanical names* are in italic type.

K. latifolia Linnaeus, Mountain Laurel

Alba Invalid cultivar name applied to plants with white or near white flowers.

ALPINE PINK (Briggs Nursery, Olympia, Washington, 1982 catalog, color photo) Selected by J. Eichelser, originally propagated and released as J-12. Rich pink in bud, opens to a medium pink with the inside center of the open corolla near white. Growth habit is good and foliage is thick, glossy, broad, and heavy. Foliage tends to be light green, last flush of growth often turns yellow, especially under good growing conditions. Stems of new growth and petioles are moderately pigmented purplish red. (Figure 3-1)

Figure 3-1. 'Alpine Pink' is notable for the two-tone appearance of the open flowers-near white in the center and pink on the outer half of the corolla. (Briggs)

f. *angustata* Rehd. (*Jour. Arnold Arb.* 26:481, 1945) Narrowly oblanceolate to linear leaves that are 1½–3¼ in (4–8 cm) long and 3/16–3/8 in (5–10 mm) wide. Rare foliage form. Under the control of a single recessive gene [w]. Common name: Willow-leaved Laurel. See 'Willowcrest'.

Apetala see f. *polypetala*

BETTINA (Dudley, *Amer. Hort. Mag.* Oct. 46: 246–248, 1967) Corolla reduced and deep purplish pink when grown in full sun, faintly pigmented in shade. Anther filaments and style exserted, normal length. Originated at the U.S. National Arboretum, S. March, 1950s. Flower form under the control of a single recessive gene [be]. (Figure 14-11)

BRAVO (R. A. Jaynes, *Kalmia, The Laurel Book* II, 1987)—Selected before 1973 by the late Edmund V. Mezitt, Weston Nurseries, Hopkinton, Massachusetts. It is a third or fouth generation pink selection. It was propagated and sold under name for several years at Weston Nurseries but not listed in their catalog. The leaves are large, rounded and glossy; new growth has red stems. The flower buds and open flowers are dark pink.

BRIDESMAID (R. A. Jaynes, *Kalmia, The Laurel Book* II, 1987) Selected about 1973 at CAES (Connecticut Agricultural Experiment Station, New Haven; crosses and selections by R. A. Jaynes) and commercially propagated and introduced by Bolton Technologies, Bolton, Connecticut, 1986. The flower is a rich, deep pink in bud as well as when open except that the center of the corolla (⅓ diameter of open flower) is white. The edge of the corolla rolls back as the flower ages, also a characteristic of 'Sarah.' Leaves are lustrous, dark green, broad, and heavily textured. The habit is somewhat spreading and semi-compact. Good annual flowering. From a 1968 controlled cross of a deep pink and a red budded selection (293 × 299). Tested as CAES ×965 plt. 15. (Figure 3-2)

Figure 3-2. 'Bridesmaid' is rich pink in bud and open flower but, like 'Alpine Pink,' has a near-white center. (Jaynes)

BRILLIANT (R. Hay & P. M. Synge, *The Color Dictionary of Flowers and Plants for Home & Garden,* Crown, New York, 1969, color photo p. 209) "... one of the finest forms with deeper pink fl., crimson in bud." [This may not be a valid cultivar. Information on origin, original description, and propagation is lacking (from Great Britain).]

BULLSEYE (R. A. Jaynes, *Int. Plant Prop. Soc. Proc.* 32: 431–434, 1982) CAES selection of f. *fuscata.* Commercially introduced by Knight Hollow Nursery, Madison, Wisconsin, 1983. Broad, purplish cinnamon band of pigmentation on the inside of corolla, white center and white edge. A good grower in the nursery with new growth often a bronze-red (Figure 3–3). Stems of new growth and petioles purplish red on the sun

Figure 3-3. 'Bullseye', like 'Sarah' and some other selections has bronze red stems and foliage on the new growth. (Jaynes)

Figure 3-4. 'Bullseye' is a broad-banded selection. Like other banded forms the band width and color will vary some from year to year and on exposure to sunlight. (Jaynes)

side. From a cross of a red-bud selection (137) with pollen of a broad-banded plant from Bristol Nurseries, Connecticut. Tested as CAES ×1144 plt. 3. (Figure 3-4)

Caes 137 (Briggs Nursery, Olympia, Washington, 1982 catalog) Invalid cultivar name. It is a test number of a selection made by R. A. Jaynes, Connecticut Agricultural Experiment Station, in the fields of Weston Nurseries, Hopkinton, Massachusetts, 1962. A red-bud selection less intense in color than similarly named cultivars, a parent of 'Bullseye', 'Carousel', 'Nipmuck', and 'Quinnipiac'.

Calico Invalid cultivar name for one or more f. *fuscata* plants propagated around 1970 by La Bars Rhododendron Nursery, Stroudsburg, Pennsylvania. See: Kalico Kal, also an invalid name.

CANDY (Briggs Nursery, Olympia, Washington, 1985 catalog) This plant flowered about 1970 and was selected and named in 1972 by Edmund V. Mezitt, Weston Nurseries, Hopkinton, Massachusetts. It is a third or fourth generation pink selection. It was propagated and sold under this name for several years at Weston Nurseries but not listed in their catalog. The foliage is broad, heavy and ovate in shape. Petioles and new stems are purplish red. Flower buds and the open corolla are dark pink.

CAROL (R. A. Jaynes, *CAES Mimeo List,* 1984) Selected 1975 and commercially propagated by Bolton Technologies, Bolton, Connecticut, 1986. A bright, intense red-bud (similar to 'Nipmuck') that contrasts well with the near white of the open corolla. Bud color of plants in warm sites, such as near a foundation wall, may be more pink than red. A compact growing plant with thick, broad, lustrous, glossy foliage; leaf blades sometimes undulate. Stems of recent growth and petioles moderately pigmented purplish red. Originated from a 1969 controlled cross at CAES of a deep pink (1161), female, and a red-bud (776c). Tested as CAES ×1049 plt. 33. (Figure 3-5)

Figure 3-5. 'Carol' was selected especially for broad habit, dense foliage, and thick, glossy leaves. The bud color may be more pink than red some years. (Jaynes)

Figure 3-6. 'Carousel' is a banded form with a very "busy" flower; color and width of band will vary some with year and exposure. (Jaynes)

Figure 3-7. 'Clementine Churchill' is a pink selection from England and first described in 1952. (Jaynes)

Figure 3-8. 'Elf' is a miniature Mountain Laurel selection, form *myrtifolia*. The flowers are within the normal color range for the species and not as reduced in size as the foliage and plant habit. (Jaynes)

CAROUSEL (R. A. Jaynes, *Int. Plant Prop. Soc. Proc.* 32: 431–434, 1982) CAES selection of f. *fuscata.* Intricate pattern of bright, purplish cinnamon pigmentation on inside of corolla. From a controlled cross of a red-bud selection (137) and a GOODRICH-like banded plant. Flower similar to GOODRICH but more white showing and pigment brighter. A good grower and relatively easy to root. Petioles and current season stems moderately pigmented purplish red. Tested as CAES ×1153 plt. 11. (Figure 3-6)

CLEMENTINE CHURCHILL (A. G. Soames, Award of Merit, *Jour. Royal Hort. Soc.* 77: 422, 1952) Originated Sheffield Park, Sussex, England. Outside of corolla is Tyrian Rose and the inside rose-red (Rose)Madder). Foliage and habit good. Flowers much like 'Pink Charm' except the latter has redder buds. (Figure 3-7)

DEN WINDOW (R. A. Jaynes, *Kalmia, The Laurel Book* II, 1987) This plant ·flowered and was selected in the 1960's by Edmund W. Mezitt, Weston Nurseries, Hopkinton, Massachusetts. It is a fourth generation pink selection. Weston Nurseries has propagated and sold the plant since 1972. The open flowers are large and light pink becoming progressively deeper pink as they mature. The plant is robust, being both wide and upright. The leaves are broad and nearly flat, but slightly folded along the mid-rib. Foliage is bluish green in color and new growth is glossy, stems are purplish red.

Dexter Pink (strain) (Greer Gardens, Eugene, Oregon, catalog, p. 58, 1981) Invalid cultivar name applied to pink-flowered seedlings grown from seedlings of plants originally selected from the C. O. Dexter Estate, Sandwich, Massachusetts. Named Dexter Pink by John Eichelser, Melrose Nursery, Olympia, Washington, to distinguish them from the clonally propagated 'Ostbo Red' he was growing. More recently a plant has been tissue culture propagated and sold under this name by B & B Laboratories, Mount Vernon, Washington (1986 catalog).

ELF (R. A. Jaynes, *Int. Plant Prop. Soc. Proc.* 32: 431–434, 1982) CAES selection of f. *myrtifolia.* Commercially introduced by Briggs Nursery, Olympia Washington, 1982. This is a Miniature Mountain Laurel, having characteristic reduced leaf size and slower growth. However, young plants are capable of vigorous growth. Unless pruned heavily when young plants may become leggy and appear stiffly branched. Form and rate of growth vary greatly with conditions. Older and more slowly grown plants develop considerable charm and grace. Petioles short, which together with stems of new growth are purplish red on sun side. Flowers are typical of wild-type, light pink in bud, near white open with a crisp, narrow ring near the corolla base. Cuttings root somewhat easier than most. From a cross (1–76) of six miniature plants caged with a bumblebee. Tested as CAES BAR-4. (Figure 3-8)

EMERALD SHEEN (R. A. Jaynes, *Kalmia, The Laurel Book* II, 1987) This plant first flowered in 1977 and was selected and named the following year by R. Wayne Mezitt, Weston Nurseries, Hopkinton, Massachusetts. The seed parent is believed to be the cultivar 'Twenty'. Plants were first sold under name in 1985. The outstanding feature of this selection is the thick textured, glossy, rounded, convex, dark green foliage borne on a dense, compact plant. It flowers somewhat sparsely; medium pink buds, open nearly white and mature to medium pink. The flowers are very large in densely packed, "frilly" clusters but sometimes hidden by the foliage.

FRECKLES (R. A. Jaynes, *Int. Plant Prop. Soc. Proc.* 32: 431–434, 1982) CAES selection of f. *fuscata*. Commercially introduced by Knight Hollow Nursery, Madison, Wisconsin, 1983. The flower buds are light pink and there are ten purplish cinnamon spots about 1/10 in (2 mm) across on the inside of the corolla at the level of and just above the 10 anther pouches. The selection has a good habit, is a good grower in containers if not over-fertilized, and is precocious. Petioles and stems of new growth sometimes lightly pigmented purplish red on the sun side. From a second generation controlled cross of 'Star Cluster' and a red-bud (187). Tested as CAES ✕1028 plt. I. (Figure 3-9)

Figure 3-9. 'Freckles' is one of the more subtle banded types and is referred to as an interrupted band. (Jaynes)

FRESCA (Greer Gardens, Eugene, Oregon, catalog p. 58, 1981; color photo in Briggs Nursery catalog, Olympia, Washington, 1982) Selected by J. Caperci 1969, introduced by J. Eichelser. A selection of f. *fuscata* with a distinct chocolate-purple band around the inside of the corolla, also described as burgundy in color. Petioles and stems of new growth purplish red in color. (Figure 3-10)

Figure 3-10. 'Fresca' a banded selection. (Briggs)

f. *fuscata* (Rehd) Rehd. (*Rhodora* 12: 2, 1910) Flowers characterized by a heavily pigmented, usually continuous, brownish, purplish, or cinnamon band on the inside of the corolla at the level of the anther pockets. It has been found at different locations in the wild since 1830 and of sporatic occurence among seedlings grown in nurseries. Under the control of a single dominant gene [*B*]. Common name: Banded Laurel. See: 'Bullseye', 'Carousel', 'Freckles', 'Fresca', 'Goodrich', 'Hearts Desire', 'Kaleidoscope', 'Minuet', 'Pinwheel', 'Star Cluster', and 'Yankee Doodle'.

GOODRICH (R. A. Jaynes, *The Laurel Book,* 1975, color photo p. 39) Selected by R.A. Jaynes and J. W. Goodrich from a native stand at Chaplin, Connecticut, 1972. Cinnamon-brown band virtually fills the inside of the corolla except for some white border on the edge of the corolla. Vigor and growth of plant in cultivation has been disappointing in several cases; foliage susceptible to leaf spot. (Figure 3-11)

Figure 3-11. 'Goodrich', a broad banded selection from the State Forest in Chaplin, Connecticut. It is a weak grower under cultivation despite its survival in natural stand. (Jaynes)

HEART OF FIRE (R. A. Jaynes, *Kalmia, The Laurel Book II,* 1987) A seedling of 'Ostbo Red' grown and selected by John Eichelser, Melrose Nursery, Olympia, Washington and named by his daughter, Lori Eichelser Gangsei in 1986. It was previously propagated and sold by Briggs and Melrose Nursery as J-1 and John's Red. It is a red-bud similar to 'Ostbo Red' but was selected for its better foliage and habit; the leaves are broader and flatter. Petioles and current season stems are purplish red. (Figure 3-12)

Figure 3-12. 'Heart of Fire' has deep red buds and opens to a rich pink. (Eichelser)

HEARTS DESIRE (R. A. Jaynes, *Kalmia, The Laurel Book II,* 1987) Selected by R. A. Jaynes and introduced by Briggs Nursery in 1987. The flower is red in bud and opens with a cinnamon-red pigment that almost fills the inside of the corolla (f. *fuscata*) (see 'Kaleidoscope'). The lip of the corolla is white (approx. 1/16 in (1.5 mm)) as is the center of the corolla. The flower truss is large and many-flowered. The foliage is dark green and the habit broad and densely branched. The stems of new growth are blushed purplish red. This plant was selected from a controlled cross of a deep pink (319) and a banded/redbud (137 × Bristol/733ap). (Figure 3-13)

KALEIDOSCOPE (R. A. Jaynes, Kalmia, *The Laurel Book II,* 1987) Selected by R. A. Jaynes from a cross of 'Sarah' and a sibling of 'Bullseye', and introduced by Knight Hollow Nursery in 1987. The flower is red in bud and opens with a rich cinnamon-red band (f. *fuscata*) that almost fills the inside of the corolla like 'Hearts Desire'. The flowers are a bit more brilliant on 'Kaleidoscope' although in somewhat more open trusses. There is a distinctive white lip (approx. ⅛ in (3 mm)) on the corolla edge and the throat of the flower is white. The foliage is dark green and plant habit characteristic of the species; petioles and stems of new growth are purplish red except where heavily shaded. (Figure 3-14)

Kalico Kal Invalid cultivar name applied by E. Amateus to banded (f. *fuscata*) plants in a native stand on land of S. Koenig, Holmes, New York. Pigment of bands largely confined to upper third of corolla, at and above the anther pockets. See: Calico, also an invalid name.

M-14—See: 'Olympic Fire'

f. *myrtifolia* (Bosse) K. Koch (*Dendrologie* 2(1): 153, 1872) A Miniature Mountain Laurel, rarely found in the wild. Habit and foliage about one-half to one-third normal in size, flowers reduced somewhat less. Plants of this form are quite distinct from the species and yet individual plants may also vary in habit and rate of growth. Under the control of a single recessive gene [*m*]. Common name Miniature Laurel, also referred to as Minor and Nana. See: 'Elf', 'Minuet'.

MINUET (R. A. Jaynes, *Kalmia, The Laurel Book II,* 1987) Selected by R. A. Jaynes and introduced by Briggs Nursery in 1987. 'Minuet' is a miniature (f. *myrtifolia*) like 'Elf' but also banded (f. *fuscata*) The flowers are large relative to the reduced plant habit. The band is broad, and a solid bright cinnamon maroon color. The pigment pattern is much like 'Goodrich' but the color redder and brighter. The buds are light pink. The leaves are glossy, dark green and narrow; growth and habit somewhat diminished compared to 'Elf'. From a cross of miniature x banded ('Star Cluster')/redbud. (Figure 3-15)

NANCY (R. A. Jaynes, *CAES Mimeo List,* 1984) Selected 1975 and commercially introduced by Bolton Technologies, Bolton, Connecticut, 1985. A clear, vibrant, pinkish red in bud opening to a bright clear pink. There is a crisp, maroon pigmented band within and near the corolla base. Foliage and habit normal for the species. Petioles and stems of current

Figure 3-13. 'Hearts Desire' combines red bud color with a broad maroon band, and large truss size. (Jaynes)

Figure 3-14. 'Kaleidoscope' selected from a controlled cross in which the red bud characteristic was combined with a broad band. The white edge on the corolla contrasts well with the band and bud color. (Jaynes)

Figure 3-15. 'Minuet' is the first miniature Mountain Laurel with a banded flower to be named; from a controlled cross. The band of 'Minuet' and 'Carousel' are derived from the same population of wild plants at Chaplin, Connecticut. (Jaynes)

Figure 3-16. 'Nancy'. The bud and open flower color is very bright and clear, being free of lavender or purple overtones. (Jaynes)

Figure 3-17. 'Nipmuck' is red in bud, has light green foliage, and cuttings are relatively easy to root. (Jaynes)

Figure 3-18. 'Olympic Wedding' has pink buds and the flowers open to a band that is usually interrupted but not as sparse as that of 'Freckles.' (Briggs)

season's growth are purplish red except in heavily shaded sites. Late flushes of growth are yellow-green. From a 1974 controlled cross of a deep pink flowered plant (319) with pollen of 'Pink Charm'. Tested as CAES ×1203 plt 1. Sibling of 'Raspberry Glow' and 'Sarah'. (Figure 3-16)

NATHAN HALE (M. Johnson, *The Plants We Grow,* 1986) Selected in 1975 and commercially introduced by L. Hoffman in 1980 as Hoffman #4. The flowers are red in bud and open pink. The growth habit is symetrical and somewhat compact. Foliage is heavy, shiny and dark green in color; petioles and stems of new growth are purplish red. It grows well in containers. Selected by the Nathan Hale Society of the Sons of the American Revolution to honor Connecticut's Revolutionary War hero, Nathan Hale.

NIPMUCK (R. A. Jaynes, *The Plant Propagator* 25(3): 11–12, 1979) Selected 1971 and introduced at the CAES. Intense red-bud color; cuttings root with relative ease. Similar to 'Quinnipiac', but the foliage color is a lighter yellow-green and growth is better; upper foliage often turns an unattractive purplish color in the fall. Petioles and stems of current season are moderately pigmented on the sun side. From a cross made in 1963 of a plant with deep pink flowers (189) and one with red buds (137). Tested as CAES ×122 plt. 9. (Figure 3-17)

f. *obtusata* (Rehd.) Rehd. (*Rhodora* 12: 2, 1910) Leaves are oval to oblong-obovate and rounded at both ends. Petioles short and internodes reduced in length. Under the control of a single recessive gene [*ob*]. Common name: Hedge Laurel.

OLYMPIC FIRE (Briggs Nursery, Olympia, Washington, 1982 catalog, with color photo) Selected and originally propagated by J. Eichelser, Melrose Nursery, Olympia, Washington. A seedling of 'Ostbo Red'. Large red bud, opens pink, heavy foliage, less breakage than 'Ostbo Red' and easier to root. Good habit and foliage color in containers, leaves undulate. Petioles and stems of new growth purplish red on sun side. Tested and sold as M14 by Greer Gardens, 1981.

OLYMPIC WEDDING (R. A. Jaynes, *Kalmia, The Laurel Book II,* 1987) Selected from a cross of 'Ostbo Red' and 'Fresca' by John Eichelser, Melrose Nursery, Olympia, Washington, 1984, and introduced by his daughter, Lori Eichelser Gangsei in 1987. The buds are pink and open to reveal a broken, maroon band. The leaves are dark green, broad, and flat. The plant has a good branching habit. It is a sibling of 'Wedding Band'. (Figure 3-18)

OSTBO RED (J. Eichelser, *Int. Plant Prop. Soc. Proc.* 22: 190–192, 1972; briefly described by R. Jaynes, *Int. Plant Prop. Soc. Proc.* 21: 366–373, 1971) Selected in 1940's by E. Ostbo from material obtained from C. O. Dexter, Sandwich, Massachusetts, and named by John Eichelser, Melrose Nursery, Olympia, Washington. Also sold as Ostbo's Red #5, Ostbo #5, Dexter 5, West Coast 5, and Red-Bud *Kalmia*. First red-budded selection to be named. Buds iridescent red, most intense when grown in the sun; color and brilliance of other red-buds should be judged against this selection. Leaves slightly smaller, undulate, and more twisted than the species. Petioles and stems of new growth colored somewhat purplish red on the sun side. A parent of 'Heart of Fire', 'Olympic Fire', 'Olympic Wedding', 'Pink Star', and 'Wedding Band'. (Figure 3-19)

Ovata Invalid cultivar name applied to plants with broad, ovate shaped leaves. See: f. *obtusata.*

Peckham's Pink Strain (Greer Gardens, Eugene, Oregon, catalog p. 58, 1981) Strain grown by George and Shirley Peckham, Pleasant Hill, Oregon. Flowers a light and bright pastel pink.

PINK CHARM (R. A. Jaynes, *Int. Plant. Prop. Soc. Proc.* 30: 427–428, 1980; color photo, cover *J. Heredity* 72(4), 1981) Selected in 1974; originated from a 1970 controlled cross of two pink selections (138 × 316) at the CAES. Commercially introduced by Briggs Nursery, Olympia, Washington, 1982. Flower buds deep pink to red, open flowers a rich pink. There is a dark, sharp reddish maroon inner ring on the corolla. Blooms annually if dead headed. Good habit and a good grower in containers. Cuttings relatively easy to root. Stems of current season growth almost entirely purplish red, petioles pigmented above. Tested as CAES ×1078 plt. 14. 'Pink Charm' was the pollen parent of 'Nancy', 'Raspberry Glow', and 'Sarah'. (Figure 3-20)

PINK FROST (Greer Gardens, Eugene, Oregon, catalog p. 58, 1981; color photo Briggs Nursery, Olympia, Washington, 1982 catalog) Selected by J. E. Eichelser, Melrose Nursery, Olympia, Washington, 1965, commercially introduced 1977. Foliage is excellent, leaves wide and lustrous; large, rich pink buds open to light pink and then blush to a deeper pink. Scorch on leaves has been a problem in the Northeast. Cuttings root better than species. (Figure 3-21)

PINK STAR (Greer Gardens, Eugene, Oregon, catalog p. 65, 1982) A seedling of 'Ostbo Red' selected and introduced by J. Eichelser, Olympia, Washington. Large, star-shaped flowers, clear medium pink in bud and lighter colored when open. Under good growing conditions shoots of this selection tend to extend continuously during the growing season in contrast to the discreet flushes of most other cultivars. Thus heavy pruning and/or reduced fertilization is required to get good branching. (Figure 3-22)

PINK SURPRISE (R. A. Jaynes, *The Laurel Book,* 1975) Selected by R. A. Jaynes, CAES, from field at Weston Nurseries, Hopkinton, Massachusetts, 1965. Commercially introduced 1979. Foliage good, vigor good with some tendency towards legginess. Has done well in containers. Stems of new growth purplish red and petioles pigmented above. Flower buds deep pink, open to medium pink. The corolla has a crisp inner ring and ten pigment flecks where the anthers are held. Cuttings relatively easy to root (that was the "surprise!"). Tested as CAES 223. (Figure 3-23)

Figure 3-19. 'Ostbo Red,' the first named red-budded Laurel. The bright, clean (no lavender) bud color is among the best. (Jaynes)

Figure 3-20. 'Pink Charm' is a strong pink of similar intensity in bud and open flower. (Jaynes)

Figure 3-21. 'Pink Frost' has good contrast between the darker buds and open flowers; leaves are broad and foliage heavy. (Jaynes)

Figure 3-22. 'Pink Star' is a deep pink in bud and open flower and was selected for the strongly lobed, star-shaped corolla. (Briggs)

Figure 3-23. 'Pink Surprise', a good pink with nice markings inside the corolla at the level of anther pockets; one of the easier selections to root from cuttings. (Jaynes)

PINWHEEL (R. A. Jaynes, *Kalmia, The Laurel Book II,* 1987) Selected by R. A. Jaynes in 1982 and introduced by Briggs Nursery in 1987. This is a banded (f. *fuscata*) selection. The buds are tinged with pink. The inside of the corolla is nearly filled with cinnamon-maroon pigment. The corolla is white in the center and the edge is scalloped white. A truss of open flowers is reminiscent of Sweet William flowers. Foliage is somewhat undulate (wavy) in full sun. The growth habit is characteristic of the species. Stems of new growth may have a purplish red blush on the south side but otherwise they are entirely green as are the petioles. (Figures 3-24, 3-25)

Figure 3-24. 'Pinwheel', a banded form with an intricate pattern of pigmentation, white edge to the corolla; trusses of open flowers resemble flowers of a Sweet William. (Jaynes)

Figure 3-25. 'Pinwheel'. Closeup of flowers from a shaded portion of the same plant as previous figure; notice the pigmentation pattern is different. (Jaynes)

f. *polypetala* (Nickolsen) Beissner, Schelle, & Zabel (*Handb. den Laubgeholz-Benennung* 386, 1903) Typically the corolla is cut to form five strap-like petals. Selections often lack vigor. Ebinger (1974) also includes other corolla types: reduced ('Bettina'), and no corolla (Apetala). Common name for the usual type is Feather Petal. It is under the control of a single recessive gene [p]. 'Bettina' and Apetala are apparently under the control of separate, single recessive genes, [be] and [ap], respectively. (Figure 2-14)

QUINNIPIAC (R. A. Jaynes, *The Plant Propagator* 25(3): 11–12, 1979) Selected 1971 and introduced at the CAES. Intense red bud color. Cuttings root with relative ease. There is a sharp inner ring in the corolla. This selection is similar to 'Nipmuck' which is a sibling, but the foliage is darker green and growth not as vigorous. Petioles usually pigmented purplish red above. Foliage is prone to purple leaf spot in the fall, especially if plants are container grown. From a cross made in 1963. Tested as CAES ×122 plt. 11.

RASPBERRY GLOW (R. A. Jaynes, *CAES Mimeo List,* 1984) Selected 1979 and commercially propagated by Bolton Technologies, Bolton, Connecticut, 1985. From a 1974 controlled cross of a deep pink flowered plant (319) with pollen of 'Pink Charm'. A deep burgundy-red in bud, opening with a great deal of color on the inside of the corolla and fading to a medium pink. Good color in partial shade. Foliage dark green, habit excellent; stems of new growth purplish red. Tested as CAES ✕1203 plt. 35. Sibling of 'Nancy' and 'Sarah'. (Figure 3-26)

Figure 3-26. 'Raspberry Glow'. Flower buds can be a deep purplish red; open flowers are usually a raspberry-pink. (Jaynes)

Red-bud Invalid cultivar name. Common commercial name for cultivars with intense red colored buds, eg: 'Olympic Fire', 'Ostbo Red', and 'Nipmuck'.

RICHARD JAYNES (Briggs Nursery, Olympia, Washington, 1984 catalogue) This plant first flowered before 1965 and was selected by Edmund V. Mezitt, Weston Nurseries, Hopinton, Massachusetts. He named it in honor of Richard A. Jaynes in 1977. Weston Nurseries originally progagated the selection by grafting and sold the plant on a limited scale for many years. The flower buds are red to dark raspberry in color. The inside of the newly opened corolla has a silvery white cast over pink. The darker color of the buds seems to "bleed through" to the inside of the corolla giving a uniform dark pink to red color in a truss of fully open flowers. Ed Mezitt considered this plant a major breakthrough in his crossing-selection program because it was a "bleeder" and the first plant to show true progress toward becoming a "red" Mountain Laurel. It is a heavy, annual bloomer. Foliage is glossy, with an undulate or twisted blade. Stems of new growth and petioles are purplish red in color. (Figure 3-27)

Figure 3-27. 'Richard Jaynes'. Shown are the late Ed Mezitt, his son Wayne, and plants of 'Richard Jaynes' which Ed named in honor of the author. The flowers are red in bud and deeply pigmented open. (Jaynes)

Rosea Invalid cultivar name applied to plants with deeply pigmented flowers.

Rubra Invalid cultivar name applied to plants with deeply pigmented flowers.

SARAH (R. A. Jaynes, *Int. Plant Prop. Soc. Proc.* **32**: 431–434, 1982) CAES selection. Introduced by Knight Hollow Nursery, Madison, Wisconsin, 1983. Flowers red in bud and pink-red open, eye-catching in bud and open; reddest selection from CAES. The markings within the corolla are good and distinct. The foliage and habit are excellent. Petioles and young stems are purplish red. Plants do well in containers except browning of leaf tips and margins occurred late in the growing season with one grower. From a controlled cross of a deep pink flowered plant

Figure 3-28. 'Sarah'. Perhaps the closest to a red-flowered Mountain Laurel to date. The inner ring in the corolla is deeply pigmented; edge of older flowers rolls back. (Jaynes)

Figure 3-29. 'Sarah' is bright and eye-catching at a distance or up close. (Jaynes)

(319) with pollen of 'Pink Charm'. Tested as CAES ×1203 plt. 77. Sibling of 'Nancy' and 'Raspberry Glow'; seed parent of 'Kaleidoscope'. (Figures 3-28, 3-29)

SHARON ROSE (R. A. Jaynes, *Kalmia, The Laurel Book II*, 1987) Selected from seedlings of deeply pigmented Laurel of uncertain source, named, and propagated by Arthur A. Wright, Wright's Nursery, Canby, Oregon. Plants have been sold under this name since about 1980. Flowers buds are bright red, fading to pink when open, much like 'Ostbo Red'. The inside of the corolla is initially near-white becoming more pink. Plant habit is good, leaves are thick, broad and flat, and cuttings are comparitively easy to root.

Sheffield Park (G. Krüssmann, *Handbuch der Laubgeholze*, P. Parey, Berlin, 1962; W. J. Bean, *Trees and Shrubs*, Vol 2, G. Taylor *Ed.*, J. Murray, London, 1973) Reported as a cultivar by Krüssmann and strain by Bean. This is apparently a strain of pink-flowered plants grown by A. G. Soames at Sheffield Park, England, which in turn came from material grown at the Knap Hill Nursery.

SHOOTING STAR (R. A. Jaynes, *The Laurel Book*, 1975, color photo p. 40) Selected in 1972 by M. & H. Rogers from a native stand, Danbury, North Carolina. Commercially introduced by Briggs Nursery, Olympia, Washington, 1982. Corolla is cut to give five distinct lobes that reflex after the flower opens. Flowers about one week later than the species. Leaves broad, new growth yellow-green and plant somewhat less hardy than the species. Tested as CAES 325. Under the control of a single recessive gene [s]. (Figure 3-30)

SILVER DOLLAR (R. A. Jaynes, *The Laurel Book*, 1975, color photo p. 41) Weston Nurseries, Hopkinton, Massachusetts, selected 1952, introduced in 1977 catalog. Flowers up to 1½ in (4 cm) across, buds white to pink blush, attractive pigment markings within corolla. Leaves large, dark, and leathery. Field grown plants have good habit but plants grown in containers may do poorly. (Figure 3-31)

SNOWDRIFT (R. A. Jaynes, *Kalmia, The Laurel Book II*, 1987) A compact, densely foliaged, white-flowered selection of R. A. Jaynes. It is thickly branched, has dark green, broad leaves and grows at least as broad as tall. The seed parent was in a planting of white-flowered plants isolated by several hundred feet from other Mountain Laurel. The flowers have good substance and on close inspection faint reddish pigment markings on inside of corolla. Micro-propagated plants should be available in 1988. (Figure 3-32)

SPLENDENS (Exhibited by J. Veitch and Sons, 1890, *Jour. Royal Hort. Soc.* 12: 1 xxxix) R. DeBelder described plants growing at the Arboretum at Kalmthout, Belgium (*Jour. Royal Hort. Soc.* 94: 91, 1969), ". . . flowers deeper shade than the type but 'Clementine Churchill' is definitely the best for flower colouring." (Figure 3-33)

STAR CLUSTER (The Holden Arboretum, Mentor, Ohio, 1983) Originated in 1940 at C. O. Dester Estate, Sandwich, Massachusetts; selected,

Figure 3-30. 'Shooting Star' is a unique flower type discovered in 1971. It flowers about 10 days later than normal Mountain Laurel. (Rogers)

Figure 3-31. 'Silver Dollar' has flowers the size of a silver dollar or almost twice the diameter of normal Mountain Laurel. The inner pigmented ring and markings at the anther pockets add to the attractiveness of the flowers. (Jaynes)

Figure 3-32. 'Snowdrift' is a multistemmed, dense, compact, white flowered selection. (Jaynes).

Figure 3-33. 'Splendens', described in 1896 in England, is the oldest named cultivar. It represents what would be considered an excellent pink if found in the wild. The pigmented ring and markings on the inside of the corolla give the flower character. (Jaynes)

Figure 3-34. 'Star Cluster'. A banded selection that has shown greater tolerance of heavier soils than we usually associate with *Kalmia*. (Bristol, Holden Arboretum)

propagated from cuttings, and released by Holden Arboretum. A selection of f. *fuscata* similar to 'Fresca' but the banding is not as interrupted. The speckled, maroon band on the inside of the corolla contrasts with the otherwise white corolla and white buds. Foliage is dark green and the plant broadly spreading. It grows in clay soil amended with organic matter; cuttings apparently amenable to rooting. It is in the parentage of 'Freckles', 'Minuet', and 'Yankee Doodle'. Louis Lipp sent a banded plant in the early 1960's to R. A. Jaynes who used it in crosses. The plant was later named 'Star Cluster'. (Figure 3-34)

Star-ring Invalid cultivar name. Descriptive term for plants bearing flowers having an intensely pigmented ring within and near the base of the corolla with five spokes that radiate up the creases between the five corolla lobes. The trait appears to be under the control of a single dominant gene [Sr]. (Figure 14-7)

Figure 3-35. 'Stillwood' is a nearly pure white selection from New Hampshire. The buds show no blush even when grown in full sun. (Jaynes)

Figure 3-36. 'Tightwad'-like. This selection has the same characteristic as 'Tightwad'; the flowers never open and remain in good condition for several weeks. Photo was taken 2 weeks after flowers had reached full bud stage. (Jaynes)

STILLWOOD (R. A. Jaynes, *The Laurel Book,* 1975, color photo p. 38) R. A. Jaynes and H. I. Baldwin selected from a native stand, Russell Abbott Forest, Wilton, New Hampshire, in 1962. Commercially introduced by Knight Hollow Nursery, Madison, Wisconsin, 1983. Flower buds are white when grown in full sun and the flowers open white. Very faint ring near base of corolla. Pigment specks within corolla and near anther pockets may be visible on close inspection. Stems of new growth are yellow to yellow-green presenting a pleasing contrast to the light green foliage. Tested as CAES 149. (Figure 3-35)

SUNSET (R. A. Jaynes, *Kalmia, The Laurel Book II,* 1987) Selected and named in 1979 by R. Wayne Mezitt, Weston Nurseries, Hopkinton, Massachusetts. Propagated and sold at the nursery since 1985. The flower is bright red in bud and near-red open. The plant habit is low and spreading. Leaves are narrow and twisted with thick blades. Petioles and new stems are purplish red.

TIGHTWAD (R. A. Jaynes, *Kalmia, The Laurel Book II,* 1987) This plant was selected by H. Wright (deceased), Highlands, North Carolina and named by C. Towe, Walhalla, South Carolina. Cummins Garden, Marlboro, New Jersey is introducing the plant. It was apparently found in the wild in western North Carolina. Its noteworthy feature is the flowers which develop to the large bud stage, remain in good condition for a month beyond the normal bloom period, but never open. If grown in the sun the flower buds are a good pink. It is pollen and seed sterile, and the pistils are often short and fasciated. A plant very similar to this was discovered by E. D. Chappel in July, 1973, at Devil's Den, Weston, Connecticut. (Figure 3-36)

TWENTY (R. A. Jaynes, *Kalmia, The Laurel Book II,* 1987)—Grown from seed germinated in the 1950's by E. V. Mezitt, Weston Nurseries, Hopinton, Massachusetts, and selected by him in the 1960s. Propagated and sold at the nursery as #20 beginning in 1965. The plant is low and compact growing. Flowers are dark pink in bud and open to a medium pink. Foliage is glossy and dark green; leaves are long with a distinct fold along the center rib. The plant grows twice as wide as high. Open pollinated seedlings of this plant also tend to be more compact than the species.

WEDDING BAND (R. A. Jaynes, *Kalmia, The Laurel Book II,* 1987) Selected from a cross of 'Ostbo Red' and 'Fresca' by John Eichelser, Melrose Nursery, Olympia, Washington, 1984, and named by his daughter, Lori Eichelser Gangsei. She is propagating it and will introduce it in 1988. The buds are pink and open to reveal a solid maroon band (f. *fuscata*) of approximately ¼ in (6 mm) diameter. The band is comparable to 'Fresca' and 'Star Cluster'. The leaves are dark green, broad, and flat. The plant has a good branching habit. It is a sibling of 'Olympic Wedding'.

WILLOWCREST (R. A. Jaynes, *The Laurel Book,* 1975, photo p. 25) Named and propagated from a làrge plant at the Henry Foundation for Botanical Research, Gladwyn, Pennsylvania; originally collected by H. Wright, Highlands, North Carolina. A selection of f. *angustata.* Leaves narrowly oblanceolate to linear, giving the plant a graceful appearance. Buds medium pink opening to a pink blush, pollen sometimes aborted and pistil fasciated, occasionally flowers do not fully open. The form is very rare and under the control of a single recessive gene [*w*]. (Figure 3-37)

YANKEE DOODLE (R. A. Jaynes, CAES Mimeo List, 1984) Selected 1975 and first commercially propagated by Bolton Technologies, Bolton, Connecticut, 1985. This is a f. *fuscata* selection with red buds. Pinkish red in bud with a narrow, interrupted maroon band within which contrasts well with the white background color of the open corolla. The inner pigmented ring of the corolla is crisp and red in color. Foliage is somewhat yellow-green; petioles and new stems are blushed purplish red on the sun side. Originated from a second generation controlled cross (1969), the F_1 was made in 1963 (a cross of a banded and a red-budded plant, 'Star Cluster' and 187, respectively). Tested as CAES ×1028 plt. 8. (Figure 3-38)

K. angustifolia Linnaeus var. *angustifolia* Sheep Laurel, Lambkill

HAMMONASSET (R. A. Jaynes, *Int. Plant Prop. Soc. Proc.* 22: 489, 1972) Selected 1961 from a native stand, Madison, Connecticut, and commercially introduced in 1972. Flowers a rich, bluish rose. Mature height about 2 ft (60 cm), somewhat less than common for the species. (Figure 3-39)

Figure 3-37. 'Willowcrest' is a willow-leaved form collected in the southern Appalachians by H. Wright. (Jaynes)

Figure 3-38. 'Yankee Doodle', a red-budded selection that opens to reveal a narrow, sometimes interrupted band. (Jaynes)

Figure 3-39. 'Hammonasset', a bright flowered selection of Sheep Laurel. (Jaynes)

Pumila Invalid cultivar name applied to various selections of dwarf or low
   habit. Like the names Ovata, Nana, and Rubra, they are descriptive and
   do not have specific botanical or horticultural rank. I received a nice low
   growing plant under this name years ago from the Royal Botanic
   Garden, Edinburgh, Scotland (Figure 8-7).

f. *candida* Fern. (*Rhodora* 15: 151, 1913) White flowered, no anthocyanin. The
   presence of anthocyanin is controlled by a single dominant gene.
   (Figure 2-20)

K. *angustifolia* var. *caroliniana* (Small) Fern. Sheep Laurel, Lambkill
   (A white flowered form is known in cultivation similar to f. *candida*
   above.)

K. *cuneata* Michaux. White Wicky

K. *ericoides* Wright ex Griseb. var. *ericodes* Cuban Laurel

K. *ericoides* Wright ex Griseb. var. *aggregata* (Small) Ebinger Cuban Laurel

K. *hirsuta* Walt. Sandhill Laurel

K. *microphylla* (Hooker) Heller var. *microphylla* Alpine Laurel

K. *microphylla* var. *occidentalis* (Small) Ebinger Western Bog Laurel

f. *alba* Ebinger (*Rhodora* 76: 342, 1974) White flowering form collected near
   Wrangell, Alaska, and Lulu Island, British Columbia

K. *polifolia* Wang. Bog Laurel, Eastern Bog Laurel

f. *leucantha* Schofield & Smith (Canad. Field Nat. 67: 94, 1953) White
   flowering form known from one collection, Hodgewater Line,
   Newfoundland.

Hybrids

ROCKY TOP, K. *polifolia* × K. *microphylla* var. *microphylla* (R. A. Jaynes, *The
   Laurel Book*, 1975) From an F_1 cross, 1974, of plants from Mount
   Washington, New Hampshire, and Mount Adams, Washington, respec-
   tively. More tolerant of northeastern growing conditions than the
   Western Laurel. Intermediate habit, mature height 1–1½ ft (30–45 cm).
   Pollen and seed sterile, triploid. Susceptible to mites and not long lived
   in eastern gardens. Easy to root. Tested as CAES ×356h; not commer-
   cially propagated.

Chapter 4_____

THE SEEDS

Although a native of our woods, the cheapest and easiest mode of procuring [Mountain Laurel] plants is to import them from England, where they are raised from seed in large quantities. (Sprague 1871)

Laurel seed is small and requires careful handling for good germination. The seed of each species has a characteristic size and shape (Figures 4-1), and specific germination requirements. The Sandhill Laurel, *Kalmia hirsuta*, has the smallest seeds, as many as five million to the ounce (28 g), even smaller than those notoriously small-seeded garden flowers Petunia, Nicotiana, and Begonia.

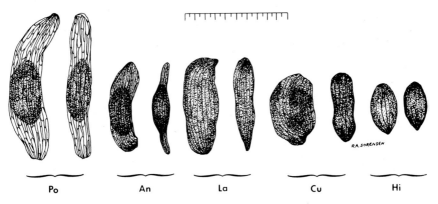

Figure 4-1. Drawings of typical seeds of 5 Laurel species. Po, Eastern Bog Laurel; An, Sheep Laurel; La, Mountain Laurel; Cu, White Wicky; Hi, Sandhill Laurel. The scale is 1 mm (1/25 in) in length. (Sorensen-Leonard)

SEED HARVEST AND CLEANING

Maturation of seed capsules, even in the same area, will vary by a few days from year to year. If capsules are harvested too soon, the seed will not be ripe or, even if mature enough to germinate, it may not shed readily from the capsule. As the capsules mature, they change from green to brown. If left on the plant too long, the capsule will dehisce (split) and scatter its seeds. Yet, with Mountain Laurel and Sheep Laurel it is often possible to extract a few seeds from capsules left on the plant in the spring or summer, six to nine months after they have ripened. The approximate flowering period, days to seed harvest, and harvest period for Connecticut are given in Figure 4-2. Each species is distinct from the others, either in time of flowering, time of seed harvest, period of flowering, or period required for seed maturation.

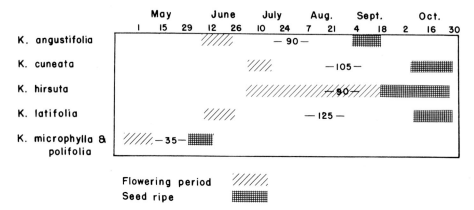

Flowering period

Seed ripe

Figure 4-2. Relative periods of flowering and seed ripening, and time from flowering to seed maturation in days. The dates are for Connecticut and will vary at other locations, but the general pattern will hold. Note an almost fourfold difference in the time required for Mountain Laurel seed to mature as compared with Eastern Bog and Western Laurel. Also note that Sandhill Laurel tends to be ever-blooming. (Jaynes)

To extract small quantities of seed, place the harvested capsules in a coin envelope or other small container and allow them to dry for a few days. The capsules will then open and seeds can be shaken loose. The seed will separate from the capsule but will be mixed with dust and chaff. Clean the seeds by gently funneling them down a trough-shaped piece of white paper and letting them fall a short distance onto another piece of paper. The chaff moves down the paper more slowly than the seed. With each pass some chaff can be discarded. Repeat the process several times and most of the chaff will separate from the seed.

I have often collected capsules from my controlled crosses too soon due to a fear of loosing seed from premature opening of the capsules on the plant. In such cases the seed is mature but it does not readily release from the capsule when dry. The solution is to crush the capsules on paper between table top and a small wooden block. The seed will have more debris in it and the cleaning will be more laborious with this method, but the seed can be recovered.

Large quantities of dirty seed can be shaken through sieves. Most Mountain Laurel seed will pass through a 0.5 mm round-holed sieve. I use a #1 (0.508) and #2 (0.610) sieve obtained from D. Ballauf Mfg. Co., 126 Lafayette Ave., Laurel, Maryland 20707. Even with this method a final cleaning on white paper is recommended, because any debris left with the seed increases chances of contamination and will support fungal growth at the time of germination.

The specific gravity of Laurel seed is taken advantage of with other cleaning methods. Seedsmen could use commercial air separators to winnow the heavier, viable seed from the dust and chaff. Alternatively, the fresh, filled Mountain Laurel seed can be placed in water, where the chaff and unfilled seeds float while the viable seeds sink to the bottom. Decant the debris and remove the good seed and dry for sowing.

SEED STORAGE AND LONGEVITY

Laurel seed maintains its viability for several years if stored under cool, dry conditions. I store seed in glassine or coin envelopes in unsealed trays in a household, frost-free refrigerator at 40°F (5°C).

Exact longevity for species is difficult to determine because of variability among seed lots, and departures from ideal storage conditions. Mountain Laurel seed is long-lived. Of 28 lots of seed stored more than 10 years, 75% had a germination percentage above 50%. It came as a surprise to me that such small seed would stay alive so long. Numerous tests suggest that Mountain Laurel seed kept dry and refrigerated remains in good condition for 15 years and possibly longer. Some seed stored 20 years is still capable of producing seedlings.

Tests with the other species were less extensive: *K. angustifolia* 1 lot, stored 16 years, 22% germination; *K. polifolia* 10 lots, stored 8–17 years, only 3 lots germinated, 8 years—51%, 12 years—27%, and 15 years—59%; *K. cuneata* 2 lots stored 3 and 10 years, 29 and 46% germination respectively; *K. hirsuta* 8 lots, stored 7–16 years, the only germination was less than 1% for each of 2 lots stored 14 years. Thus, except for *K. hirsuta*, the evidence suggests that seed of these other species can, like Mountain Laurel, also be stored for many years and remain viable.

GENERAL REQUIREMENTS FOR GERMINATION AND EARLY GROWTH

The best temperature for germination and initial growth is between 70–75°F (21–24°C). Constant temperatures above 80°F (27°C) reduce survival, whereas temperatures below 70°F (21°C) slow growth dramatically (Figure 4-3). A cool, wet germination and growing medium, especially during cloudy, low-light periods in winter may result in ammonia buildup and root injury.

Various media can be used for germination, including pure peat moss or milled sphagnum moss. I prefer the following for small batches

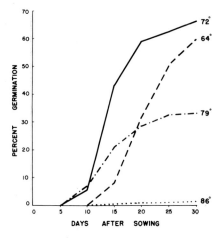

Figure 4-3. Seed germination of Mountain Laurel at 4 temperatures: 64, 72, 79, and 86°F (19, 21, 23 and 25°C). Note particularly the low germination percentage at the two high temperatures. (Jaynes 1971e)

of seed germinated in closed, but not airtight, plastic boxes (proportions by volume):

3 parts Canadian peat (screened ¼ in (6 mm))
2 parts perlite (screened ⅛ in (3 mm))
3 parts milled sphagnum moss

This mix has a pH of about 4.2. If milled sphagnum is not available use a mix of 2 to 3 parts peat to 1 part perlite. By using a medium without soil one minimizes the danger from soil-borne pathogens, and, in adddition, the peat and sphagnum moss contribute some antibiotic activity. Clear plastic boxes, 3½ × 7 × 1¾ in (9 × 18 × 4 cm) high and placed 9–12 in (23–30 cm) below fluorescent lights have served me well. Certainly, a variety of other metal and plastic containers can be substituted. Trays without clear tops can be placed in clear plastic bags. A few pencil sized holes will allow for air exchange without excessive drying. Large quantities of seed can be germinated in standard flats.

These and other mixes exhibit an unusual property; when stored they do not support good seed germination and growth. Though difficult to believe, this virtually aseptic, nonsoil mix, stored nearly dry, deteriorated as a germination medium in a few months. I have observed this deterioration of the medium time and again, and one of my colleagues, who uses a quite different medium for germinating gloxinias, has had the same difficulty with his stored mixes. Possibly the natural antibiotic qualities of the sphagnum moss and peat oxidize and deteriorate when mixed with other materials. This could account for the growth of fungi and a marked decrease in germination and initial vigor of seedlings. So, my advice is not to prepare more germination mix than will be used within two months.

The mix used in the small germination boxes is not entirely satisfactory for seed germination in flats, for in the larger, deeper trays greater compaction occurs resulting in less internal drainage and aeration. This deficiency of seedling mixes is common and typically indicated by rapid growth of seedlings around the edge and stagnation in the center of the container. Here are two mixes that have worked well for germination of seed in flats:

2 bu (70 l) peat
1 bu (35 l) perlite
½ bu (17 l) coarse sand (optional)
1 oz (28 g) hydrated lime
    and
1 bu (35 l) peat moss
1 bu (35 l) milled sphagnum moss
1 bu (35 l) perlite
1 oz (28 g) hydrated lime

After filling the flats, gently firm the surface with a board. Wet the medium thoroughly prior to sowing by setting the flats in a shallow tray of water (you can make one with a sheet of plastic placed on a level surface and bounded by 2-in (5 cm)-high boards). If you water the mix directly from above, it may compact and leave a layer of perlite on top. If the surface appears too rough, sprinkle a thin layer of milled sphagnum on it.

Germination problems occur with *Kalmia* seeding mixes containing high portions of vermiculite. If you use vermiculite in the mix keep the proportion to 15 % or less by volume.

The seeds should be sown on the surface of the mix and *not covered*. They need light and will not germinate in the dark. A moist medium and high humidity are necessary for germination. Once the seed is germinated and well rooted, the surface of the medium should be allowed to dry occasionally to retard algal and moss growth.

It is not necessary to fertilize the mix until true leaves are formed. Then sprinkle on a solution of soluable fertilizer, such as 20-20-20 prepared at the rate of 1 t/gal (5 g/4 l). After the first application, sprinkle more on at 2- and 3-week intervals, testing the mix from time to time to prevent overfertilizing and to detect a possible imbalance of nutrients or a pH change.

The seedlings can be left in flats for more than 2 months if they do not become too crowded or matted by algae and moss (Figure 4-4). Remember that, once the seeds have germinated and developed roots, the surface of the medium should be allowed to dry every few days. Dithane M-45 (6 oz/1000 sq ft or 1 t/13 sq ft (1.8 g/sq m) can be used to control algae, but use it sparingly. Heavy applications may injure the seedlings. Should a heavy mat of algae and moss form, it is best to transplant the seedlings, leaving behind as much of the algae and moss as possible.

Most seeds will germinate in 10 to 21 days. Light intensity should

Figure 4-4. Flats of Mountain Laurel seedlings being grown in a commercial green-house. Recently sown seeds at left are covered with newspaper to give shade and lessen drying. (Jaynes)

be a least 110 foot-candles (50 einsteins/m /sec). A pair of closely spaced standard fluorescent tubes with a white reflector will furnish this much light when placed 9–12 in (23–30 cm) above the seeds. The bulb length will depend on the area to be covered. Intensity of fluorscent tubes drops sharply near the ends, thus distribution of light is better with an 8 ft (2.4 m) fixture than with two 4 ft (1.2 m) fixtures.

When growing the seedlings indoors, I have used 16 hours of light, from 8 am to midnight. In the greenhouse during the winter I extend the day length with 75-watt floodlights from 10 pm to 2 am. These incandescent lights are used not to increase growth (by photosynthesis) but to keep the seedlings from becoming dormant. The reflector bulbs are spaced every 4 ft (1.2 m), 30 in (75 cm) above the plants, so that the plants receive only 8 to 10 foot-candles of artificial light in the middle of the night. To save energy the lights can be set by timers to "flash" on 5 seconds every minute. The plants will still per-ceive that the days are long as in the spring and grow accordingly.

Experiments with Mountain Laurel and Sheep Laurel seed demonstrate that germination can be hastened by starting the seeds under an atmosphere enriched with carbon dioxide (CO_2). The benefit of CO_2 on increasing plant growth is well-known and is discussed in the next chapter, but its effect on stimulating germination is less well under-stood. The translucent seed coats of laurel allow the seed leaves to green up, and in the presence of high CO_2 levels their development and growth is speeded up, resulting in faster germination.

Time of Sowing

Seeds from even late-maturing species can be harvested and cleaned by late fall. They should be planted indoors under lights by December 1 so that by late spring husky seedlings will have developed. Then they can be moved outdoors and will continue to thrive throughout the normal growing season.

An alternative is to sow the seed outdoors in the spring after the soil warms up. The seed should still be sown in flats and shaded from full sun. Protect the plants from extreme cold the first winter by placing the flats in a cold frame or covering them with conifer branches. If the seedlings are large enough (1 ½+ in (4 cm) tall) they can be bedded out the following spring.

MYCORRHIZA—FUNGI ASSOCIATED WITH THE ROOTS

Many species, especially in the Ericaceae, have fungi that are intimately associated with the roots, and are called symbiotic mycorrhiza. These fungi are dependent on the plant, and in turn they may in some way assist the plant in assimilating nutrients and water or in preventing attacks by other fungi. Indeed, *Kalmia* plants have been described as normally having mycorrhizal associates within (endophyte) and outside (ectophyte) the roots. They are not carried in the seed or on any other parts of the plant growing above ground.

A helpful paper by William Flemer of Princeton, New Jersey, deals with isolating these fungi and growing Mountain Laurel seedlings with and without them. Under sterile conditions he isolated pure cultures of various root-associated fungi and then inoculated the root area of aseptically grown seedlings with them. He observed a positive growth response by the seedlings to the presence of the most commonly isolated endophyte. On the basis of Flemer's work one may conclude that there is an important mycorrhizal association beneficial to the growth of Mountain Laurel.

I have not repeated Flemer's experiments and take no special measures to inoculate seedlings. In fact, I do not use soil, a possible source of mycorrhizal inoculum, in the germinating mix, because it is also a source of pathogenic fungi. However, the beneficial organism may be present in peat or sphagnum, and the plants may thus become naturally inoculated. It is also possible that mycorrhizal association does not occur and/or is less important to seedling growth in more complex media than in the sterile defined environment of the laboratory. More research in both laboratory and field is needed to determine how to manage these fungi to our benefit in growing seedlings.

THE SEEDS AND THEIR GERMINATION

Western Laurel, *K. microphylla;* Eastern Bog Laurel, *K. polifolia;* and Sheep Laurel, *K. angustifolia*

These three species are the easiest to germinate, because their seed has no strong dormancy requirement. There has been just a hint of partial dormancy in Sheep Laurel seed from plants of the southern part of the range. Interestingly, these species, with no special pregermination requirements are the ones with elongated and wing-like seeds (Figures 4-1). Dormancy may be related to the tighter, harder-appearing seed shape, but then the relationship may be entirely coincidental. The number of seeds per capsule varies from a few up to about 200 in the Western Laurel and Eastern Bog Laurel and 300 in Sheep Laurel. The number of seeds per capsule is less when pollination is poor or when there are an excessive number of flowers on a plant.

Mountain Laurel, *K. latifolia*

Fresh Mountain Laurel seed will germinate without any special treatment. However, cold stratification for 8 weeks or merely soaking the seeds overnight in 200 ppm (parts per million) gibberellin (a naturally occuring plant hormone) increases germination 50%. Seed stored for a year or two will germinate even better than fresh seed, because simple dry storage overcomes the partial dormancy requirement of fresh seed.

Dormancy requirements probably evolved as an adaption to prevent all the seed from germinating at once in the wild. For example, if there were an extended warm period in the fall after the seed capsules had split, then only the seed without a dormancy requirement would be able to germinate; the rest would remain quiescent during the winter until favorable conditions occurred in the spring.

Treatment of Mountain Laurel seed is necessary or valuable only when seed is in short supply, as that from controlled crosses, or when the expectation is that germination percentages of fresh seed will be abnormally low. Untreated fresh seed usually has a 20–50% germination rate in 3 to 4 weeks. By treating with gibberellin, germination is greater and a bit faster, and emergence is more uniform (Figure 4-5).

Mountain Laurel seed has a ribbed or striated surface. It weighs more than Sandhill and White Wicky seed, about 1.4 million seeds per ounce (28 g). Even seeds from one plant may vary considerably in size, and most capsules contain between 100 and 250 seeds, but some with more than 400 seeds have been observed.

In the wild, Mountain Laurel seeds germinate on bare mineral soil or on low growing moss. Since the soil cannot be allowed to dry, seedlings are commonly found on north-facing slopes of road cuts with mature plants above; the source of the seed that is dispersed by gravity and wind. Some long distance spread occurs from the release of seed in winter when it is blown across the surface of hard packed snow.

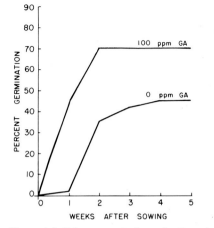

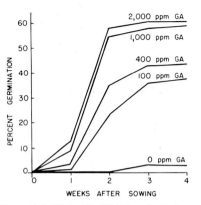

Figure 4-5. Enhancement of germination of Mountain Laurel seed with gibberellin (GA). Note 45% of the untreated seed germinated while about 70% of the GA treated seed did so. As with the White Wicky seed, gibberellic acid substitutes for the effect of longer cold stratification that occurs in nature. Rates of GA higher than 100 to 200 ppm cause excessive elongation of the seedlings. (Jaynes 1971c)

Figure 4-6. Gibberllin (GA) breaks the dormancy of White Wicky seed. It is a substitute for the effects of cold stratification that occur in nature during winter. Instead of treating the seed for 8 weeks with moist cold, it can be treated for 24 hours on blotting paper wetted with a solution of GA. (Jaynes 1971c)

White Wicky, *K. cuneata*

Freshly harvested seed of White Wicky has a poor rate of germination, usually less than 5%. However, seed treated in a moist-cold environment (stratified) for 8–16 weeks shows a tenfold germination increase. To stratify such fine seed, mix them with a small quantity of moist sand and place them in a refrigerator at a constant temperature of 40°F (4°C). Or simply sow the seed on the moistened germination mix, and refrigerate at 40°F (4°C). The latter technique works well for small quantities of seed sown in small plastic containers taped shut to prevent evaporation during the cold treatment. Seed harvested in late fall or winter has often been naturally stratified enough to satisfy the dormancy requirement.

A short treatment with giberellin can be used instead of the stratification procedure. A solution of 500 to 1000 ppm of gibberellin is effective (Figure 4-6). Before sowing the seeds, place them on a piece of filter or blotting paper saturated with the gibberellin solution for 12–24 hours. The effect on germination is the same as if they had received 8 weeks of moist-cold treatment. Since it is difficult to remove the seed from the wet paper immediately after treatment, let the paper and seeds dry. Then the seed simply will roll off the paper and can be handled normally.

The White Wicky seed capsules (Figure 4-7) hold as many as 200 seeds; the average is closer to 100. They are so small that aproximately 1.7 million seeds weigh only 1 oz (28 g).

Figure 4-7. White Wicky in late fall after the leaves have dropped. The seed capsules are suspended on gracefully curved peduncles. (Jaynes)

Sandhill Laurel, *K. hirsuta*

This species exhibits the most unusual requirement for germination, and its seed is the most difficult to germinate. The seed is incredibly small; as many as 5 million to the ounce (28 g). There are only a few other plants in the world with such minute seeds. Yet, because they are round they roll easily on paper and so can be readily separated from the chaff. The difficulty with this seed is in fulfilling the dormancy requirement to insure germinatiion. Seed sown on the usual mix will not germinate for 3 or more months, often with less than 20% success.

I have improved success by treating the seed with heat-humidity prior to sowing. Seeds were placed in small open vials set in a closed jar containing ½ in (12 mm) of water. These jars were then heated in an incubator or constant-temperature water bath. The higher the temperature, the shorter the treatment time (Figure 4-8). At the unusually high temperature of 176°F (80°C), the seed need only be treated for 10–20 minutes. Yet at 140°F (60°C) the treatment had to continue for about 12 hours. Treatments up to temperatures of 194°F (90°C) were effective but dangerous, because boiling kills the seeds. Seed treated with a solution of gibberellin (2000 ppm) for 48 hours had a positive effect on the germination of both untreated and heat-treated seeds.

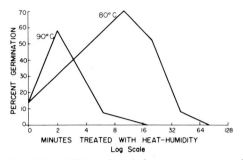

Figure 4-8. Germination of Sandhill Laurel seed after treatment at near-boiling temperatures (90°C = 194°F and 80°C = 176°F) and high humidity. Even with this treatment, seed of Sandhill Laurel germinates slowly. The data shown are 11 weeks after sowing. Germination of the other laurel species, by comparison, is usually complete within 3–4 weeks. (Jaynes 1971c)

This heat-humidity treatment that stimulates *K. hirsuta* seed germination would surely kill seeds of most other plants. During the early stages of these seed germination experiments I corresponded with T. S. Shinn of Leicester, North Carolina, who had been frustrated in his many attempts to germinate Sandhill Laurel. I explained what we were doing and, using his oven, he treated the seed at about 176°F (80°C) for 20 minutes. And, thus, he succeeded in germinating Sandhill Laurel for the first time. I was delighted to learn that we were not dealing with a mere laboratory effect.

Heat-humidity treatments with Sandhill Laurel have been performed many times, and, although often successful, they are unfortunately not always effective. Therefore other treatments need to be worked out that will assist us in obtaining maximum, fast, reliable germination with this species. One thing I have noted is that untreated seed, which has a low germination rate in plastic boxes under lights, will often germinate after several weeks on the surface of the same medium when watered regularly in a flat in a greenhouse. Perhaps either sunlight, bacterial action, or leaching of water triggered germination.

This unusual dormancy requirement of Sandhill Laurel seed could have evolved in the natural envirmonment as a response to recurrent ground fires. During a fire, soil temperatures in the upper ¼ in (6 mm) often reach 170°F (77°C). Humidity and vapor pressure in the top layer of soil increase as the fire passes, because water vapor is forced downward from the burning litter and condenses there, like vapor in an inverted still. A seed adapted to germinate after a fire would find itself on a seedbed of bare mineral soil. It would be relatively free of competition, since the fire would destroy seeds of most other plants on or near the soil surface. Yet, after a ground fire, shade from large shrubs and especially trees would frequently be present. This shade would lessen temperature extremes and moisture stress on young seedlings and thus benefit their survival.

Fire is accepted in the southeastern coastal plain as a natural part of the environment. Other plants in the area are adapted to fire, although often not in the same way. Longleaf Pine, for example, loses its competitive advantage unless there are occasional ground fires which kill many plants but neither the very young pine seedlings nor large pine trees. Giant Sequoias with their fire-resistant bark are also at a disadvantage without occasional ground fires to destroy competition. Lodgepole, Jack, and similar pines depend on the heat of fires to open their cones for seed release.

The unique dormancy requirement of Sandhill Laurel seed may have been a key factor in the spread of *Kalmia* onto the coastal plain. If this is true, then the Cuban Laurel, *K. ericoides,* which represents a further extension of the genus, might have a similar seed dormancy requirement.

*Chapter 5*_____

GROWING THE SEEDLINGS

. . . the annual growth of 20 wild seedlings under a forest cover averaged only 10 mm [3/8 in]. (Kurmes 1961)

With Laurel, especially Mountain Laurel, the time from sowing to flowering may seem interminable. Improved techniques to speed growth of the seedlings and to bring about early flower bud formation are always welcomed. Yet, too much kindness, such as the high fertilizer rates used for faster growing plants, will do Laurel in.

MEDIUM AND SPACING

To insure the best growth, seedlings should be transplanted 2–6 months after germination. However, nurseries commonly leave their plants in the flats for a full year after germination which probably delays time until flowering an additional year. If the seed is sown in late fall in a greenhouse or indoors under lights, the seedlings should be ready for transplanting in mid-winter. I generally prick them off with forceps when they have 2–3 true leaves and space them 1½–2 in (4–5 cm) apart in a flat. I use a dibble board the size of the flat with 60 to 80 nails equally spaced to mark the position for planting each seedling. The choice of mix varies from grower to grower; I have found both of the following satisfactory for small transplants:

> 1 bu (35 l) peat moss
> 1 bu (35 l) perlite
> 1/5 bu (7 l) soil (Vapam treated)
> 1–2 T (15–30 g) hydrated lime
> 1 T (15 g) 20-20-20 soluble fertilizer watered in
>   or
> 2 bu (70 l) peat
> 1 bu (35 l) perlite
> ½ bu (17 l) coarse sand
> ½–1 oz (15–30 g) hydrated lime
> 1 T (15 g) 20-20-20 soluble fertilizer watered in

(Sprinkle approximately every 3 weeks with 1 t/gallon (1.2 g/l) of 20-20-20 fertilizer)

The small amount of lime adds some calcium and raises the pH of the mix a bit above the 4.2 of the peat moss. The hydrated lime is more active and faster acting than regular limestone. When using limestone, use one-third more material than for hydrated lime. Soil is a highly variable component and introduces certain risks for that reason; however it does increase the exchange and buffering capacity of the media.

OPERATION HEADSTART—FERTILIZING THE AIR

Enrichment of the atmosphere around seedlings with carbon dioxide (CO_2) is an economical means of achieving a dramatic increase in plant size. Carbon dioxide is an essential raw material for plant growth, and its low ambient concentration is often the critical factor limiting plant growth. Ambient air contains 300–350 ppm CO_2, but some plants may use up to ten times that amount. An increased Laurel seed germination rate and a large increase in seedling size were achieved by exposing the sown seeds for 7 weeks to an atmosphere of 2000 ppm CO_2 (Figure 5-1).

Figure 5-1. Mountain Laurel seedlings 7 weeks from sowing. The plants on the left were exposed to normal air and most have only one true leaf, whereas the plants on the right, exposed to 2000 ppm CO_2, are much larger and many have 4 true leaves (white line is 0.4 in or 1 cm). (Jaynes)

Greenhouse operators have used enriched CO_2 atmospheres for many years, and therefore several techniques are available to increase CO_2 concentration. CO_2 generators burning propane gas are used in large greenhouses. One of three methods are used in greenhouses smaller than 20×50 ft (6×15 m): dry ice, compressed gas, or combustion (Mastalerz 1969). Each has its advantages and disadvantages. The source of the CO_2 makes no difference to the plants, unless, of course, it contains toxic impurities, something not likely with any of these methods. Plants themselves give off CO_2 at night or on dark, overcast days and utilize a CO_2 enriched atmosphere only on bright or sunny days. The CO_2 source therefore need be operated only during the day and only on days when the greenhouse vents are closed most of the time. Generally winter is the most practical time to add CO_2 to the atmosphere of growing plants.

An increased concentration of CO_2 alone will not stimulate plant growth. Other conditions—light, nutrients, and temperature must be equally favorable. We have found that 600 foot-candles (250 einsteins/m^2/sec at 400 to 700 nm) are required for good growth with CO_2 enrichment. This level was attained in the laboratory with high-output fluorescent tubes and in the greenhouse by supplementing natural daylight in winter with fluorescent light to extend day length and to supplement daylight on cloudy days. Somewhat lower light intensities are adequate in normal air, but of course growth is reduced. Low light intensity produces spindly seedlings.

The most advantageous time to expose Laurel to an enriched CO_2 atmosphere is from seed germination until after several true leaves are formed—that is, from December until March. Many seedlings can be handled in a relatively small space, and the rapid increase in plant size in the first few months is of utmost importance in reducing the time until the plants reach flowering age. Obtaining a 3-in (7.5 cm) plant from seed outdoors under natural conditions takes 2–3 years, whereas the same size can be realized in a single winter and spring under controlled greenhouse conditions. With a winter headstart the young seedlings are already "one-year-size" or more in May and are ready to take advantage of the full growing season outdoors.

Dry Ice

Dry ice is CO_2 in the solid state. It is more expensive than some other means of providing CO_2, but it is pure and relatively easy to handle. For example, it can be stored in a home freezer. The daily requirement for each 100 sq ft (9 sq m) of greenhouse floor space is about 1¾ lbs (0.8 kg). To obtain even distribution, place the required amount in equal portions on the walkway three or four times during the day, or use an open insulated box which allows slower evaporation and requires only a single placement in the morning.

Compressed Gas in Cylinders

Carbon dioxide may also be purchased as a compressed gas in cylinders. The gas itself is relatively inexpensive, but the required flow meter, pressure regulator, solenoid valve, and time clock add up to a considerable initial expense (Figure 5-2). The system is usually regulated by a time clock which opens the valve shortly after sunrise and closes it an hour before sunset. Large cylinders contain 60 lbs (27 kg) of CO_2 or about 522 cu ft (150 kl). A flow rate of 1½–2 cu ft (40–55 l) of CO_2 per hour per 1200 sq ft (110 sq m) of greenhouse will yield about 2000 ppm CO_2. If CO_2 is fed for 9 hours a day at this rate to an area of 100 sq ft (9 sq m), then a large cylinder will last 4–6 weeks.

Figure 5-2. Experimental equipment for passing CO_2-enriched air over germinating seedlings: air pump, CO_2 tank, mixing valve, flow meters, and plastic covered chambers containing seed flats. (Jaynes)

Alcohol Burning

The least expensive and perhaps simplest means of supplying CO_2 is to burn methyl or ethyl alcohol. To obtain 2000 ppm CO_2 per 100 sq ft (9 sq m) of greenhouse space, 2–3 fluid oz (60–90 ml) of ethanol or 3–4 oz (90–120 ml) of methanol must be burned per nine-hour day. To lessen the danger of fire, a kerosene lantern or similar device is used to enclose the alcohol flame. A small lamp with a ¼ in (6 mm) diameter wick and low flame burns about 1 oz (30 ml) of alcohol in nine hours. One disadvantage of the combustion method is the production of heat and water vapor. Neither ia a serious problem, unless the heat necessitates increased ventilatiion which would disperse the CO_2. In large greenhouses it is practical to partition off, with clear plastic curtains, the area where CO_2 enrichment is desired.

The actual concentrations of CO_2 achieved with any one of the preceding methods will vary somewhat depending on the height and tightness of the greenhouse. Anything between 400 and 3000 ppm will help the plants. If the 2000 ppm is maintained, you should have no qualms about working in the enriched atmosphere.

Most laboratory devices for measuring CO_2 concentration are expensive and cumbersome. However, there are moderately priced gas detectors adequate for greenhouses. (The Bendix Gastec Detector is distributed by Lindy Division) Union Carbide and the Kitagawa Kit is distributed by Matheson; see "Gas-industrial" in the Yellow Pages for local addresses of distributors.) Growers of large numbers of plants should consider such a device.

Carbon dioxide provides only one of the needs of growing plants. The others should not be neglected, especially in the enriched atmosphere. In fact, when the CO_2 concentration is increased, plants are able to utilize more light and nutrients. So take full advantage of the enriched atmosphere by paying careful attention to supplying sufficient light, maintaining the right temperature, and adding adequate nutrients and water. With careful management the grower enjoys substantially larger grown plants in much less time. Check with the floriculture specialist in a nearby state university for more information and suggestions on the use of CO_2 to stimulate plant growth.

A Tonic for Laggards

Despite attempts to provide the proper environment, growth of Mountain Laurel seedlings may stagnate two or three months after germination. Such seedlings can be stimulated to elongate and grow by spraying them once or twice with a 200 ppm water solution of gibberellic acid (Gibrel—80% potassium gibberellate, Merck Chemical Division). But locate and correct the cause for the poor growth. Likely causes are low temperature, crowding, insufficient nutrients, low light, short days.

GROWING IN CONTAINERS

For the nurseryman, growing plants in containers has proven one of the best ways to obtain optimal growth of plants. Containers are easy to plant; digging and burlapping are eliminated; and the mechanics of the operation become almost independent of weather. In addition, more plants can be grown per unit area. However, mass growing of plants in containers is relatively new and certainly in its infancy for Laurel. Growing in containers allows less room for error than field growing. The plants have to be watched and tended more closely. For every nurseryman who has been successful with Mountain Laurel in containers, there are two who have had problems. The requirements, in general, are the same as for other ericaceous plants with only slight modifications in media, fertilizer, and watering. The medium must be well drained and have an acid pH. Nutrients must be available but not in high concentrations. The problem of yellowing of the last flush of growth in the early fall is common and can be reduced, if not eliminated, by maintaining good aeration, adding chelated iron (e.g., Sequestrene), and keeping a good balance between available nitrogen and potassium.

There is little agreement about a proper container media for Laurels. Media used vary from straight peat moss to straight pine bark. Either of these are likey to make it difficult to establish the plants in the landscape in soil.

The work of Dr. Henry DeRoo of the Connecticut Agricultural Experiment Station confirms the need for good drainage and aeration. This statement is so often repeated in horticultural literature that it has lost its impact, but growers of Mountain Laurel had best heed it. DeRoo found that the standard container media for growing Ericaceous material in two large nursery firms caused chlorotic Mountain Laurel plants within two months. The basic ingredients of these mixes were:

(A)   2 parts Canadian peat moss
    2 parts native peat (muck)
    1 part sand
    1 part perlite
(B)   1 part native peat
    1 part sand.

Rhododendrons and Azaleas grew in these mixes. A third commercial medium to which the Laurel responded much more favorably was:

(C)   1 part Canadian peat moss
    1 part sand
    2 parts bark (mixed hardwood)

The bark assured good drainage. The experimental mix that proved best of all was:

(D)   2 parts Canadian peat
    1 part sand
    1 part bark

Additional nutrients were added to each cubic yard (0.75 cu m) of this mix as follows:

2 lbs (0.9 kg) dolomitic limestone
3 lbs (1.3 kg) gypsum (landplaster)
2½ lbs (1.1 kg) 20 % superphosphate
1½ lbs (0.7 kg) ureaform
1 oz (28 g) New Iron (chelated iron)
2 oz (56 g) trace elements.

All the mixes in the experiment had a pH of 5.0 to 5.5 and were fertilized weekly according to need as determined by a soil test. A mix intermediate to C and D, having equal parts of peat, sand, and bark was also satisfactory.

Note that all of the mixes are what is called "artificial", that is none of them contain soil. The drawback to any medium containing soil, other than drainage and pathogens, is the difficulty in obtaining soil of the same quality from year to year. For these reasons soil is best avoided in commercial production.

Fertilizer requirements depend on the medium and local growing conditions. Nutrients can be supplied through the irrigation water, applied on top of the medium, or mixed in the medium at the time of potting. Slow-release fertilizers such as Osmocote (14-14-14) last longer and require less frequent application. Laurel is not a "heavy feeder"; hence apply less, perhaps one-fourth of the label-recommended application which is generally based on heavier-feeding, faster-growing plants. The soil should be tested regularly and the pH kept at about 4.8 to 5.5.

Follow the methods outlined in Table 5-1 to grow handsome, budded plants in 3 years: one winter inside and 3 growing seasons outdoors (Figures 5-3, 5-4, 5-5, 5-6).

Figure 5-3. Cutting grown Mountain Laurel after the second growing season and over-wintered in a hoop house. (Jaynes)

Table 5-1 Schedule from Sowing to Flowering

I. Indoors—greenhouse or bank of lights needed
  A. Sow before December 1 (at least 150 foot-candles of light and a temperature of 70–75°F (21–24°C) required).
  B. Enrich with CO_2 within 2 weeks (light intensity of 500–2000 foot-candles suggested).
  C. Transplant seedlings after 8 weeks (February).
  D. Maintain enriched CO_2 for another 4–8 weeks.
  E. Transplant 1–2 in (3–5 cm) seedlings about June 1 to:
    1. lath house or protected bed; or
    2. place in containers. (20–50% shade for 1+ months)
  F. Prune in late winter, early spring to get low branching.
  G. 1. After 2 years in lath house transplant in early spring to field.
    2. Where winters are harsh, overwinter containers in unheated, plastic-film-covered shelters and transplant to larger containers in spring if necessary.
  H. Leave until budded and then transplant to permanent location or sell.
  Time span for Mountain Laurel from seed to budded plants should be 3–5 years, depending on how carefully optimum conditions were maintained.

II. Outdoors
  A. Sow in early spring on bare, mineral soil, shaded to prevent the surface from drying, or sow on mix in flats.
  B. Cover seedlings with straw or conifer branches in late fall or protect flats of seedlings in cold frame.
  C. Transplant from seed bed or flats in spring when plants are 1+ in (2.5+ cm) tall and space out in protected beds or plant in containers (see E–H above).

Figure 5-4. Temporary structures for overwintering evergreen plants grown in containers in cold temperate climates. They are pipe-hoop houses covered with plastic sheeting put on in November or early December and removed in spring. Plants can be shipped any time during the year, and winter burn of foliage is virtually eliminated. (Jaynes)

Figure 5-5. Mountain Laurel propagated from cuttings and growing in containers. (Jaynes)

Figure 5-6. Two-year-old Mountain Laurel seedlings transplanted in early spring and mulched with wood chips. To aid in weed control, granular simazine was applied at a rate of 3 lbs (1.4 Kg) active material per acre (0.45 hect) with a cyclone spreader after a few heavy rains had settled the soil and plants. (Jaynes)

PRUNING SMALL PLANTS

Pruning is an integral part of growing seedlings. Attractive structure of mature plants is dependant on branches formed near the ground. This is accomplished in the case of most Mountain Laurel by pruning young plants. Pruning during the cold-dormant season just before growth starts in the spring is the most effective means of stimulating multiple breaks. Pruning is preferably done at the end of the *first* dormant season. However, in the case of tissue culture started plants, or seedlings grown under lights in a greenhouse for up to 18 months, it is advisable to prune before that first dormant phase, i.e. when the plants are 1–2 in (3–5 cm) tall. Successive "pinchings" are usually required to obtain multiple breaks on growing plants. The amount to prune-off depends in part on legginess and height of the plant. Leave a few leaves below the pruning cut. On tall, spindly plants prune low enough so that the newly formed branches will be within a couple of inches (5 cm) of the soil.

GROWTH REGULATORS

Many growth regulators which improve habit or increase flowering are used in the commercial production of ornamental plants. Little is known about the effect of these compounds on the Laurels. At least the more promising should be tested on Mountain Laurel because of their potential value.

Off-Shoot-O, a chemical pinching agent, has been used successfully to "prune" the tips of Azaleas. This or a similar compound might be useful in preventing legginess in Mountain Laurel. Other growth retardants are capable of limiting vegetative growth and stimulating flower bud production. These should be particularly useful with plants that have been pushed hard for several years to obtain maximum size.

I had some success with Phosphon and CCC (Cycocel), growth retardants, when applied to Mountain Laurel seedlings in their third year of growth. The experiments were conducted using plants in containers and also in the field. Although more tests are needed, the following observations and tentative conclusions appear valid:

1. Phosphon at rates between 0.4–0.8 g per plant is effective in stimulating flower bud formation on seedlings in containers and in the field (Figure 5-7).

2. Combinations of Phosphon and CCC (0.4–0.6 g and 0.3 g, respectively, per plant) also were promising. Higher rates of CCC caused discoloration or injury to the leaves.

3. There was a dramatic difference in response depending on the pedigree (genotype) of 3-year-old plants. Seedlings of some crosses

produced no flowers regardless of treatment, whereas seedlings of the same size from different parents were quite responsive. As with other species, a certain minimum size has to be reached before flowering can be induced and that is dependent on genetic makeup. The plants had reached the critical size for Laurel, 8–10 in (20–25 cm) in height, early in their third growing season.

Figure 5-7. Mountain Laurel plants 2 years after treating with phosphon on the left and untreated on the right. Reduction of growth and increase in flowering was excessive. (Jaynes)

*Chapter 6*_____

VEGETATIVE PROPAGATION: TRADITIONAL METHODS

*In the woods its . . . shoots extend laterally to take advantage of the
side light and are often bent down by the dead leaves and branches
falling from the tree tops. Where the snow lies deep, it tends further to
weight them down, until finally many of them lie in contact with the
ground. Dead leaves and litter soon cover them and after a few years,
when the debris has rotted and become part of the soil, they take root
and give rise to new shoots. Where the contact with the parent is
broken new plants are formed. This is the process of natural layering.
Often, however, the contact is not broken, and thus the soil becomes
filled with a dense, widely ramified set of laurel roots, and the surface
becomes covered with a tangled mass of branches to the height of a
man's knees. This tangled mass excludes almost all other vegetation
from under the trees. (Buttrick 1924)*

Means to propagate plants at times seems only to be limited by the
imagination. We have discussed seed or sexual reproduction and in the
next chapter will describe tissue culture propagation. Here are covered
the age old methods of rooting cuttings, grafting, and layering.

PROPAGATION BY CUTTINGS

One of the most satisfactory means of multiplying selected woody
plants is to root stem cuttings. This popular method is used with Rhododendrons, Azaleas, and other ericaceous plants. Some Laurel species
root readily, but, unfortunately, Mountain Laurel is most intransigent.
But it can be done and refinements in technique promise continued
improvement. The situation is perhaps similar to that faced by Rhododendron propagators 30 years ago. Of the many cultivars available, only
a few responded to the commonly used techniques. Adaption and
more sophisticated use of auxins, mist, plastic tents, fog, plus improvement of stock, have greatly increased our ability to mass-produce
Rhododendron cultivars from cuttings. Some of these same techniques are applicable to Mountain Laurel, and progress will continue as
increased efforts are devoted to this species.

Facilities, Media, Temperature

Cuttings are most often rooted in a greenhouse, although a small "cold" frame with heating cables will do, and even an indoor case, where plants depend entirely on artificial light, can be used. Since cuttings obviously have no roots to absorb water, they must be exposed to high humidity. Most commonly, humidity is supplied as mist or fog over the cuttings or by enclosing the propagation bench with clear plastic film to form a humid chamber.

MIST PROPAGATION   The successful operation of an intermittent mist system depends on a good supply of non-alkaline water. Low-volume atomizing nozzles spaced 1–2 ft (30–60 cm) above the cutting bench insure good coverage of the cuttings (Figure 6–1). An electric valve (solenoid) can be regulated by any one of a number of available devices to control the mist and keep the foliage moist, without allowing the medium to become soggy.

Electic time clocks, electronic leaves, and evaporative pans can be used to regulate the cycling of the mist. One of the most satisfactory controls uses a photocell which makes the amount of mist dependent on the amount of light available. Thus when a cloud passes, the control immediately compensates by calling for less mist. Time clocks are insensitive to light and weather conditions; electronic leaves salt up; evaporative pans tend to stick or are too readily affected by air currents. The one disadvantage of photocell control is the initial expense; but if it prevents even one failure, it more than pays for itself. When a mist

Figure 6-1. Mist propagation of Laurel cuttings in a commercial greenhouse in winter. Heating pipes are under the bench, and the side walls trap the hot air and force heat up through bench and rooting medium. (Jaynes)

system must be left unattended for a few days, the photocell control is the most reliable.

Whatever control device is used, the correct amount of mist must be determined by observation and testing. On a sunny summer day the typical requirement would be 6 seconds of mist every 3 minutes, whereas on a winter day 6 seconds of mist every 15 minutes is usually adequate. These times vary with different facilities.

Mist applications are especially valuable with soft or semihard cuttings in the summer when outside temperatures are high. Mist has the inherent disadvantage of leaching nutrients from the plant and the medium which adversely affects slow rooting material. After 2–3 months in mist, unrooted cuttings tend to become "hard" with leaf surfaces covered with a thin layer of salts; yet in a plastic tent I have succeeded in keeping Mountain Laurel cuttings in good condition for as long as 2 years with some rooting occurring throughout the entire period. It must be admitted, though, that some growers are successfully propagating *Kalmia* from cuttings in the fall and winter using mist.

FOG OR VENTILATED HIGH HUMIDITY PROPAGATION This method is very similar to mist propagation except that droplet size is smaller. As a result moisture stays suspended in the air longer and less water is needed to maintain high humidity. Dr. Daniel Milbocker of Virginia Truck and Ornamentals Research Station, 1444 Diamond Springs Road, Virginia Beach, Virginia 23455, has been instrumental in developing this method since 1974. It is proving to work well with many plants and several firms now produce fogging devices. Yet, despite the availability of equipment there is little experience in rooting Mountain Laurel cuttings. Foggers are being used to humidify plants immediately after removal from tissue culture laboratories and, there is every reason to believe that fogging should compare favorably with mist, especially for summer propagation.

PLASTIC TENT One of the easiest and most reliable means of providing high humidity for cuttings is to cover the bench with a light frame of 1 × 2-in (2.5–5 cm) boards or wire mesh which is in turn covered with 4-mil clear polyethylene (Figure 6-2). The edges of the plastic are tucked inside of the bench to allow condensation inside the plastic to drip back into the medium. This is essentially a closed system with only drain holes under the bench to allow for the exchange of air and the elimination of excessive moisture. Such a "sweat box" requires little care. Once cuttings are stuck, watered in, and the tent closed, no further care is needed for about 4 weeks. At that time the medium should be checked to see if additional water is needed. If the mix, bench, and cuttings were clean at the start, then fungal pathogens should be no problem.

It is important to monitor the temperature, especially on sunny days. If the temperature goes above 90°F (32°C), then additional shading is necessary. The trick with a tent is to get as much daylight as

Figure 6-2. Plastic tents for rooting Laurel cuttings in fall and winter. Shade placed over tent prevents overheating on sunny days. (Jaynes)

possible without overheating. So, of course, shading adequate in November is inadequate in June.

MEDIA   As with other aspects of propagation, there is no concensus on the best medium to root cuttings. One commonly used for Rhododendrons is also good for Laurel:

2 parts fibrous-sphagnum peat moss
1 part coarse perlite

Many propagators are now substituting less expensive ground styrofoam for perlite. The ratio may be altered to equal parts of each. Many propagators formerly insisted on fibrous German peat, but its scarcity has led to the substitution of Canadian peat, which has proved satisfactory. The peat moss/perlite mix provides an acid, light, porous medium of high water-holding capacity. Normally the medium should be spread 6–8 in (15–20 cm) deep in the bench. Do not use the mix for successive batches of cuttings; this often leads to problems with pathogens and reduced rooting. Other media mixes used for Laurel cuttings include:

1 part fibrous-sphagum peat moss
1 part coarse perlite
2 parts sand

TEMPERATURE   Between 70 and 80°F (21–27°C) is the best temperature for root formation and growth. In summer the problem is holding the temperature down to this level, while in winter the problem is maintaining this temperature range. Do not assume the rooting medium is the same as the air temperature. In an open bench the mix will be from 5–10°F (3–6°C) *cooler* than the air temperature.

"Bottom heat" refers to heating from below the medium, and is provided in several ways. The first and most common is installing electric heating cables or mats under the mix. A similar but less expensive method is passing hot water through small diameter, flexible tubes placed under the medium much like electric cables (Biotherm System). (Biotherm Engineering Inc., P.O. Box 5007, Petaluma, California 94953) Another directs greenhouse heat (hot air, hot water, steam) under the propagation benches trapping it there with side curtains of plastic or felt paper. Whatever the method used, the heat radiates up through the rooting medium. In all cases the temperature should be regulated with a sensor in the mix at the level of the base of the cuttings. As long as the medium is 70–75° (21–24°), it really does not matter if the air temperature is considerably lower. In fact, if foliage is kept cool until roots are formed, the cuttings will more readily flush into growth when the air temperature is later raised.

PREPARATION OF CUTTINGS Summer cuttings should be taken while they are turgid. Do not collect any past mid-morning on sunny days. In the fall or winter, the timing of collection is less important; however, collection when temperatures are much below freezing should be avoided. Cuttings which are not immediately stuck in the bench can be stored in the refrigerator at 40°F (4°C) for a few days in the summer and for a few weeks in the fall or winter.

One of the mysteries of plant propagation is that some obviously mistreated cuttings root, whereas coddled ones may not. Nurserymen tell of cuttings forgotten in the trunk of the car or under the work bench for a few days that surprisingly root when finally stuck in the bench. On occasion I have been amazed and delighted to root cuttings of Mountain Laurel that were badly mauled and delayed in transit. And so the mystery remains regarding the proper pretreatment of cuttings.

Wounding of Rhododendron cuttings is a common practice and appears to be of benefit with Mountain Laurel, but with the other laurel species it is not worth the extra effort. To wound the cutting, remove a sliver of bark with a bit of wood from either side of the cutting. Each cut should be about ¾ in (18 mm) long and extend to the base or stop ¼ in (6 mm) above the base.

Some propagators routinely rinse their cuttings in a water bath containing a fungicide, insecticide, and/or antidesiccant. I lean towards spraying the cuttings immediately after sticking with a fungicide (Benlate at 1 t/gallon (0.1 g/l) and miticide. Hobbyists can skip the additives and just rinse the cuttings in cool water. However, a clean bench and a clean mix are essential. Several days before the benches or flats are to be filled, all traces of old mix should be removed; the benches should be rinsed with water, doused with a nonresidual disinfectant like sodium hypochlorite (Clorox), and allowed to dry.

LIGHTS   Extend the daylight period to 16 hours during the short days of fall and early winter because long days benefit rooting and subsequent growth. In practice, the day length can be extended by turning on the lights at dusk for a few hours. The same effect is achieved more economically by having the lights come on for less time in the middle of the night. Physiologists, working with other plants, have found that the length of the *dark* period is the critical factor. Hence, light in the middle of the night more efficiently breaks the period of continuous darkness. One 75-watt incandescent reflector floodlight every 12 sq ft (1 sq m) of bench space should be adequate if placed 30 in (75 cm) above the plants.

Western Laurel, *K. microphylla,* and
Eastern Bog Laurel, *K. polifolia*

Unlike other Laurels, the soft or semihard cuttings of these species are easy to root (Figure 6-3). No special cut, wound, or leaf removal is necessary. Cuttings need be only 1–2 in (2.5–5 cm) long. They can be handled in a tent or under mist, and with no auxin treatment roots will appear within 3 weeks. Under lights and warm (70–75°F (21–24°C)) conditions, they will continue to grow. The young plants may require pinching to encourage good habit—these pinched shoots make excellent cuttings.

Figure 6-3. Cuttings of Bog Laurel after 3 weeks in a plastic tent. (*K. polifolia* and *K. microphylla* are the only Laurel species easy to root.) In 4 more weeks these plants could be cut back to obtain more cuttings for propagation and to force branching. (Jaynes)

Mountain Laurel, *K. latifolia*

Few horticulturists agree on the best time to take cuttings; whether wounding is beneficial; the best medium to use; or even how long rooting will take. For example, investigators have reported January; March, June and July; and August to December as the "best" times to take cuttings.

Perhaps it is best to report the results of my own experiments. A plastic tent works better for me than mist, in large part due to the length of time required for rooting. I prefer mist or fog for soft or semi-hard cuttings taken in summer when temperatures are high as the water droplet cooling effect is extremely beneficial. The same cooling effect in the fall and winter months tends to reduce the medium temperature below 70°F (21°C) and so delays rooting. Humidity chambers have the advantage for amateurs or part time growers of not having to be watched as closely as mist and fog systems. The cuttings can be left for a few days without worrying about faulty controls or clogged nozzles. Having said that, I must report that experiments of R. F. Williams and E. E. Bilderbach, at North Carolina State, Raleigh, showed no differences between intermittant mist and polyethylene tent in the propagation of Mountain Laurel stem cuttings taken in the fall.

I have had best success with cuttings taken in October, just before a hard freeze; yet cuttings taken from mid-September through November performed nearly as well. Make cuttings about 2–3 in (5–7.5 cm) long from the current season growth. If cuttings are not well hardened, delay taking them until later in the fall or winter. Well fertilized plants, especially in containers and nursery beds, tend to harden later, and cuttings from such plants may root best in January. Less vigorous cuttings from within the plant crown often root better than the outer thick, vigorous cuttings. At least one commercial grower shades his stock plants to improve success in rooting cuttings. Most commercial growers wound the cuttings on one or both sides as previously described.

I have not been able to demonstrate a positive and consistent response to the auxins, fungicides, and other materials which reportedly aid rooting in other ericaceous plants. A 5-second dip in an ethyl alcohol solution of 5000 ppm each of NAA (2-naphthalene acetic acid) and IBA is beneficial with some clones. A commercial preparation of this material called Dip-and-Grow (10,000 ppm IBA and 5,000 ppm IAA) is available (Alpkem Corporation, P O Box 1260, Clackamas, Oregon 97015) and is used at a 1:5 to 1:15 dilution depending on the cultivar and hardness of the cuttings. One of the difficulties in evaluating auxins is that different clones respond differently to the same auxin treatment and the same clone may respond differently in different years or under different propagation regimes. Most growers use auxins and research supports the positive effect of NAA, IBA, and 2,4,5-TP (2,4,5-trichlorophenoxypropionic acid) with some clones. Growers would do themselves and others a favor if, along with the auxin treated cuttings, they would leave some untreated cuttings of the same cultivar for comparative purposes.

John McGuire at the University of Rhode Island had excellent success (96%) in rooting 'Pink Surprise' from semi-hardwood cuttings in the summer under outdoor intermittant mist. The cuttings were dipped in a talc dust of Hormex 45 (4.5% IBA) and placed in flats of peat moss and vermiculite. They were heavily rooted in 8 weeks.

Alfred Fordham, former propagator at the Arnold Arboretum, has successfully rooted softwood cuttings forced into growth in winter. A note in an old gardening magazine indicates that a nursery in New York, as long ago as 1893 (Trumpy), was rooting cuttings from young wood of plants grown indoors. The rooting of cuttings from forced plants has worked extemely well with Exbury azaleas and has several advantages. The technique is particularly suitable for container-grown stock plants. Stock plants are allowed to go into their usual fall dormancy until mid-January, when they are heated and forced into growth. The new shoots are then rooted under mist or plastic, with these advantages: 1) Cuttings root more readily, 2) Unlike fall cuttings, the cold treatment requirement has been fulfilled, 3) Once rooted, they have a full, normal growing season ahead. However, despite the promise of this method, my attempts to root cuttings of Mountain Laurel from plants forced into growth in February and March have been unsuccessful.

STOCK PLANT AGE   One important and often overlooked factor in rooting Mountain Laurel and other difficult-to-root species is the age of the stock. It has been known for years that cuttings from young plants generally root more readily than those from older plants. The classic example is the difference in the rooting ability of "juvenile" and "mature" English Ivy, *Hedra helix*. The juvenile vines form roots readily, but the mature, shrub-like form is difficult to root.

Several years of experimentation have demonstrated that the same is true in rooting Mountain Laurel cuttings. Indeed, the percentage of rooted cuttings of 1-year-old seedlings, receiving no auxin treatment was 90% while the rate of rooting dropped off rapidly with older plants, diminishing to 20% for flowering plants. In addition, the speed of formation and quantity of roots on a cutting are greater from young seedlings, and such cuttings will flush into growth more rapidly than cuttings from older plants. Cuttings from flowering plants have the disconcerting tendency of producing flower buds in the propagation bench. These flower buds occupy the sites where vegetative growth should occur and are best removed.

Cuttings from rooted cuttings and cuttings from young grafts also root more readily than cuttings from the original stock plant. Data given in Table 6-1 show this effect rather dramatically for a red-bud clone. Cuttings taken from cuttings rooted the previous year rooted much better than cuttings from flowering plants of the same clone, 94% versus 30%.

Table 6-1 Comparative rooting of cuttings of one clone (137) of Mountain Laurel taken from stock plants of different ages. No auxin or fungicide treatment.

Age of stock plant	Number of cuttings	Number rooted, Oct to Feb	Percent rooted
15-year-old original plant	10	3	30
8-year-old plants from rooted cuttings	16	5	31
1-year-old plants from rooted cuttings	34	32	94

Cuttings from young tissue culture started plants are another source of material that has been shown to root more readily than cuttings from the parent plants. The process of tissue culturing appears to make the plantlets more juvenile than comparable plants started from normal stem cuttings.

Clones vary in their ability to form roots on cuttings. Select clones that root more readily and then continue to take cuttings from recent propagations, rather than the original or other flowering plants.

An example of a clone that roots readily is the pink selection, 'Pink Surprise', which has consistently rooted 80% or better from fall cuttings for 6 consecutive years Figure 6-4. Once rooted plants are

Figure 6-4. Typical rooting response of an easy-to-root cultivar, 'Pink Surprise', *left*, and most Mountain Laurel selections, *right*. Photo taken 12 weeks after October sticking of cuttings in a humidity case. (Jaynes)

obtained, cuttings should be taken from these and not the original plant to maintain as much juvenility as possible. Cuttings can be taken if necessary from 1–2-year old seedlings if the seedlings are of known pedigree and flower color.

Cuttings, especially those from older plants, taken in the fall may show a reluctance to flush into growth after rooting. If possible, give such cuttings a cold period, 35–50°F (2–10°C) for 6 weeks, with no artificial light to extend day length. For cuttings taken in October, try this dormancy treatment during February and March. Then in April, when the rooted cuttings are warmed, they should burst into growth. When it was not possible to cool the greenhouse because of the other plants, I have moved flats of rooted cuttings into a cold (dirt) cellar where they received 8 hours of incandescent light daily. After 6–8 weeks of this "winterization," they were brought back into the greenhouse to resume growth. Another alternative is to take cuttings in the first half of January after the stock plants have received some cold. About the time the cuttings root they begin to flush new growth.

By carefully selecting and manipulating the stock and then treating the cuttings properly, you will succeed in rooting this difficult species. It does take patience and perseverence. Other things being equal, the most important decision is the cultivars chosen to propagate—some are much easier to root than others. Some of the best for rooting are 'Bullseye', 'Carousel', 'Nipmuck', 'Olympic Fire', 'Pink Charm', 'Pink Surprise', and 'Quinnipiac'. As for the other factors: timing, wounding, auxin, fog or tent, media, etc., no one recipe is guaranteed better than another.

Sheep Laurel, *K. angustifolia*

Sheep Laurel is somewhat easier to root then Mountain Laurel. Softwood cuttings taken during the summer can be rooted, but firmer cuttings taken in late summer, or fall and into January are easier to handle and to root. Treat them with the same 5-second auxin dip as Mountain Laurel cuttings (Dip-and-Grow, 1 : 7 dilution).

Whenever possible, choose cuttings without flower buds. They are easier to root and they flush into growth more readily. Cuttings should be 2–3 in (5–7.5 cm) long and have two leaf whorls. Strip off the lowest leaves, and wound lightly on each side. Newly rooted cuttings will begin growth without first receiving a cool rest period.

White Wicky, *K. cuneata*, and Sandhill Laurel, *K. hirsuta*

There is limited experience with rooting these two undomesticated species. Greenwood cuttings and semi-hardwood cuttings taken in late summer or early fall will root. Auxin treatment is beneficial. Cuttings of White Wicky taken too late in the fall will lose their leaves. Extension of the day length with light in late summer and fall will extend the rooting and growing period. As with Mountain Laurel, use juvenile wood when possible.

PROPAGATION BY GRAFTING

Outstanding Mountain Laurel specimens which are inordinately difficult to root, are candidates for grafting. Mountain Laurel can be grafted with little difficulty, and suckering of the stock is not a serious problem on established grafts. Late winter or early spring is the normal grafting time. Stocks should be placed in pots or flats in the fall and then exposed to cold temperatures until about the first of February, when they can be warmed up and forced into growth. Vigorous seedlings 4–8 in (10–20 cm) tall make good stocks, but they should not be grafted until clear signs of root activity are observed by tipping the plant out of the container and looking for new white rootlets on the surface of the root ball. This should occur 2–3 weeks after they are given heat.

Dormant scions should be either whip, cleft, or side-veneer grafted onto the stock as low as possible (Figures 6-5, 6-6). Wrap the graft firmly but not tightly with a rubber band or a rubber budding strip. The grafted plants must be kept under humid conditions until new cells knit the stock and scion together. A plastic tent makes for the easiest and best environment. Individual humid chambers can be created merely by enclosing each potted and grafted plant in a plastic bag. After 4–6 weeks, the tent can be gradually ventilated for a week or two for the plants to adjust to the less humid growing condition of the greenhouse. When there is no longer any danger of frost, plant the grafts outdoors. An advantage of late winter and early spring grafting is that the grafts put out one flush of growth before the normal growing season even begins.

June grafting can be successful and is most valuable for propagating new selections identified in flower or in cases where it may be inconvenient or impossible to obtain scions the next winter. For June grafting use scions of the current season's growth, firm but not woody. Stock should be chosen from small plants which grew vigorously the previous year.

Graft scions onto last year's growth on the smooth part of the stem with few leaves. Tie the unions with budding strips or cut rubber bands, and handle the grafts the same as in early spring grafting. Approximately 7 weeks after grafting, the plants can be set outside in shaded beds. Since June-grafted clones often do not put out a flush of growth until the following spring, the only advantage over grafting the same plants next spring is to serve factors of necessity or convenience.

One rooting method used with difficut-to-root Rhododendrons and certain other plants is to graft the difficult-to-root scion onto a stem section of an easy-to-root selection. Then treat the graft like a cutting

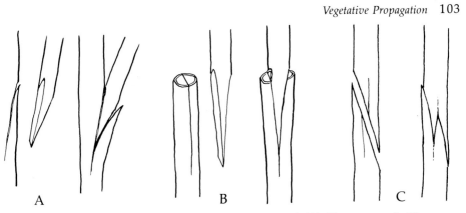

Figure 6-5. Three kinds of grafts used with Mountain Laurel: (A) side veneer graft, (B) cleft graft, (C) whip graft. A sharp knife to make smooth cuts and good matching of the cut surfaces are essential. (Jaynes)

Figure 6-6. A cleft-grafted Mountain Laurel wrapped with a rubber band. The union should be made as close to the ground as possible. The example is grafted higher than necessary or desirable (Jaynes)

placing the union below the medium surface in the propagation bed. The easy-to-root "stock" will form roots while the graft knits, and months later the scion itself roots. With some combinations a delayed incompatibility will cause the graft union to fail eventually, but not until after the scion roots. It is a promising approach that I tested by grafting Mountain Laurel selections onto Eastern Bog Laurel and Sheep Laurel. Several of the grafts on sections of underground stems of Sheep Laurel were successful, but on the whole the method is unreliable and impractical.

PROPAGATION BY LAYERING

Laurels spread and propagate in the wild by natural layering. Bent-over branches are covered with leaf litter and humus, eventually rooting along the portion covered and in contact with the soil. All species will layer, but, since Mountain Laurel is the slowest to respond, let us look at it. Heavy snows and other woodland events bend the branches of Mountain Laurel down so that layering occurs. If the process happens repeatedly for many years, small thickets arise which have their origin in a single plant. I have observed clumps of banded Mountain Laurel, readily identified by their unique flowers, which measured nearly 20 ft (6 m) edge to edge. It is easy to imagine a single plant spreading over a much larger area.

To layer a selection of your own, remove an inch (2.5 cm) or so of soil beneath a low-lying stem and then bend it to the ground (Figure 6-7). Rooting can be facilitated by girdling: firmly bind the stem where it comes into contact with the soil with one or more loops of wire; bend the stem to break it partially; or make several shallow encircling knife cuts. Then peg the stem down and cover it with leaf mold or peat moss and soil. Finally, water and mulch. Do not allow the layer to dry out. If started in the spring, roots may have formed by fall, but a second growing season is often necessary for good rooting. Once roots have formed, sever the layer from the mother plant and move it to a protected location. If the roots are not strong, prune back the top when you transplant it to reduce the stress on the new plant.

Layering is a laborious and slow method, yet one that fascinates many gardeners. To propagate just a few plants the technique is as practical as any; however, it has little or no appeal for the nurseryman who needs a more efficient method.

Figure 6-7. Layering. A lateral branch is placed and pegged into a depression dug along-side the plant. The branch is wounded, covered with a mix of peat moss and soil, and kept moist. After rooting (6–18 months for Mountain Laurel), the layer is cut from the mother plant and transplanted. The number of layers per stock plant is determined by the number of branches that can be pulled to the ground. (Jaynes)

Chapter 7

MICROPROPAGATION OF MOUNTAIN LAUREL

Keith E. Jensen, PhD, President, Evergreen Cloning Nurseries, 30 Trumbull Road, Waterford, Connecticut 06385

The rate of multiplication appears adequate for commercial purposes. Producing an average of 30 shoots per culture in 8 weeks yields at least 7000 shoots per 1 sq ft [900 sq cm] of culture shelf space per year. With a 73% rooting success, this represents approximately 5000 useable propagules [per square foot per year] (Lloyd and McCown 1980). [Imagine devoting 1 acre (0.4 ha) to such a method: 200,000,000 plantlets could be produced in 1 year!]

The fascination in propagating plants by microculture methods may be due, in part, to seeing miniature, primitive, organized structures form shoots that later develop into stems, leaves and roots. But equally awe-inspiring is the realization that from one piece of plant tissue, so many exact duplicates (potentially millions) of the plant can be made. Now that good methods have been worked out for *Kalmia*, it has become easier for beginners to have the pleasure of successes after a relatively short period of learning. Upon hearing about these techniques, commercial producers sometimes begin to have visions of marketing thousands of plants from each of their best cultivars.

Rather than present a full, scientific review of the subject, the purpose of this chapter is to inform the novice and encourage others to try Mountain Laurel propagation by culturing shoots in sterilized medium. Included is information about needed equipment and techniques that have worked well for several of us. We are a group of people who have had experience (ranging from 3–10 years) in getting *Kalmia* cultivars into meristem propagation and rooting the microcutting shoots. First drafts of the manuscript were by Keith Jensen; subsequently constructive criticism and/or editing was provided by Les Clay, (Clay's Nurseries, Langley, B.C.); Charles Fink, (Herman Losely and Son Nursery, Perry, OH); Nancy DePalma, (formerly with the Connecticut Agriculture Experiment Station, New Haven, CT); Steve McCulloch, (Briggs Nursery, Inc., Olympia, WA); and Deborah McCown, (Knight Hollow Nursery, Madison, WI). Technical information was also provided by Charles Addison, (Bolton Plant Technologies, Bolton, CT);

Randy Burr, (B&B Laboratories, Mt. Vernon, WA); Sylvia Pidacks, (Weston Nurseries, Hopinkton, MA); and Gerald Verkade, (Verkade's Nursery, New London, CT).

Several excellent books describing methods generally in use for growing plant tissue under sterile conditions in artificial media are available. One of the best for beginners is *Plants from Test Tubes: an Introduction to Micropropagation* by Lydiane Kyte (Timber Press, Portland, Oregon, 1983).

Historically, micropropagation of broad-leaved evergreens was not very successful, nor widely practiced, until after two new experimental blends of chemicals were formulated and introduced. Such chemical recipes for synthetic media were the scientific results of biochemical experiments to discover the essential components required for rapid replication of plant cells and differentiation into organized tissues. The old standard preparations of mineral salts and vitamins—like that of Murashige and Skoog (referred to as MS medium and published in 1962) which have continued to serve so well for culturing of tobacco, orchids, small fruits, vegetables, herbaceous perennials and other plants—always failed the experimenters when tried with various species of Ericaceae (such as Azalea, Rhododendron and *Kalmia*). This difficulty was duly noted by Anderson and in 1975 he published a new formulation that was a significant improvement. He found also that among the cytokinins (plant cell growth regulators) tested, the one called 2iP—which has the full chemical names of N6-(2-isopentenyl)-adenine or 6-(gamma-gamma-dimethyl-allyl) amino purine—was a clear choice over other available cytokinins to induce shoot formation in Rhododendron cultivars. A few years later other very important modifications in medium formulation were made by Lloyd and McCown (1980). Their new medium worked exceptionally well for *Kalmia* propagation so they drew attention to the fact that shoot tip culture of Mountain Laurel was a commercially feasible means of propagation. Their "woody plant medium" (abbreviated as WPM) has since become the standard formulation used for *Kalmia*. In addition to the Ericaceae, many other families of plants have been cultured successfully with this medium.

FACILITIES AND EQUIPMENT NEEDED TO GET STARTED

Space

The area required depends upon the size of operations anticipated, but in any case it should be in a clean environment, apart from greenhouse activities and preferably where the walls and floors can be scrubbed on a regular basis. Beginners at home have converted basement rooms and small bedrooms to house the benches and sterile-containment hoods, and made closets into "grow rooms" with shelving, lights and temperature controls suitable for incubating the tissue cultures. The laboratory work involved in the making of media and cleaning/sterilizing containers can be done in a kitchen. As with most such endeavors it seems to take more room than was originally thought by most beginners; so plan auxiliary space for the storage of supplies and refrigeration.

Commercial growers, thinking about arranging for new facilities in which to do micropropagation, may want to consider the use of a remodeled house-trailer of about 700 sq ft (65 sq m). Implementation of this idea has yielded a near ideal space for start-up operations at the Prides Corner Farms, Lebanon, CT; Further details about that option can be obtained by contacting K. Jensen.

Sterile Air Hood

Because all plant microculture media will also support growth of many kinds of bacteria, yeasts and molds, everytime the containers are opened presents a good opportunity for microbes in the air to enter the media and form colonies. To reduce the chance of contamination, all sterile (aseptic) operations should be performed in a hood or box cabinet. Several laboratory equipment suppliers offer "laminar-flow" hoods in which all the air flowing into the working area of the hood has been passed through filters which remove all microbial particles. Commercial hoods are somewhat expensive, so a cheaper alternative is to build your own (as some of us have done) by acquiring the components and designing plans or using published descriptions. Interested readers should consult the paper by Martin Meyer in *HortScience,* August, 1986, (volume 21, pp 1064–1065). Although most laboratories doing plant tissue culturing employ hoods, an alternative is a box cabinet made with a rigid, clear plastic or glass top and three sides enclosing a space large enough to permit easy manipulation of containers and apparatus. Lydiane Kyte's book provides sketches of such cabinets.

Grow Rooms

Grow rooms are used to grow the cultures and plantlets under controlled conditions. Two kinds of rooms or cabinets should be planned: one for incubating the cultures when in sterile medium and the other for rooting the microcuttings in a peat mixture (which is not sterile). The special conditions needed for care of plantlets in the rooting stage include high humidity and controlled lighting, but can be done in a greenhouse.

These rooms or cabinets (which should be separated from other operations) should be designed so they can easily be scrubbed periodically to reduce microbial contamination; maintain temperature in the range of 70–80°F (21–27°C); and illuminate with fluorescent tubes (cool-white seems to be as good or better than Gro-lux for this purpose). Some propagators provide timer switches to provide 16 hr light and 8 hr dark periods; others use 24 hr continuous lighting. During the micropropagation phases most Mountain Laurel cultivars prefer light intensity not exceeding 1000 lux or 100 ft candles which can be obtained by means of defusing light through opaque white plastic sheets or setting the light source at the correct distance. Shelving should be constructed of materials that permit free air flow as is obtained with expanded metal screens or 0.5 in (1.2 cm) grid "egg-crate" panels for fluorescent light fixtures. Care should be taken to avoid overheating of cultures close to lighting fixture ballasts. Some propagators remove the ballasts and wire them outside the room.

Rooms for rooting have less strict requirments, but shelving should be of greater strength to hold the weight of boxes containing moist peat moss mixtures. Generally the light intensity can be greater than is supplied during shoot microculturing, but rooting plantlets also need no more than 200–300 ft candles. Too much light may produce toxic changes (reddening) in some cultivars.

Sterilizers

Complete decontamination of containers and culture media is best achieved with autoclaves or pressure cookers. All microbes and spores are killed by heating at 250°F (120°C) obtained with 15 lbs (7 kg) pressure for 15–30 min. Larger volumes of fluid require the longer periods of heat. A special "autoclave" tape that changes color after the correct temperature has been reached can be used on containers or wrapped apparatus to indicate sterilization has occurred.

Forceps, scissors and scalpels used in working with the plant tissues can be disinfected by immersion in 70% ethyl alcohol; the alcohol is removed by flaming so an alcohol lamp or a propane burner is needed in the hood. Alternative methods include immersion in disinfectant solutions or use of electrical heaters like the trade-marked product "Bacti-Cinerator."

Containers

Although glass test tubes (usually 25 mm dia, 150 mm length with plastic caps) are a time-honored means of holding media and cultures, several kinds of jars (baby food or home-canning), and autoclavable plastic vessels of various shape and design are now in common use. These containers should have a tight fitting closure that also permits exchange of air but blocks microbial passage. Several of us have used polycarbonate, egg-shaped containers; they are now available in 500 unit lots from J. P. Bartlett Co. The square boxes 3 × 3 × 3 in (7.5 × 7.5 × 7.5 cm) manufactured by Magenta Corp. have become favorites for larger-scale production in several nurseries. Single-use, disposable plastic PlantCon boxes 9.5 cm sq are available from Flow Labs.

PROPAGATION MEDIA

Formulation

The woody plant medium described by Lloyd and McCown is now standard for *Kalmia* propagation. It can be procured by special order from GIBCO or other tissue culture media supply houses; however, most commercial and experimental propagators make their own using the formulation given in Table 1. A recent change in formulation subsitutes KNO3 (at 1150 mg/liter final) for the K2SO4 and is known as modified WPM. It is preferred by several of the micropropagators. L. Clay finds that Anderson's medium (containing some cystine) works well with some Laurel cultivars.

Table 1   Components of Woody Plant Medium (Lloyd and McCown)

Stock	Chemical	gm in stock	ml/liter	mg/liter in medium
A	NH4NO3	10.0	20	400
	Ca(NO3)2+4H2O .	13.9		556
B	K2SO4	24.75	20	990
C	CaCl+2H2O	3.84	5	96
D	KH2PO4 .	6.80	5	170
	H3BO3	0.248		6.2
	NaMoO4+2H2O	0.010		0.25
E	MgSO4+7H2O	14.8	5	370
	MnSO4+H2O	0.892		22.3
	ZnSO4+H2O	0.344		8.6
	CuSO4+5H2O	0.010		0.25
F	FeSO4+7H2O	1.114	6	33.36 .
	NaEDTA	1.49		44.76
G	Thiamine HCl	0.04	5	1.0
	Nicotinic acid	0.02		0.5
	Pyridoxine HCl	0.02		0.5
	Glycine	0.08		2.0
H	Myo-inositol	4.0	5	100.0

Stocks A and B are made in 500 ml volumes; stocks C through H in 200 ml volumes. They can both be stored under refrigeration (4°C) for 6–8 weeks. Inspect periodically for visible signs of microbial contamination, expected in organic stocks G and H, discard when seen.

To prepare stock F make 100 ml of each component, add several drops of 0.1 N HCl to each to acidify, then while stirring the EDTA, add the FeSO4 slowly. A pale golden color should develop. This complex provides for slow release of iron to the plants.

Sugar (sucrose) is used at 20 gm/liter. The stocks are then combined in the indicated volumes of each. After adding antibiotics and growth regulators, distilled water is added to produce the final volume. The pH is next adjusted with 1N KOH or NaOH to bring to pH 5.3. If the medium is to be gelled, the weighed amount of agar or other gelling agent is then added and stirred while heating to bring to mild boiling for a few minutes to obtain a clear solution. Media must then be autoclaved to sterilize.

Growth Regulators

The most important, variable additives to the media are the growth regulatory substances called cytokinins and auxins. Early in the history of Mountain Laurel micropropagation there was good reason to be concerned about which cytokinin to use, but currently most propagators rely on the synthetic form called 2iP. Usually stock solutions (for example 1 mg/ml) are prepared by adding small amounts of dilute acid (0.1N hydrochloric) to weighed amounts of the powder, gently heating while stirring to obtain a clear solution, then bringing the concentrate up to proper volume with distilled water. Batches of media are made with different quantites of 2iP by using varied volumes of the stock solution. The stocks can be stored under refrigeration or frozen in appropriate containers until needed. Before each use the refrigerated stock solutions should be carefully examined visually for evidence of microbial contamination (cloudiness, floating masses or particulates).

Although some very successful propagators use only 2iP, and no other stimulant, others skilled in this art prefer to include additional growth regulators during the initiation stages. L. Clay finds that certain culivars respond better by alternating medium containing combinations of either 2iP and IAA (indole-3-acetic acid) or BAP (benzylaminopurine) and IBA. GA3 and zeatin are sometimes helpful. Among the many gibberellins isolated, the one called GA3 (because it was the third one found) is most commonly used for this purpose. Stock solutions can be made by using a few drops of a dilute base (such as NaOH or KOH) to get a clear solution, then bringing to appropriate volume with distilled water. Portions can be distributed to vials and heat sterilized for subseqent freezing and storage.

In contrast, the naturally occurring cytokinin, zeatin (which is quite expensive) requires acidification to go into solution and is less heat-stable. Some techicians sterilize it by ultrafiltration through single-use filter devices which are available from many laboratory supply companies; filter pore size of 0.22 micron is the best choice. Others simply add 10% more to allow for the loss of potency during heat-sterilization.

When an auxin is added to *Kalmia* media, the choice is usually indol-3-butyric acid (called IBA). It is heat-stable. Stock solutions are made by adding the powder to a small volume of dilute base (like KOH). After gentle heating/stirring, the clear solution is brought to proper volume with distilled water. Again, the standard practice is to store frozen vials of the compound until needed.

The quantities of cytokinins and IBA added to the initiation media are almost a matter of personal preference; every propagator has had a different experience and deals with this matter from their own point of view. For example, some propagators when handed a new cultivar use multiple lots of media, each with slightly different concentrations of cytokinins and auxins. At the other extreme, some depend upon a standard concentration of 2iP and use no other hormone. A more conservative strategy is to try the combination that often succeeds, and if the trial fails, then move on to favored alternatives. Some of us use a fluid medium containing 2.5 micrograms (ug)/ml of 2iP; 0.1 ug/ml of IBA; and 20 ug/ml of GA3. (Another way to express concentrations is based on weight of substance contained per liter of medium; therefore in the above example there are 2.5 milligrams (mg)/L of 2iP.)

Failure to realize active growth and new shoot formation, suggests that the cytokinin level is not high enough or that naturally occuring zeatin is needed. Accordingly, the next experiment might be conducted with the 2iP increased to 5 or 10 ug/ml or zeatin (1.0 ug/ml) added. In short, it becomes a game to learn those conditions that optimize vigorous initial growth for each cultivar. After the tissues are well-established and shoot proliferation is occurring rapidly, a typical propagation medium has no other growth regulator than 2iP in concentrations ranging 0.4 to 2.5 ug/mg.

Other Additives

In starting cultures the medium may be liquid or gelled, but subsequent transfers are made to gelled medium using 4.5–8.0 gm/liter of agar. The brand of agar and its concentration varies with individual growers; some prefer to use the highest purity grade—such as Phytagar, the trademark product sold by GIBCO—while others believe that good grades such as that supplied by Sigma Chemical Company are entirely satisfactory. Concern about impurities in agar has led to the use of Gelrite, which is not an agar, but a gellan gum produced by Kelco. One of us (D. McCown) recently began to use a mixture of agar and Gelrite; others are beginning to follow this practice.

As a part of the effort to control microbial contamination introduced by the plant tissue, some workers add small amounts of an antibiotic, such as gentamycin (20 mg/liter) and/or a fungicide, like benomyl (10 mg/liter) to the culture medium.

Sterilization and Storage

Both fluid and gelled medium absolutely require sterilization. Sterilization is best achieved by holding at 250°F (120°C) under 15 lbs (7 kg) of steam pressure in an autoclave for 15–30 minutes. The period of time is varied depending upon the volume and kind of materials being sterilized. Some laboratories sterilize the medium after it is put into the containers used for culturing; others prefer to sterilize media and containers separately and put the media in the containers, as needed, under the sterile air hood. Media can be stored under refrigeration for periods of 6–8 weeks without significant loss of potency; however precautions, such as storing in plastic bags, can be taken to avoid drying media out if held for extended periods. Aliquots of fluid medium can be frozen, but once agar is added freezing should be avoided because the gelling properties are changed.

PLANT SPECIMEN HANDLING

This section has some suggestions and directions about how to start initial cultures and perform the critical processing of plant materials selected for culture.

Collection

Cuttings taken any time of year are a good source of axillary buds, but soft, green wood with good apical vigor is more successful than dormant shoots. This could be due to the levels of endogenous hormones in the shoot tips. Some propagators use only the apical shoots. Flower bud shoots can also be used, but generally are not as easily disinfected as the stem branches and microbial contamination frequently appears weeks after initiation in culture.

Storage

Immediately after cutting, the specimen should be placed in a container to prevent drying, for example a plastic bag, containing moistened paper. When held in a refrigerator "crisper" drawer, most samples will remain viable for several weeks.

Disinfection

Thorough cleaning is absolutely essential to success. The amount of tissue to be cleaned can be reduced by trimming off the leaves and cutting the twigs into segments that contain 1–3 nodes (buds) each. The methods for treating these pieces of plant tissue vary with every lab, but a typical sequence is as follows:

1) Shake or stir in a mild detergent solution (add a few drops of Tween 20, Woolite or Ivory detergent to 100 ml of water) for about 5 minutes.
2) Rinse with sterile demineralized water.
3) Hold in 70% ethanol for 10 seconds.
4) Shake or stir for 15–20 minutes in a 10–15% liquid bleach solution (the common washday products contain 5.25% sodium hypochlorite, an excellent oxidizer-disinfectant).
5) Rinse in sterile demineralized water with three changes of water.
6) Hold in sterile demineralized water until dissected.

The conclusion of step 4 and both steps 5 and 6 should be carried out under the sterile hood. A simpler method successfully used by some propagators employs no pre-treatment steps but a small amount of detergent is added to the bleach solution; after exposure to the disinfectant, the plant pieces are washed as in steps 5 and 6. For tissue in deep winter dormancy some of us have extended step 1 to 45 minutes and for step 4 used up to a 50% bleach solution for ½ hour.

Dissection Methods

Again there is much diversity in techniques followed by different propagators. Some avoid any cutting of tissue after disinfection and place the segments on gelled medium without any further manipulations. Others skilled in the art wish to work only with the meristematic tissue in the center of a bud. To do so they transfer the disinfected pieces, one at a time, into Petri dishes or onto sterilized paper toweling tacked to plywood blocks. While holding the stem with a sterilized forceps or hemostat, the petiole stub is grasped with another forceps and pulled carefully to remove the petiole, thereby revealing the small axillary bud embedded in the stem (Figure 7-1). This vegetative bud contains meristematic tissue, that is, cells which will respond to cytokinins and auxins by multiplying and differentiating into shoots. The stem section with its bud intact is placed on liquid or gelled growth media and in successful trials some buds will begin to show shoots in a few weeks. An alternative technique, first described and successfully practiced by Dr. Hindera Palta at the New York Botanical Gardens and more recently taught to us by C. Addison, is to cut out the bud carefully with a sharp-pointed #11 blade scalpel, and after momentary drying, to float the bud on the surface of a liquid medium.

I have had some success using flower buds. In this approach segments of the flower bud are cut into lengths of about 10–15 mm and put on gelled media or floated on "rafts" of non-woven fabrics, such as Pellon or Lelux, sold by fabric stores for garment interfacing.

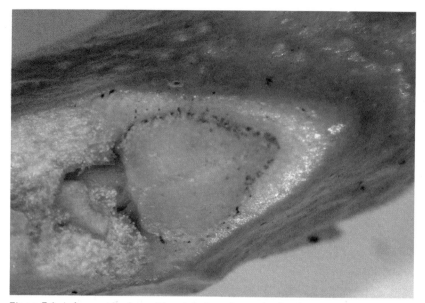

Figure 7-1. A dormant bud on a Mountain Laurel stem that has been uncovered by removing the leaf petiole. The bud, about 1/25 in (1 mm) in diameter, is all that is needed to initiate propagation of a new selection in culture. (Jaynes)

TISSUE CULTURE TECHNIQUES

This part of tissue culturing may be the most difficult to describe because the lessons to be learned come largely through experience. Go ahead and try, you'll like it!

Initial Cultures

The critical factors in successful initiation of Mountain Laurel cultures are still not completely understood at a scientific level. Large measures of luck and art are required in helping the buds survive the trauma of decontamination and dissection and then respond well to the stimuli furnished in the growth medium. Perhaps it is most important to emphasize the necessity of doing several (3–10) explants (specimen pieces) from each cultivar in each batch of experimental medium. Starting with a floating bud specimen less than 0.5 mm, success is signalled when those floating specks swell with green growth to a size that is soon (within weeks) 6–8 times the original bud dimension. If stems with axillary buds left intact have been cultured on fabric rafts in liquid medium, visible green shoots from several of the buds will be evident in a few weeks. At that time they can be transferred to gelled medium, left longer as floaters, or moved to liquid medium with fabric

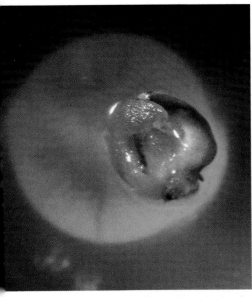

Figure 7-2. This is a bud that had been isolated on liquid medium and is now growing on solid (agar) medium; the green meristematic tissue has begun to divide and enlarge. (Jensen)

Figure 7-3. A stem segment that included a bud at the base of the still attached petiole. Shoots have formed from that bud. (Jensen)

Figure 7-4. Seen here is a small cluster of flower buds in sterile culture. Emerging from under them are shoots which will become fully formed stems and leaves. (Jensen)

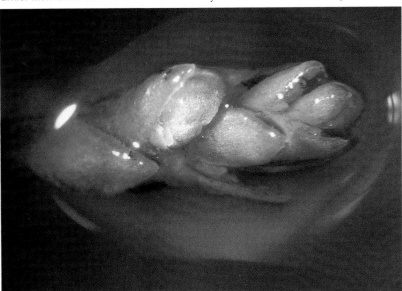

rafts. The latter alternative provides the advantage of supporting the greater tissue mass while still maintaining optimum conditions for the free exchange of nutrients and toxic wastes. Figures 7-2, 7-3, and 7-4 show various tissues, including a vegetative bud, stem segment, and flower buds in the early stages of isolation and development.

Transfers to Secondary Media

Once shoots have formed well, the next stage of culturing begins. This is the stage in which the numbers of shoots/plantlets in the containers are rapidly increased. In a sense this stage is like farming in that the cultures become miniature gardens or fields to be watched and cared for. Any browning or dead tissue from old stems should be cut away and discarded as the toxins produced by dying tissue poison healthy neighboring tissue. Plant cultures with colonies of yeast, bacteria or fungi growing on the agar surfaces or in the medium should be discarded. Occcasionally the tips of the shoots can be "rescued" from contaminated cultures by dipping the pieces in a mild disinfectant such as 2% bleach solution and transferring to a new container of medium.

Standard practice is to transfer the shoots with leaves at intervals of 3–4 weeks to keep them growing vigorously. Multiplication is encouraged by stripping the leaves and petioles from the shoots and then laying the shoots on a new agar surface. New shoots will start from each stripped petiole base. Alternatively, shoot clumps 3–5 mm in diameter are moved together and the ends pressed into the agar medium. When the cultures are in a good state they will form new masses of shoots that are soon ready for further sub-dividing into new culture containers.

Technicians in the D. McCown lab cut the shoots into mid-sections and tips; the mid-sections are laid on their sides (pressed slightly into the gelled medium), without removing leaves, from which new shoots emerge from axillary buds. Tips are put into other vessels because they grow at a faster rate and do not have the same multiplication potential. The bases are discarded. L. Clay uses an 8 week cycle for large-scale production and transfers only clumps producing viable shoots.

Shown in Figure 7-5 is a step in the process of trimming prior to transfer to a new medium. Note that the containers (polycarbonate eggs) are labeled with color-coded tape and experiment number. The taller plantlets in Figure 7-6 can either be harvested for sticking or used for further shoot propagation by laying the stem down on new medium. The remaining clump can be divided for transfer to another egg.

For large scale production, some of us move shoot clumps into the $3 \times 3 \times 3$ in ($7.5 \times 7.5 \times 7.5$ cm) autoclavable plastic boxes (Magenta Corp.). A clear single-use plastic box marketed by Flow Labs may also

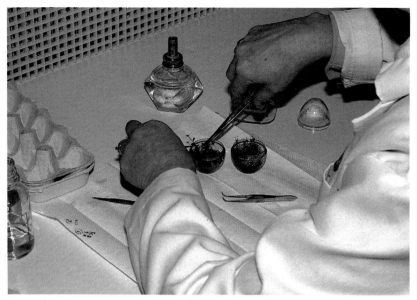

Figure 7-5. Trimming and making transfers in a laminar-flow hood. Note the egg-shaped container in which the plantlets are growing. (Jensen)

Figure 7-6. Shoots that have become large enough to harvest for sticking and rooting. The remaining clump could be subdivided into other containers for growing on. (Jensen).

Figure 7-7. Close-up of Mountain Laurel in a baby food jar at Knight Hollow Nursery, Madison, Wisonsin. (McCown)

be used. A glass circular container 7 cm in height and 8 cm in diameter covered with a 9 cm glass Petri dish is also useful when the tops are sealed with Parafilm to permit air exchange and inhibit contamination or water loss. Baby food jars fitted with a clear plastic lid (Magenta Corp) are excellent containers. Most of the major commercial micropropagators have relied on them (Figure 7-7, 7-8).

Figure 7-8. Racks of tubes and baby food jars in the new and large scale production facility at Briggs Nursery, Olympia, Washington. (Briggs)

ROOTING

Now that you have many shoots growing well in microculture you must learn how to get them rooted and have plantlets growing in the "real world." Here are some tips that may help.

Culture Media to Encourage Root Growth

Some cultivars will begin to form root hairs if left for long periods in woody plant medium, but this is a rare event. C. Addison has found that better root formation is obtained by reducing the macro-mineral concentration of the medium formulation to half strength; the sugar is reduced to 10 gm/liter (using glucose rather than sucrose); 2iP is left out; IBA is increased to 3 mg/liter; and activated charcoal at 0.6 gm/liter is added to absorb cytokinins produced by the plantlets.

Several cultivars respond in this kind of medium by forming roots after 4–6 weeks, but others do not root and may even show toxic symptoms. However, it is worth experimenting with those cultivars, which are otherwise not readily rooted in peat mixtures, to learn if improved rooting occurs after transfering through media containing charcoal prior to harvesting. "Harvesting" is the term used for cutting shoots from clumps grown in culture which are to be "stuck." "Sticking" is the process of putting the cut stems into a peat mixture for rooting and growing the plant on.

Sticking in Peat Moss Mixtures

Commercial propagators differ on the ideal length of shoots harvested. Some prefer to cut only after the shoots have reached 3–5 cm. G. Verkade has good luck with smaller shoots of 1–2 cm lengths. In either case there is agreement that the shoots must be kept moist or immersed in water after cutting and until they are stuck. Some add benomyl to the water (10 mg/liter) to inhibit fungus growth. Cuttings can be held for at least 24 hours under refrigeration prior to trimming and sticking.

Media composition varies greatly from straight peat moss, milled spagnum to composted and screened pine bark or washed pine sawdust, vermiculite, styrofoam, to assorted mixes thereof. Wetting these mixtures is enhanced by adding small amounts of mild detergent (like Ivory liquid soap) or the commercial wetting agent called Aquagro at about 2 ml/liter. Of major concern is that the medium not be too wet and so encourage rotting. Usually the moisture content should be much less than "squeezable", and just feel moist to the touch.

G. Verkade uses rooting containers of clear plastic, 4 x 5 in (10 × 2.5 cm) "sandwich" boxes with 1 in (2.5 cm) of peat mixture in the bottom to root 35 to 50 microcuttings (Figure 7-9). A larger 5.5 × 7 in (14 × 18 cm) box is now favored with about 2 in (5 cm) of medium as it permits sticking 200 plantlets. Both containers manufactured by Ekco Products Inc. come with tightly fitted lids to reduce moisture loss. These containers may be held in cabinets furnished with fluorescent tubes for lighting and plastic sheets at the sides to reduce air movement and help maintain high humidity. Bottom heat may be beneficial but is not critical.

Alternative methods include using wooden or plastic seeding flats (10 × 21.5 × 2.5 in high (25 × 42 × 5.5 cm)) holding 200–260 cuttings. The flats or pots are placed on greenhouse benches lined with wet

perlite and covered with a wire mesh frame supporting sheet plastic t(
inhibit water evaporation.

Sticking small cuttings requires using forceps (tweezers) to hol
and guide each cutting into the medium. Most technicians trim th
lower leaves from the cutting with a scalpel or fingers and the
grasping the stem gently with small forceps, push the cutting into tt
rooting mixture a fraction of an inch.

Figure 7-9. A variety of small containers used to root microcuttings under a 4 ft (1.2 m)
fluorescent light fixture in the basement. (Jaynes)

Dipping

The practice of dipping the microcuttings in a solution containing
IBA or other auxin is not usually followed with Mountain Laurel. But in
the case of unusually difficult cultivars which do not root well some
advantage may be realized in using a diluted, liquid commercial dip
such as Wood's or Dip-and-Grow, diluted about 1:15. If used, place the
solution in a very shallow container and dip only the cut end of the
microcuttings before putting the stem into the peat moss mixture.

Transfer of Rooted Plantlets

With any of the above methods some good roots will be evident in
3–6 weeks, though some cultivars may take a little longer. As the plants
grow larger "harden" them gradually to lower humidity conditions. In
closed containers open the lid a fraction more each day until the lid is

removed entirely in about a week. If all the plants under a tent can not be hardened at the same time by opening the enclosure a bit more each day, then individual boxes are first removed part of the day and, after several days of such handling, removed completely.

When hardened off the small plants are transplanted into 2 in (5 cm) pots or similar containers and moved to greenhouse conditions for further growing. Handling is then identical to that of seedling Mountain Laurel (Chapter 5).

SOURCES OF MATERIALS

Most of the apparatus and chemicals required for tissue culturing can be obtained from companies selling laboratory or greenhouse supplies. The following addresses may be useful:

J. P. Bartlett Co. Inc., 578 Boston Post Rd., South Sudbury, MA 01776

Carolina Biological Supply Co., 2700 York Rd., Burlington, NC 27215

Cole-Parmer Instrument Co., 7425 N. Oak Park Ave., Chicago, IL 60648

Ekco Products, Inc., Clayton, NJ 08312

Flow Laboratories, Inc., 1710 Chapman Ave., Rockville, MD 20852

GIBCO, 3175 Staley Rd., Grand Island, NY 14072

Kelco, 8355 Aero Dr., San Diego, CA 92123 Magenta Corporation, 3800 N. Milwaukee Ave., Chicago, IL 60641

Sigma Chemical Co., P.O. Box 14508, St. Louis, MO 63178

Chapter 8

LANDSCAPING AND GARDEN CARE

A soil of a peaty nature is best, but in gardens consisting of pure loam they may be grown well by trenching deeply and mixing plenty of well-decayed leaf-soil and as much peat as can be afforded with the top spit [the depth of a blade of a spade]. They can have the same antipathy to lime at the roots, which renders the cultivation of so many ericaceous plants in chalky soils a difficult and expensive matter. A cool and continuously moist soil is an important desideratum, and this is why deep trenching is recommended. In hot, sandy soils the ground should be removed to a depth of 2 feet and placed at the bottom with the best of the natural soil mixed with a heavier loam, filling the upper part with a mixture of peat, leaf-soil, and loam. This may be a troublesome and perhaps costly business, but it is cheapest in the end, and saves much labour in watering during the hot summer weather. (Bean 1897)

LANDSCAPING

Although the Kalmias can and do fit in many garden styles including formal, rock, and Japanese, they are particularly suitable to a naturalistic garden style. This style involves adopting the better features of wild or natural landscapes and incorporating them into managable and condensed form around our homes, parks, and places of work. The naturalistic garden style stresses, according to Professor Sally Taylor, Connecticut College, New London, Connecticut,

1) free-flowing curves, not straight lines; asymmetrical balance, not symmetrical plant placement.
2) knowledge of plant growth habits, to avoid heavy pruning needed to create a desired shape; prune to tidy up only.
3) selection of plant combinations which are found growing together in their natural habitat; plants which are pleasing together often grow together.
4) appropriate ground covers to face down and finish plantings, blending the edges of beds and lawn.
5) consideration of the landscape value of plants at all seasons, not just the short season of floral display.

Curves are an essential ingredient to an informal and naturalistic garden. They add a feeling of motion, depth, and intrigue to a landscape. Curves should be bold, not weak and hesitant. Visualize a falling drop of water, swollen at one end and pointed at the other. Lay the tear drop on its side and divide in half:

On one end you have a bold outward curve and the other a gentle inward curve. The outward curve needs the tallest plants, the inward the shortest. Use the outward curve to enhance a view or screen something undesirable. Face tall plants down with smaller ones and ground covers. The curves should reflect the angles on building; never use an outward curve on an inward corner and vice versa. In an open or lawn area do not place outward curves opposite each other. Outward curves should in general refect inward curves, but formal symmetry wants to be avoided.

There are many elements in a well executed landscape as indicated in the following quote from Fred Galle's book on *Azaleas:*

A well-planned garden, like a beautiful painting, has its effects on the viewer as the result of careful design and composition. Throughout the garden there should be a sense of unity and orderly arrangement of landscape features and plants in relation to their architectural surroundings. Scale in the landscape relates to the unity of the planting, tree and shrub groups, the land form, and the architechtural features. The plants, as well as the architectural features, should be in scale with one another. Throughout the garden there should be unity and harmony achieved with an understanding of the natural forms, and a repetition and dominance of plant textures. A garden does not need to be of large dimensions. It may be a small terrace, a part of a natural woodland, or it may flow into an open stretch of lawn. A garden should exist for the enjoyment of the owners and be a place for retreat from the perplexities of the day. A garden of charm has the appearance of being casually refined and well organized, but is not created without time and effort.

Texture is an important facet of the landscape and is often referred to as the subtle thread or theme running through a well conceived design and should complement the overall texture determined by the foliage of the trees and shrubs. The texture of the evergreen leaves of Kurume azaleas would be considered fine, while many of the deciduous azaleas and many evergreens such as the Glenn Dale azaleas [and Mountain Laurel] would be considered as medium texture in contrast to the leaves of White Oak or Southern Magnolia, which are coarse textured. One should be able to sense the beauty of a garden at any season. Azalea gardens [and laurel] that are irresistible in the spring should display year-round beauty through a skillful blending of plants and other components of varied texture. A beautiful landscape is a tasteful blending of the ever changing seasonal forms and textures of plants.

Among the elements in a landscape plan are the overall design, plant composition, scale, and texture. Periods of bloom, fall color, mixes of deciduous and evergreen plants, annuals and perennials, needled and broad-leaved, bring about both subtle and dramatic changes in the garden from season to season. The Laurels are low maintenance plants and can be an attractive major element in most gardens. Like many of their Ericaceous relatives, they are relatively easy to transplant. So, if the initial attempts at locating them are not just right, they can be moved.

Despite contrary attitudes of landscape architects, I feel that as long as some of the basic elements of landscape design are understood it is possible to walk around the garden with one or a few plants and set them in different locations to get a feel for where they will do and look best. As long as you have a general scheme in mind, locating individual plants can be done just as well with a shovel in hand as with pencil and paper. To be sure a collection of specimen plants "dropped" at random is not pleasing to most of us, nor does a perfectly organized and manicured garden reflect reality for most of us (Figures 8-1 to 8-10). Have fun, create what you think is best and remember you are really the only one who must to be satisfied with the result. For more information on landscaping consult some of the numerous books on the subject such as *Garden Design Illustrated,* by J. A. and C. L. Grant (Timber Press, Portland, Oregon, 1983).

Figure 8-1. Naturalized Mountain Laurel planted at the border of woods and lawn. (Jaynes)

Figure 8-2. Each individual plant may develop its own form and character. Here the stem and seed capsules add charm through the dormant season. (Jaynes)

Figure 8-3. A collection of Mountain Laurel color selections in a private garden, Connecticut. (Redfield)

Figure 8-4. Mountain Laurel 'Pink Charm' in front of Redvein, *Enkanthus campanulatus,* with a ground cover of Bellwort, *Uvularia sessilifolia.* (Jaynes)

Figure 8-5. Selected Mountain Laurel seedlings used to screen a greenhouse and shed. (Jaynes)

Figure 8-6. A garden specimen of native Mountain Laurel. (Redfield)

Figure 8-7. Sheep Laurel used as a ground cover next to a porch and bounded by a low stone wall and walkway; a low selection referred to as var. *pumila*. (Jaynes)

Figure 8-8. Vigorous, attractive Mountain Laurel growing in a garden in Japan. (Suzuki)

Figure 8-9. Montain Laurel used as a ground cover instead of a lawn to mow. Annual pruning is required to keep plants from becoming too tall. The low ground cover overhanging the stone wall is Bearberry, *Arctostaphylos uva-ursi.* (Jaynes)

Figure 8-10. Mountain Laurel pruned as a hedge on perimeter of front lawn. Flowering dogwood trees add accent. (Jaynes)

SITE SELECTION

It is discouraging to purchase, or be given, a valuable plant only to have it decline and die in the garden. But anyone who has enjoyed success with Azaleas and other Ericaceous plants should have little trouble with Laurel. Their requirements are, in fact, similar.

An initial consideration is whether the plant will be hardy. This can be determined by knowing where the species normally grows and how other specimens have done in your area. Locally grown plants have the advantage of having been exposed and acclimated to the local environment. Species like Mountain Laurel with extensive north and south range vary greatly in their hardiness. Plants native to the southern end of the range are not adapted to the shorter growing season in the north and will not adapt to it.

Most of us are limited in our choices of planting sites, so we must survey the conditions around our homes carefully before selecting a planting location. None of the Laurels will thrive in an exposed location where the soil is left bare and the ground freezes deep in winter or where there is no snow protection; but with protection against winds, all do well in full sunlight. In fact, the more sun they receive, the more dense their growth and the more prolific their flowering. On the other hand, partial shade, from an overstory of widely spaced trees, is beneficial in prolonging the life of the flowers and extending the blooming period, especially in the case of Mountain Laurel (Figure 8-11). Shade becomes even more important with Mountain Laurel in the mid to southern part of its range where the combination of summer sun and heat is particularly harsh.

Avoid planting Mountain Laurel in low, open areas which are frost pockets. This species, adapted to high country, is susceptible to frost injury when planted in low pockets, but the other Laurels are more resistant, as would be expected from their natural habitat which includes low, wet areas. On clear nights heat is radiated to the open sky from the ground, plants, and air. If there is no breeze, the cold air settles and moves downslope where it collects in depressions, valley bottoms, and along steams, or so-called frost pockets. A change of just a few feet in height may mean a difference of several degrees in minimum temperature. Because a canopy of trees, even with bare branches, will moderate the effects of heat loss, sites below trees offer good locations for Mountain Laurel and other ericaceous plants.

You may assume that the southern side of a house is a preferred location for Laurels. Not so. Plants on the south side of a building are exposed to the full winter sun and reflected heat in the day and then cruelly and suddenly subjected to the cold-air temperatures of night.

Excessively high daytime temperatures and frozen ground can literally be death to broad-leaved evergreens, because water is lost from the leaves and can not be replaced from the roots (Figure 8-12). But a

Figure 8-11. A natural stand of Mountain Laurel enhanced by thinning the trees and removing lower branches to allow more light to reach the plants. (Jaynes)

Figure 8-12. (A) The rolled and drooped leaves of a Rhododendron on a cold day with the temperature below freezing. (B) Mountain Laurel leaves seldom roll but will droop as the temperature drops to the teens. Note flower buds on both plants. (Jaynes)

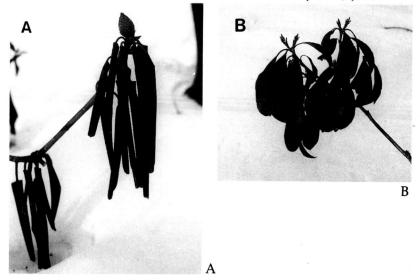

A

B

southern exposure can be tempered to the plant's benefit if it is moved several feet away from the building or if overhead trees break up the sun's intensity. The angle of the sun changes greatly during the year, so do not be fooled: trees that shade a bed in June may not do an effective job in December.

The northern side of the house is one of the best locations for Mountain Laurel. Here the plants are shaded in winter because of the low sun angle, daytime temperatures are moderated, and the ground is subjected to less freezing and thawing. In summer they receive early morning and late afternoon sun but are shaded from the intense midday sun. They will receive adequate light, even if they receive no direct sunlight but are exposed to the open sky. On the other hand, if they receive no direct sunlight and the sky is blocked by a canopy of tree foliage then flowering will be limited.

Ground slope is not of concern as long as other conditions are met. A southern slope is warmer and dryer than one facing north; hence on the former a good mulch is essential.

Eastern Bog Laurel, Mountain Laurel, and Sheep Laurel are all found in the wild fairly close to the coastline, but only the Eastern Bog Laurel and Sheep Laurel can be considered salt-tolerant. Mountain Laurel can not withstand salt and in the Northeast, where roads are kept clear in winter with applications of sodium chloride, plants close to the road have often died. Where Mountain Laurel survives along such roads it is either up a bank or beyond the splash or drainage zone of the road bed.

SOIL

Laurels prefer a well-drained, acid soil and suffer in heavy, poorly drained, alkaline soils. Bog Laurel and Sheep Laurel can tolerate wet soil but do better in well-drained locations. Fortunately, inhospitable soils can be modified. Peat moss, up to 50% by volume, and coarse sand can be mixed into clayey soils and the planting bed raised a few inches to improve drainage and aeration. Peat moss will improve most soils and aid in establishing new transplants.

In clayey soils, prepare an area much larger and deeper than that required for the root ball and work in peat moss, leaf mold or other partially decayed organic matter. A shallow, dish-like hole in such soils acts as a catch basin for rain water and the roots will rot. Thus an alternative on heavy soils is to set the plant on the soil surface and bring good, well drained soil up to and around the plant root ball.

Plant growth depends on soil moisture; soils vary greatly in their water-holding capacity and their ability to release water to plants. Coarse, sandy soils admit water rapidly but have limited storage capacity. Fine textured soils, on the other hand, have a much larger capacity, but, when compacted, water infiltration is slow and surface runoff increased. In addition, water is tightly held to fine clay particles, and therefore less moisture is released to plant roots in clayey soils than in sandy soils.

Established Laurels are tolerant of drought conditions but do best when soils are kept moist, but not wet. Conditions vary, but during the growing season plants need at least 1 in (2.5 cm) of water per week; if not released by the soil or provided by rains, then irrigation is necessary. Since daily waterings may waterlog the soil, and sprinklings may be superficial, a good soaking every 1–2 weeks during dry periods is preferred.

pH is the term applied to the chemical measure of the hydrogen ion concentration of the soil solution. Neutrality is pH 7.0. Acid soils have a numerical value lower than 7.0; while alkaline soils have a numerical value higher than 7.0. Few natural soils are more acid than pH 3.5 or more alkaline than pH 9.0. The pH of wild Laurel stands generally ranges between 4.0 and 5.5.

If the soil pH is 5.6 or higher, an acidifying material such as aluminum sulfate, ferrous sulfate, or finely divided sulfur should be added to lower the pH. The following table gives approximate amounts needed to increase the acidity (lower the pH) for silty loams. On coarse, sandy soils, 50% less material should be applied.

To change pH			Pounds of material per 100 sq ft (9 sq m)		
Start		*Desired*	*Aluminum sulfate,*	*Ferrous sulfate,*	*or Sulfur*
8.0	to	5.5	13.5	25.9	5.5
7.5	to	5.5	11.5	23.5	5.0
7.0	to	5.5	9.0	16.5	3.5
6.5	to	5.5	6.5	11.8	2.5
6.5	to	5.0	10.5	18.8	4.0

If aluminum sulfate is used excessively, aluminum toxicity may occur in some soils. David Leach, in his book, *Rhododendrons of the World,* strongly recommends ferrous sulfate, but the average garden center or nursery supplier does not stock this material. It is available from chemical supply houses. The price is often more than for aluminum sulfate. Both sulfates are quick-acting, 2–3 weeks, compared with 6–9 weeks or more for sulfur. Although slower acting, sulfur is less expensive and longer lasting, but more difficult to apply. Keep sulfur dust out of your eyes.

Soils are formed over long time periods from various kinds of rock. Parent rocks determine the soil pH so, even though additives can modify it, the soil always tends to return to its original pH over a period of time. Soils around building foundations often build a pH too high for ericaceous plants, because calcium leaches from the concrete walls or because plaster or other limestone material was left in the soil at the time of construction. Even the careless application of lime to an adjacent lawn can have a similar effect.

Some soils are very low in available calcium. In such cases lime is added or calcium sulfate (gypsum, landplaster) can be applied. The latter material should not effect pH.

FERTILIZER

Normal plant growth depends on at least 14 elements supplied by the soil. Of these, nitrogen (N), phosphorus (P), potassium (K), calcium (Ca), magnesium (Mg), and sulfur (S) are required in sufficient quantities to be called major or macronutrients. The remainder, including iron (Fe), boron (B), and zinc (Zn), are utilized by plants in smaller quantities and are called minor or micronutrients. Deficiencies or excesses in either major or minor nutrients can cause abnormal growth and may even be fatal to plants.

Most soils contain less than optimal amounts of one or more of the elements. Such deficiences must be determined to know when fetilizer is needed. Fertilizer is likely needed if the amount of new growth and color of foliage are poor. Plants in good, nutritious soils have a lustrous green to blue-green color, good growth, and good leaf retention. Those in poor soils grow slowly, have poor color, and lose their leaves prematurely. An excess of one or more nutrients may cause leggy, "floppy" growth and eventually injure the roots, leaves, and shoots. Composition and vigor of weeds are also good indicators. Or better yet the soil or leaves may be chemically analyzed.

Soil testing, although not an exact science, is the easiest and most reliable means of measuring soil fertility. Soil testing services are available through most universities or horticultural experiment stations, as well as private firms. Kits are also available for do-it-yourself testing. Information on soil testing labs and the procedure for gathering soil samples can be obtained from local agricultural agents or the nearest agricultural university.

Laurels can exist in very infertile soils but thrive with moderate fertilization. Applications should never exceed the amounts recommended for Rhododendrons or Hollies. Err in the direction of too little, because more Laurels have been injured by excessive fertilization, expecially nitrogen, than from starvation. Those who test your soil will suggest the kinds and amounts of fertilizer to apply. If plant growth suggests the need for fertilizer and a soil test is not readily obtainable, then apply at about one-fourth the rate suggested on bags of commercially available fertilizers for acid-loving plants. Were you to use one of the common evergreen plant foods containing 8% nitrogen, 4% phosphorus and 4% potassium (8-4-4), the recommended rate of application is 3 lbs (1.25 kg) per 100 sq ft (9 sq m) of ground. I recommend reducing the rate to ¾ lbs (350 g) per 100 sq ft (9 sq m) (300 pounds per acre) but apply this rate 3 times a year: early spring, June and August. Sixteen percent of the 8-4-4 fertilizer is active ingredients (three macronutrients) while the remaining 84 % is inert. Cottonseed meal has an analysis of 7-3-2 and can be applied at the same rate as the 8-4-4 fertilizer. I find that a total of 50–100 lbs (25–45 kg) of actual nitrogen per acre (0.4 ha) per year is adequate for good growth in my laurel fields. Two or three light applications of fertilizer at intervals are preferable to a single heavy application, especially when the nitrogen is in a readily soluable form. Even the "slow-release" fertilizers must be applied conservatively around Laurel.

TRANSPLANTING

Early fall and early spring are the best times for transplanting Laurel, although with certain precautions they can be moved any time that the ground is not frozen. Fall transplanting has some advantages over spring transplanting if the move is made early. Fall plantings put in at least a month before the ground freezes will have well established roots when spring shoot growth occurs. For, despite the dormant top, the roots remain active as long as the soil temperatures are above 40°F (4.5°C). Nurserymen and experienced gardeners have long taken advantage of this phenomenon to give their plants a head start. Take the following precautions to prevent frost heaving: choose a site with well-drained, porous soil and use a wood chip or other mulch.

All plants suffer some degree of shock from transplanting, since no specimen, whether field or container grown, can be transplanted without some disturbance to the roots. Container-grown plants suffer less root loss, but they must adjust to a greater difference between the texture of the mix within the container and the soil in which they are placed. Such differences between mix and soil inhibit water exchange and root growth. To facilitate the outward growth of the roots and the assimilation of water, make several shallow vertical cuts into the root ball of container-grown plants before placing them in the planting hole.

Next to fall transplanting, early spring is best. Winter transplanting is possible in regions where the ground does not freeze solidly. Take extra care whenever transplanting to obtain a good root ball, and never let the ball dry out. When there is a large amount of soft growth or the roots have been severely disturbed, prune the top growth to reduce water loss through the foliage.

MULCH

Native Laurels usually grow where they have at least some natural mulch around them, and a good mulch is advisable for Laurels in the garden. Mulches limit the growth of weeds, conserve soil moisture, reduce leaching and erosion, moderate soil temperature, prevent compaction, and, as organic mulches decompose, they release nutrients to the soil.

Wood chips and pine bark are two excellent mulches, but many others are often available locally, such as sugar-cane bagasse or buckwheat hulls. Peat moss is usually not satisfactory, because the surface dries and mats, becoming almost waterproof, and worse, if fluffed up, it blows away. Hays and straws are good, but weed seeds in them can cause a serious nuisance. (I stopped using salt marsh hay after one particularly weedy bale cost me many hours of backbreaking work.) The leaves collected by municipalities are an inexpensive substitute for bark or wood chips. I have truckloads dumped at my home in the fall; by spring they are quite usable. One drawback is that they do not last as long as chips and some blow away in windy locations. But if you grind them up, they have a more uniform appearance and do not blow around as readily. Inorganic mulches such as stone and gravel may be desirable in formal settings. Fresh sawdust or wood chips work well if not used too heavily, but initial bacterial action on them may tie up free nitrogen. So, if you use fresh organic mulches, add a light side dressing of nitrogen. As organic mulches decay (compost), they release the nitrogen that was earlier unavailable.

Soil pH may be raised , lowered or unaffected by mulch. The pH of sandy soils with low organic content are most easily changed. Organic mulches rich in calcium, magnesium, and potassium (such as maple leaves) tend to increase pH, whereas mulches rich in tannins or other organic acids (such as oak leaves) decrease it. However, such changes are normally very gradual and can be ignored. By contrast, the leaching of calcium from masonry walls has a more significant effect on changing pH.

Mulches control weeds and evaporation, and they permit more water to percolate through the soil. But, despite this potential for increased leaching, organic mulches increase available nitrate nitrogen, potassium, magnesium, and phosphorus. Fungi and bacteria increase under a mulch; apparently beneficial types prosper more than pathogenic ones. In addition, mulch protects and feeds earthworms (valuable garden allies) against freezing and desiccation. Of course, the downside is that grubs of Asiatic and Japanese beetles also do well at times under organic mulches and they will feed on Laurel roots. Moles may then come and feed on various insect grubs and worms, but then the mice take over the mole runs and the mice will feed on Laurel roots. Mulch, yes; the benefits outway the risks, but like everything else that's good and useful there are some associated drawbacks.

WEED CONTROL WITH HERBICIDES

A good mulch can solve many of the worst weed problems, and regular, but sparing, hand weeding will complete the job. I do not recommend chemical weed killers for most home gardeners. Yet, selected herbicides are necessary in large gardens, and commercial growers would find it difficult to continue without them. Their importance is indicated by the greater expenditure of money on herbicides than on either fungicides or insecticides.

A short overview will acquaint you with some of the herbicides that can be used around Laurel. Since no single herbicide will control all weeds safely, your choice will depend on many factors, including size and type of plants, kinds of weeds, and time of year. Some products are designed for the home gardener; others should be used only by professionals. New materials enter the market constantly, and preferences and the laws governing use change. Because of this, before you purchase any herbicides, check with your horticultural service or other agricultural authority for the latest information on materials and proper usage in your locality. An article by Robert C. Ticknor on "Weed Control Around Rhododendrons" in the January, 1987 *Journal American Rhododendron Society* contains much of the information applicable to *Kalmia*.

Classification of Herbicides Based on Activity

PRE-EMERGENCE HERBICIDES   Because their action affects the weeds at such an early stage of growth, these chemicals are referred to as pre-emergence herbicides. They are selective in their effect on different kinds of plants. Crabgrass killers used on established lawns and applied in the spring are a pre-emergence type. They are long lasting, having an effect for a few months to a year or more depending on the material and rate of application.

Simazine (Princep) is one of the most useful pre-emergence herbicides and is sold as an 80% wettable powder (80W), a 90% dry flowable (Caliber 90), a flowable liquid (4L), or a 4% granular preparation (4G). It kills many weeds as they germinate and is also effective on many established weeds and grasses when applied during the dormant season. Simazine is safe when used around established plants if applied properly but may lead to injury when applied around new transplants or small seedlings. It has a residual action throughout the growing season and a small persistent residue into the second year. The effect of simazine can be improved by applying it together with other pre-emergence herbicides such as DCPA (Dachthal), diphenamid (Dymid or Enide,), trifluralin (Treflan), oryzalin (Surflan), and metolachlor (Dual). The latter are more effective on grasses and some of the annual, broad-leaved weeds and are packaged in wettable, liquid, or granular forms. Like simazine, DCPA, diphenamid, oryzalin, and metolachlor are applied on the soil surface before weed germination. Trifluarlin, on the other hand, is volatile and must be mixed into the soil for best results. These materials possess moderate residual activity but when applied at the proper rates will not leave soil residues harmful to the growth of Laurel. Metolachlor is particularly effective in controlling annual grasses and nutsedge.

POST-EMERGENCE HERBICIDES   As the name implies, post-emergence herbicides control weeds after they have emerged. Dichlobenil (Casoron) is effective on established perennial weeds in established plantings with pre-emergence activity usually lasting until early summer. Nurserymen use it, but, unfortunately it injures the roots of newly planted Laurel. Applications are usually made on the soil surface during the late fall, winter, or early spring when soil and air temperatures are low, preferably just before a rain.

NONSELECTIVE HERBICIDES   Paraquat (Paraquat, Gramoxone) is a chemical hoe, in that it kills only green foliage on contact and is rapidly detoxified in soil. It is effective in preparing new plant beds formerly in sod or annual weeds. One or two sprays kill the existing weeds without spading or cultivating so planting can be done within a day.

Paraquat is used commercially and is effective in combination with residual herbicides such as simazine and Dacthal. Applied as a directed spray, it kills established annual weeds and the tops of perennial grasses on contact, while the other two chemicals prevent regrowth of grass and kill germinating seed. I used this combination successfully for many years applying it as a directed spray from a 3½ gal (12 l) backpack sprayer, though I prefer Roundup now. Paraquat can cause serious injury to lung and eye membranes; hence, caution must be used in applying it. For this reason Paraquat is registered for use in commercial plantings but not for use around homes.

Glyphosate (Roundup, Kleenup), like paraquat, is quickly inactivated in soil and so safe to plant into soon after treatment. Unlike paraquat, however, glyphosate is systemic and is moved from foliage to roots to kill rhizomes and underground plant parts. It also is much lower in toxicity to mammals and therefore safer to use. Glyphosate may also be used as a directed spray around established plants with care to avoid spraying the plant foliage. Most annual and perennial weeds and deciduous woody plants are controlled by glyphosate applied at the proper stage of growth and at the proper concentations. Woody plants, including poison ivy and brambles, are most susceptible to glyphosate sprays from mid-summer to early fall. Like paraquat, glyphosate provides no residual control of weeds from seed and must be combined or used in sequence with a pre-emergence herbicide for best results. A combination of Roundup at 1 fl oz (30 ml) plus Surflan 75W at ⅓ cup (160 ml) per gallon (3.8 l) as a directed spray on weed growth 4–6 in (10–15 cm) tall has given excellent kill and long residual control in landscape plantings of woody shrubs.

FUMIGANTS   These are general sterilants used for treating soil. Fumigants such as metham (Vapam) and methyl bromide (Dowfume) have value in sterilizing soil for mixes or in treating beds prior to planting seedlings. They kill not only weed seeds but also perennial root stocks, fungi, and nematodes. The expense of fumigation generally precludes treating large areas. For information on their use consult local agricultural authorities.

ENHANCING FLOWERING

As a rule, the more sunlight the plants receive the faster they will grow and the heavier they will bloom. However, in southerly latitudes and warm temperate regions some high shade is required to moderate the effects of the hot summer sun. Mountain Laurel is, fortunately, shade tolerant and may even bloom well with little or no direct sunlight. Individual plants vary in their capacity to bloom. As yet, we do not know enough about the named cultivars to say which will do best in sun and/or full shade. Generally, a plant that does not bloom needs more light. Thin and prune the overstory trees and shrubs to allow the plants "to see" some sky light, even if not direct sunlight.

Plants in some shade and under excellent growing conditions may produce excessive growth with few if any flower buds. A little more stress on such plants in the summer; i.e. no fertilizer and less water, will likely stimulate flower bud production.

Some plants bury their flowers in new growth. Although this may be a cultivar characteristic, it most often occurs on vigorously growing, young plants. Reducing soil fertility and simple aging of the plants will reduce this problem, as will transplanting. Typically the stress of transplanting reduces new vegetative growth and enhances flower bud formation, so that plants transplanted one spring bloom heavily the following year.

DISBUDDING (DEADHEADING)   Flower buds for the following year's bloom form in August and September on the current season's growth. Hence, cultural methods that increase the number of new shoots increase the potential for flower bud set. Flowers left on a shoot normally produce seed capsules and inhibit new growth on that shoot. Disbudding or deadheading, removal of the flower cluster immediately after flowering, generally results in the formation of one or several new shoots, on which new flower buds may form (Figure 8-13). New growth does not guarantee flowers the next year, but without new growth there will be no flower bud set at all. The developing seed capsules not only limit new shoot growth, but evidence from work with other plants suggests that they produce a hormone which, when trans-

Figure 8-13. The effect, by the end of summer, of "deadheading" in June. Flowers on left were allowed to form seed capsules: no new shoots and no flower buds for next year. On right, flower cluster was broken out of the branch immediately after flowering. Four shoots developed, and two have flower buds for the next year. (Jaynes)

located to vegetative shoots, inhibits the formation of flower buds. Thus Mountain Laurel tends to produce good floral displays every other year unless the developing seed capsules are removed to enhance annual flowering. Deadheading is not as important with the other Laurel species, for the presence of seed capsules does not as strongly inhibit flower bud formation.

Some people find plants with seed capsules unsightly, whereas others see them as an attractive feature of the plant. The species hybrids may or may not have special merit, then, depending on your point of view, for they all, except for a few crosses of Western Laurel and Eastern Bog Laurel, are sterile and fail to develop large persistent seed capsules.

Occasionly a Mountain Laurel will produce flower buds on all the shoots when transplanted, or the shock of transplanting will subsequently result in an over-abundance of flower buds. When this occurs, too much of the plant's energy goes into flower and seed production and not enough into producing new growth for maintaining the plant in good condition. At least some of the flower buds should be removed to stimulate vegetative growth. If this cannot be done in the spring, the faded flowers should be removed immediatedly after flowering. Removal of flowers at the base of the plant stimulates branching and fullness at the base. Removal of flower buds only on top of the plant stimulates height growth.

PRUNING MOUNTAIN LAUREL

One of the most common questions is, "My foundation planting has become leggy; how and when do I prune it?" The answer is, "In early spring, before growth starts." This is the best time, although some flower buds will inevitably be removed. A second choice is immediately after flowering, still early enough in the growing season to obtain at least one flush of growth subsequent to the pruning.

Pruning is an art; each plant has to be handled a bit differently, but there are some general rules. First, try to imagine what you want the plant to look like, and then prune with this design in mind. Do not prune back to naked, unbranched stems. Pruning cuts should be made at forks and where small laterals exist as sources of additional growth. There is little problem on plants with dense foliage all the way to the ground. Plants 4–6 ft (1.2–1.8 m) tall lacking lower branches present a problem. There are two approaches, neither ideal, but both better than cutting the tops off and leaving 2–3 ft (60–90 cm) naked stems. One is to remove the plants and replace them with smaller bushes of desired size; this is drastic but gives immediate results. The other approach is to cut the overgrown plants to within 2–3 in (5–7.5 cm) of the ground, best done in early spring. The plants will resprout and become dense and multistemmed, but it may take 3–4 years for them to reach flowering size again.

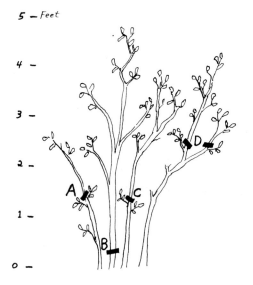

Figure 8-14. Heavy pruning is preferably done in late winter or right after blooming. (A, C, D) Moderate to severe pruning cuts to reduce height of plant and stimulate growth nearer ground; note all cuts are just above lateral branch with foliage. (B) Severe cut to stimulate basal sprouting. Generally all branches on one plant should be pruned in a similar manner. (Jaynes)

Judicious pruning every year is the easiest way to prevent plants from becoming leggy or too large. Since Laurel foliage is attractive at all times of the year in flower arrangements and especially at Christmas time in decorations, you have enough excuse to prune the plants regularly. Thinning out or removal of odd branches can be done any time of the year with no harmful effects on the plant. Mountain Laurel is normally a graceful and informally shaped plant; older plants take on an exotic or oriental character. But they are also amenable to shearing and shaping so can be grown in dense mounds or in formal hedges. Such pruning should be done immediately after flowering to permit new shoot growth and flower bud formation for the next year. However, in most situations the more natural, informal appearance that results from occasional, judicious pruning is far more attractive (Figure 8-14).

HARVESTING OF MOUNTAIN LAUREL FOLIAGE

Fifty years ago, Buttrick estimated that 20 million pounds (9,000,000 kg) of Laurel foliage were used annually in the United States for decorations during the holiday season. Since the estimated average yield per acre (0.4 ha) was as low as ¼ ton (250 kg), nearly 40,000 acres (16,000 ha) were cut over annually for Laurel foliage. A new crop could be harvested from the same land every 5 years. Thus, a total of 120,000 acres (48,000 ha) would grow indefinitely all the Laurel required by the trade. Obviously this is but a small fraction of the total area where Laurel is presently growing.

Buttrick wrote:

The growing of laurel for the sale of its foliage would be quite different from its cultivation for ornamental use in gardens. Its production for market could best take place in woodland, [where] advantage would be taken of its sprouting power. No attempt would be made to grow it from seed or produce large and handsome clumps.

The cutting of laurel so that it will sprout satisfactorily and produce further crops is quite simple. Ordinarily collectors cut or break it off at about eighteen inches [45 cm] back from the tips of the branches. Inferior branches are apt to be left growing. A good second growth seldom follows such a cutting. To secure a good second crop the cut should be made close to the root and those parts of the plant not useful for decorating purposes should be discarded.

I take exception to some of Buttrick's observations. Plants growing in sunny locations could certainly be harvested more often than every five years. In exposed locations, such as on the edge of woods or under power lines, it could be harvested every 2–3 years. Further, regrowth is quite thrifty when 18 in (45 cm) branches are taken from large, established plants Management of native Laurel stands for greens is something that a few landowners might wish to consider. Other than harvesting, labor would be required to remove competing vegetation. In some situations, the spraying of foliage with a fungicide for control of leaf spot might be considered.

No statistics are available, but Laurel greens are still used extensively in florists' arrangements throughout the year. In the southern Appalachians collectors of Laurel are called "Ivy Breakers", derived from the local name for the plant, Ivy Bush. The trade in Laurel foliage appears to have diminished considerably since Buttrick's time, in large part because of high labor costs for harvesting and certainly due to restrictive and misunderstood state laws. Most states prohibit pruning and digging of Laurel on state lands and public rights of way. Laurel is specifically mentioned in the laws of Pennsylvania, New Jersey, and North Carolina and is protected by more general statues in other states. Connecticut recently repealed some of the laws protecting specific plants including Mountain Laurel, not so they would be less protected

Figure 8-15. Mountain Laurel can be forced to bloom indoors after approximately 3 months of cold dormancy. (Jaynes)

but to get the word out that all plants on public lands should be respected. By designating specially protected plants the implication that the other plants are available for cutting and collecting is created.

Misunderstanding of these laws is widespread. Some private landowners, for example, wonder whether or not they have the right to move, or even prune, Laurel on their own property. Of course they do! In fact, the judicious harvesting of Laurel foliage for floral decoration could well supplement a landowner's income. Discretionary pruning does no harm and often helps the plants. Pruning is recommended to keep cultivated plants in bounds.

There are other interesting uses of Laurel. A century ago in England, Mountain Laurel was forced in the greenhouse as a pot plant. There is no reason why today the several species, their hybrids, and the newer selections should not be tried for pot culture and possibly forced for cut flowers. However, for Mountain Laurel a means to foreshorten the cold dormancy requirement of approximately 100–120 days at 45°F (7°C) is likely needed for commercially acceptable forcing. Exhibitors

Figure 8-16. Splashes of color can be created in the garden with selections of Mountain Laurel. (Jaynes)

in the Boston and Philadelphia spring flower shows (held in March and April) often have Mountain Laurel in bloom. Such plants are usually brought into a cool enclosure around Christmas and are gradually exposed to increasingly higher temperature over a period of many weeks. Plants can be forced into bloom in 6–8 weeks after the necessary cold treatment (Figure 8-15). Daytime forcing temperatures can be high but cool night temperatures are required to maintain the pink and red colors in the flowers.

Rules of the National Council of State Garden Clubs once added to the mystique and taboo surrounding Laurel use, for they stipulated that Mountain Laurel flowers and foliage could not be used by their members in arrangements which were entered for competitive judging. Fortunately, in recognition of the cultivated varieties which became available this rule was dropped. What better, more pleasing way to appreciate and enjoy this handsome plant than to use the foliage and flowers for decorative purposes; whether from cultivated plants or from native plants on one's own property (Figures 8-16, 8-17).

Figure 8-17. An attractive, well grown *Kalmia latifolia* in the Cecil and Molly Smith Garden, St. Paul, Oregon. In front is a single plant of *Trillium ovatum,* foliage in upper right is *Acer macrophyllum* and to the right is *Gaultheria shallon* or Salal. (Bluhm)

*Chapter 9*_____

INSECTS, DISEASES, AND OTHER MALADIES

> *They [Mountain Laurel] are perfectly hardy, although in exposed situations the foliage sometimes gets browned in winter.*
>
> *No insect attacks them, and they are subject to no diseases.*
> *(Sprague 1871)*

Every plant is subject to the ever-present threat of harm from insects and diseases; and while the Laurels, when grown under the proper conditions, are relatively free of such threats, problems do occur. So, here are described the common threats to Laurels and methods to control them. I shall concentrate on Mountain Laurel pests but will not neglect those with a preference for the other species.

Since things change rapidly, the materials listed here for control may or may not be available at the time you read this book, so always check with local authorities. Consult agricultural experts in your area for current registered uses of pesticides, and be sure to read and follow instructions on pesticide labels.

INSECTS AND MITES

Lacebug, *Stephanitis rhododendri* and *S. pyrioides*

Adults and nymphs of the lacebug feed by inserting their mouth parts and sucking sap from the undersides of the leaves (Figure 9-1). Their feeding shows on the upper leaf surface as a mottle of numerous whitish specks, not unlike the damage caused by leafhoppers and mites on other plants. On the undersurface the leaf becomes brown-spotted with excrement. The lacebugs pass the winter in the form of eggs attached to the underside of the leaf, usually near the midrib. They hatch in May, and the nymphs mature in June. Eggs for the second brood are laid in June and July and hatch in August. This generation of nymphs matures late in the season, and the adults lay eggs on the leaves; these eggs overwinter there and hatch the following spring. Mountain Laurel and Sheep Laurel grown in full sun are the most commonly attacked. Fortunately lacebugs are seldom a problem of the magnitude for Laurel that they are on the related species Japanese

Andromeda, *Pieris japonica.*

Control these pests by spraying the undersides of the leaves with Sevin, which kills both nymphs and adults. The first spraying should be in late May before Mountain Laurel flowers and the second in July or whenever lacebugs are noticed. It is sometimes advisable to include a miticide with Sevin since mites often build up after Sevin is used.

Figure 9-1. Lacebug on the underside of a Sheep Laurel leaf. Excrement spots on leaf surface are characteristic of lacebug infestation. (Jaynes)

Blackvine and Strawberry Weevils, *Otiorhynchus sulcatus* and *O. ovatus*

Blackvine Weevil larvae are present in the soil for much of the year. They devour small roots and gnaw the bark of larger roots, often girdling them and ultimately killing the plant. Nocturnal adult weevils start emerging from the soil in late May and continue to emerge through most of the summer. They spend daylight hours resting under loose soil and plant litter around the base of plants. At night they climb to the foliage where they chew notches in leaf margins (Figure 9-2). Large populations can cause notches to coalesce and the leaves will present a very ragged appearance. The serious damage, however, is done at the very destructive larvae or grub stage.

Since the banning of chlordane for use on ornamental plants, control of this pest is almost entirely concentrated on reducing adult populations before eggs are laid. Adults must feed for at least 3 weeks

Figure 9-2. Notching
on edge of leaves
caused by adult black
vine weevils. (Jaynes)

before laying eggs. Therefore an effective method of control is to spray foliage, branches, and stems and soak litter directly under plants where the adults seek refuge during the day. In southern New England the first spray is applied in early June and treatments are repeated at 3 week intervals throughout August. June and July applications are the most critical since most egg production takes place during these 2 months. Acephate (Orthene), fluvalinate, ficam, and permethrin are registered for control of black vine weevel adults.

Mulberry Whitefly, *Tetraleurodes mori*

This insect attacks Mountain Laurel as well as numerous other species, including Mulberry. The oval nymphs or larvae appear on the undersides of the leaves and are dark brown or black, fringed with a whitish border composed of a waxy secretion. In the wild they may become so numerous that they are a real bother when walking in Laurel patches, but the plants seem to suffer little from their presence. The extent of damage by these insects does not usually warrant control measures, but they can be destroyed with a synthetic pyrethrin (SBP-1382, Resmethrin, fluvalinate).

Cankerworms, Gypsy Moths, Other Leaf Eaters

Inchworm, cankerworms, caterpillars, specifically gypsy moths (*Porthetria dispar*), and elm spanworms (*Ennomos subsignarius*) are not supposed to "enjoy" Laurel foliage. However, dietary preference goes out the window when populations of these insects reach epidemic levels. Laurels under trees which have been defoliated by the larvae are soon attacked. Control with sprays of Sevin, methoxychlor, or the bacterium *Bacillus thuringiensis* (Dipel) at 10 day intervals when the larvae are present.

Rhododendron Borer, *Ramosia rhododendri*

This borer prefers Rhododendrons but also attacks Mountain Laurel. The larvae bore under the bark on main stems, leaving scars and sometimes girdling or weakening branches. The moths appear in May and June when the females lay their eggs on the twigs. The moth has clear wings spreading about ½ in (1.2 cm). Injured stems should be removed and burned. To prevent damage, the larger stems can be sprayed or painted with an insecticide (check on registration of lindane, endosulfan, and chlorpyrifos) at 20 day intervals starting in mid-May. Apply two or three treatments.

Leaf Rollers or Leaftiers, *Archips* species

The larvae roll the young leaves around themselves, hold the leaf in place with webbing, and then proceed to feed on it. They also enter the flower buds and eat pollen from the anthers, disfiguring the flowers and making them shorter-lived. This is a particularly vexing pest when one is attempting to cross-pollinate and finds nearly every bud injured and the pollen eaten. The same materials listed for other leaf eaters will control them. Apply spray several days before the flowers open so that flower-visiting bumblebees will not be affected.

Seed eaters and Other Insects

In addition to the leaf roller that thrives on the pollen of laurel flowers, another larva or later generation of the same leaf roller is a notable feeder on the seeds in developing capsules, a particularly cursed beast for the plant breeder. Repeated dustings of the developing seed capsules with an insecticide such as malathion at 10 day intervals control the damage.

Aphids, *Neoamphorophora kalmiae* and Others

Aphids are sucking insects and generally are only a problem on succulent new foliage. If large numbers are present, they stunt and deform new growth. They have been a problem for me occasionally on young greenhouse-grown plants of Bog Laurel and Mountain Laurel. They can be controlled with malathion or acephate applied as a spray or with some of the systemics applied as drenches.

European Red Mite, *Metatetranychus ulmi*

Mites are not usually a problem on Mountain Laurel but they do occur, in fact regularly on Western and Eastern Bog Laurel cultivated in the East. The most serious problems occur on cuttings of Mountain Laurel placed in polyethylene-covered propagation cases. Such extremely humid conditions are not normally associated with mite infestations so their buildup in propagation beds might be explained by the lack of natural predators.

Mature mites are extremely small and are best seen using a magnifier (Figure 9-3). They feed by sucking plant juices. The adult female European red mite is dark red with white spots. Mites pass the winter in the egg stage on bark. Several generations develop each summer with peak infestations occurring in mid- to late summer. Mites have tremendous reproductive abilities and can rapidly reach epidemic proportions. In 4 weeks at 80°F (27°C), a female mite is capable of giving rise to well over 13 million offspring. Infested foliage takes on a mottled, bronze cast, and affected leaves may drop prematurely. Several miticides, including Plictran and Tedion, can be applied as a spray. Systemics are also effective applied as a soil drench.

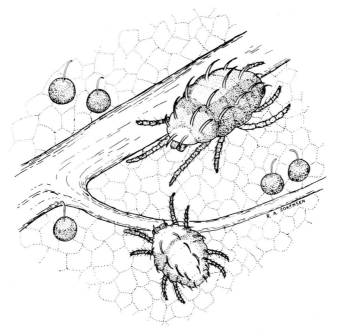

Figure 9-3. Mites and eggs on the underside of a Laurel leaf. The adults are only about the size of the period at the end of this sentence and often go unnoticed until leaves become discolored. (Sorensen-Leonard)

Miscellaneous

Other insects and mites may cause problems from time to time. Local agricultural agents will help in identifying them and in suggesting controls.

DISEASES

Leaf Spot

The fungus, *Mycosphaerella colorata,* also referred to by its conidial stage, *Phyllosticta kalmicola,* causes irregular, light gray spots with a red to purplish brown border. At first the spots are red and small but increase up to ½ in (1.2 cm) in diameter. Tiny black pustules (fruiting bodies) are scattered over the infected areas. The leaves are unsightly and, when severely infected, fall prematurely. The disease is most common on Mountain Laurel when the bushes are crowded or shaded; under such conditions humidity can be high, and moisture on the foliage does not evaporate readily after rains or heavy dews. Similar conditions may also exist in blocks of container grown plants that are irrigated often.

Whenever possible, collect all fallen and infected leaves and burn or remove them from the area. (This is a commonly recommended practice for plant diseases, but there seems to be little evidence that it really works.) Increase the amount of light and air circulation around crowded, shaded plants by removing low overhanging tree branches and competing vegetation. Where leaf spot was serious the previous year, spray new growth when half developed with a fungicide and repeat the spray when the leaves are fully developed. Use benomyl (Benlate), captan, ferbam, thiram, or zineb. On irrigated plants, apply the water in the evening or night so that the foliage can be dry during the day.

Leaf Blight

This fungal disease is caused by *Diapothe kalmiae,* also known in the conidial stage as *Phomopsis kalmiae.* The symptoms are circular brown zonate areas that become irregular in shape as they increase in size (Figure 9–4). They may eventually run together, covering the entire leaf blade. The blight also attacks stems and causes branches to die. The disease appears most commonly, like leaf spot, when new foliage remains moist for long periods. Control this the same way you would leaf spot (as explained above).

Numerous other fungi cause spotting and blighting of Laurel foliage. These include: *Cercospora kalmiae, C. sprasa, Septoria angustifolia, S. kalmicola, Venturia kalmiae, Physalospora kalmiae,* and *Pestalotia sp.* The last has been found on petioles and leaves of Sandhill Laurel cuttings kept in a humidity case. Control of these leaf-attacking fungi is the same as that given above for leaf spot.

Figure 9-4. Characteristic leaf spots, *left,* and leaf blight, *right,* on Mountain Laurel leaves. Both diseases are caused by fungi. (Jaynes)

Petal Blight

Primarily a disease of Azaleas, petal blight sometimes attacks Mountain Laurel flowers during warm, humid flowering seasons. The fungus, *Ovulina azalea,* attacks the flower corolla, which goes limp when covered by the frost-like bloom of spores of the fungus. Control measures are not necessary unless the season is abnormally wet. Zineb (Dithane Z-78), sprayed several times before and during flowering, will prevent petal blight.

Wilt or Root Rot

This is typically a seedling or nursery disease, caused by *Phytophthora cinnamomi,* which attacks the roots of young plants. It is soil-borne. The most noticeable symptom is wilted foliage, which is easiest to detect in the early morning when healthy plants are turgid. Foliage becomes discolored and acquires an olive-green cast. At first only one or two branches show symptoms. Tissue of the stem near the ground level will be dead and brown. If you scrape the bark along the stem, you will see a characteristic reddish band traveling up the vascular tissue. The band may be either thread-like or up to ½ in (1.2 cm) across. *Phytophthora* wilt is almost always fatal to infected plants. It can occur among seedlings in the cutting bench and also in older plants grown in containers or in the field.

The disease is most active in warm weather and is common in cases where aeration of the roots is poor and soil pH is high. Although the plants may grow best at pH 5.5, the fungus can be combated by increasing acidity to pH 4.5. Roots killed by water-logging or injured during transplanting or other root damage opens the way for infection. Container-grown plants allowed to sit in puddles of water suffer not only from insufficient drainage but are susceptible to the motile spore stage of the fungus which travels in the water from diseased to healthy plants.

Infected plants should be removed and destroyed. Soil and benches in greenhouses should routinely be fumigated or sterilized before any planting. Since freezing of the soil apparently destroys the disease, infected fields should be left fallow over winter. But diseased plants should be destroyed because the fungus winters over in infected plant tissue. Several fungicides have been recommended for control of the disease, but none has as yet proven to be consistently effective. *Phytophthora* is widespread and attacks many different plant genera, including *Rhododendron,* Yew (*Taxus*), and Chestnut (*Castanea*). Selection of resistant varieties may be one of the best long-term solutions. We have much to learn about the susceptibility of Laurel selections to *Phytophthora* and the means of developing resistant cultivars.

Damping-Off

The fungus *Rhizoctonia solani (Pellicularia filamentosa)* causes stem rot or "damping-off" at the ground line. It can be very serious with young seedlings, especially when they are planted in mixes containing soil. The disease can to a large extent be avoided through the use of non-soil mixes containing milled sphagnum and peat moss, which contain natural antibiotics that prevent, or limit, the growth of this fungus. Larger plants are also susceptible, notably where soil aeration is poor and when overwatering has occurred. As with wilt and some other soil pathogens, *Rhizoctonia* is associated with soils or mixes having a relatively high pH. The pH normal for Laurel should not exceed 5.5, and lower if damping-off or other diseases are a problem. The symptoms of *Rhizoctonia* are similar to those of *Phytophthora*. Roots are destroyed, but the reddish vascular streaks beneath the bark are not present. The disease can be controlled by drenching the soil with a fungicide such as benomyl.

Phythium is another damping-off fungus which attacks young seedlings. It often occurs on seedlings grown in closed, humid chambers where they have been over-watered. Aeration and a less moist medium will help check its spread. Control with fungicides may be necessary, but apply them sparingly on the young seedlings.

My two serious experiences with damping off fungi in transplant beds occurred during rainy periods of several weeks duration and in soils that did not drain quite as well as they should have. I am convinced that Laurel has fewer problems if the soil is allowed to dry almost to the point of wilting every few weeks.

Other fungi may attack Laurel roots and cause symptoms similar to those of *Phytophthora* and *Rhizoctonia*. One example is Shoestring Root Rot, *Armillaria mellea*. The causes for these diseases are often similar, but the most common cause is injured roots resulting from poor growing conditions such as overfertilization, winter injury, overwatering, and lack of aeration, any of which provide an opportunity for the diseases to take hold.

Necrotic Ringspot

The causal agent is apparently a long rod-like virus, one of the few virus diseases of *Kalmia*. Necrotic, reddish brown rings occur on the leaves which may turn entirely red and drop prematurely. Symptoms do not occur on current seasons' growth but rather on 2-year-old *Kalmia latifolia* leaves (Figure 9-5). It is not a common problem but has been reported in England, the Pacific Northwest, and Connecticut. Neither the means of transmission of the virus from plant to plant, nor a means of control is known. Economic losses due to the disease have not been reported so it does not presently pose a serious threat. In Rhododendrons the problem is associated with progeny of R. *campylocarpum* and R. *griffithianum*. In *Kalmia* it may also be found to be associated with certain cultivars.

Figure 9-5. Necrotic ring spots on 2-year-old leaves of Mountain Laurel from a Connecticut nursery. This is a virus-caused disease. (Jaynes)

MISCELLANEOUS AFFLICTIONS

Winter Injury

This nonparasitic disease is characterized by browning of the leaves at their tips and around the edges. When severe, entire leaves and even branches may be killed. At first the foliage changes from the normal dark green to a light, dull green and subsequently to brown (Figure 9-6). Severe damage occurs when the roots are frozen and strong freezing winds dessicate the leaves. Injury is not confined to the coldest periods in mid-winter but often occurs in March, after warm periods, while the ground is still frozen. A good mulch applied over the roots in November to insulate the soil is one of the best preventative measures. Windswept locations should be avoided as planting sites. Such unfavorable locations are observed as snow-free patches after a blustery snow storm. Plants exposed to the buffeting of winter winds should be protected with snow fencing, pine boughs, burlap, or other means. Remove killed and injured portions of winter-damaged plants. If in doubt as to how much to prune off, wait until the new growth begins in the spring, and then prune back to the new shoots.

Native plants of southern origin, but grown in the harsher northern climates, are particularly susceptible to damage from hard freezes in late fall and to winter injury. These same plants adapted to mild winters are more prone to droop and even curl their leaves than the native Laurel when temperatures drop below freezing.

Container-grown plants in unheated, plastic overwintering structures may, like Rhododendrons, suffer from water soaking of the leaves when well watered and kept warm and humid. Plants in this condition are then susceptible to damage by freezing. Good aeration around the plants during warm spells in the fall and conservative watering are the two best preventatives.

Figure 9-6. Winter injury on Mountain Laurel foliage with characteristic browning and dieback of leaf tips. (Jaynes)

Sunscald

Sunscald typically occurs on either newly transplanted or established plants acclimated to shade and then exposed to full sun and an inadequate water supply. It may also occur on field grown plants after several rainy and over-cast days followed by a bright, sunny day, during the period when new shoot growth is expanding. The symptoms include bleaching of the chlorophyll on the upper surface of exposed leaves and eventual browning. Affected leaves and branches should be pruned. Acclimatization, through gradual exposure of shaded plants to full sun, is one preventative measure; another is intermittant irrigation during the hottest part of the day.

Frost Damage

Unusually low temperatures in the spring or fall may damage plants. An early fall hard frost will injure plants that have continued in growth and failed to "harden off." Normally the shorter days of fall and cool weather signal the plant to stop growth and prepare for winter. However, a moist, rich soil and mild fall weather, especially after a hot, dry summer, may delay normal dormancy and stimulate plant growth. Over-fertilization in late summer and early fall also contributes to delayed hardening of plant growth. Mulched, field-grown plants in low areas are particulary susceptible to frost, because the mulch slows up heat and water loss from the ground and helps maintain root growth. As previously noted, cold air on still nights flows down the slopes to the low areas. Thus, the normally beneficial effects of a mulch are detrimental on a clear, still, frosty night. The air above the mulch supercools, because heat from the ground is trapped by the mulch. A similar problem occurs in the spring as was dramatically illustrated to me a few years ago. A field of tomatoes was planted adjacent to my field of established Mountain Laurel mulched with wood chips. On a clear evening late in May, the weather station recorded a low of 35°F (2°C). The tomatoes in bare soil came through the night with no damage, while new growth on most of the Mountain Laurel was killed. The heat rapidly radiated off the wood chips; the air actually cooled to the freezing point, causing the Laurel shoots to freeze, but the air around the tomatoes over the bare, moist soil was kept warmer by a constant supply of heat escaping upward from the soil.

The moral of this story is that heavy organic mulches may lead to frost injury in low pockets with poor air drainage. Such frost damage seldom occurs under a canopy of evergreen, or even deciduous, trees, because the canopy reflects radiated heat back to the ground.

An early hard, fall freeze may not only destroy succulent branch tips but also actually split the bark on stems and kill the plant to the ground. Such damage is often not noticeable until the following spring when the top of the plant dries up. Fortunately, Laurel are much less susceptible to this kind of damage than evergreen azaleas. Measures to acclimate plants in the fall include removal of heavy mulch until after a hard freeze and reduce fertilization and watering in late summer and early fall.

Yellow Leaves, Chlorosis

The sudden appearance of yellow leaves in the fall is often viewed as a sign of severe plant stress and cause for immediate action. Most likely it is merely the onset of the annual loss of the previous year's foliage (Figure 9-7). If the yellow leaves show up about the time the leaves on hardwood trees are turning color, and if the yellowing is confined to older foliage, despair not. Given a little wind, rain, and a week or two they will be gone and forgotten.

On the other hand if yellowing (chlorosis) occurs on the *current* year's leaves it is a sign of one of the most common troubles encountered with Laurels. The symptoms appear first on the youngest leaves; the leaf veins typically remain green but the main body of the leaf turns yellow (Figure 9-8). On severely affected plants the leaves may turn white before drying up. The problem is usually caused by soil with a pH of 6.0 or higher, which converts iron into a form that is unavailable to the plant. Lowering the pH with aluminum sulfate is relatively simple (see page 132).

Chlorosis symptoms can also result from causes other than high pH, including fertilizer root-burn resulting from too much nitrogen; winter injury to roots; heavy, poorly drained soils; and even black vine weevil root damage. Immediate reversal of symptoms can often be achieved by applying iron in the chelated form (such as Sequestrene) either as a drench or foliage spray. But the actual cause of the chlorosis should be determined by examining the growing site and the plant, testing the soil, and taking additional corrective measures when necessary.

Figure 9-7. The yellowing of older leaves of Mountain Laurel seen during a brief period in the fall is natural and occurs just before they fall off. This photo was taken in Connecticut on October 1. (Jaynes)

Figure 9-8. Chlorosis shows yellowing between veins, which remain green. Chlorosis may result from root injury, heavy or wet soils, or growing plants in neutral or alkaline soil. (Jaynes)

Moles, Rabbits, and Deer

Moles are insectivorous (non-vegetarian) and are commonly believed to cause no garden problems. Wrong, they love grubs and earthworms and in beds of small plants can raise havoc. Their apparent random, subterranean tunnels lift up plants exposing the roots to air and desiccation. Their presence around older plants is less objectionable unless the tunnels are taken over by voles and mice. These latter invaders have a habit of eating bark off of plants during the dormant season when the animal populations are high and food is scarce. Beds of small plants can be treated with materials such as Diazinon or Oftanol to eliminate the food source (grubs) of the moles. Lacking a food source, the moles will search and dig elsewhere for food.

If rabbits and woodchucks were given a choice of food most *Kalmia* species would rank very low. As described in the next chapter, the foliage is quite toxic to domestic animals. However, rabbits will seek out foliage of the Bog Laurels, *K. polifolia* and *K. microphylla*. If young plants of the other species are in their pathways they will clip them and leave the shoots. For a small plant this may result in "pruning" right to the ground. Several potential methods exist to control these animals, such as repellants, fencing, and shooting, but all are fraught with difficulties. If damage is serious, check with neighbors and local game authorities for control means effective in your area.

Deer have become a nuisance and a prime cause of damage to nursery stock and ornamental plantings in many areas. Were deer to list their preferred species, *Kalmia* would not be in the top ten, but will browse on it as do rabbits. Reduction of herd size should be an overall goal. Repellants, including human hair and compounds containing rotten eggs and thiram (e.g. Big Game Repellant, BGR) have some value but must be renewed regularly and their value is lessened as herd size and food requirements increase. One deer needs to consume the equivalent of 500–800 ft (150–240 m) of apple wood per day just to maintain its weight in winter. That translates into all the new growth on 10–20 moderate sized apple trees per deer per day. If deer are a persistant problem fencing may be required. There are several schemes available now, including electric and staggered, multistrand configurations. Check with state agricultural and game officials for assistance in determining practical control measures.

Despite the preceding list of a multitude of problems and pests, be assured that they are not often serious in the case of Laurel. However, awareness of potential problems and their control is important in limiting serious depredations.

Chapter 10 _____

MEDICINAL USES AND TOXICITY OF LAUREL FOLIAGE

Professor John E. Ebinger, Botany Department
Eastern Illinois University, Charleston, Illinois 61920

> *From Pehr Kalm's entries in his journal, which he started publishing in 1753, we know of many early uses of the mountain laurel, most of which the settlers learned from the Indians. When Kalm was in America, the laurel was already being grown in colonial gardens as an ornamental. The evergreen branches of this shrub were used as church decorations at Christmas and New Year's Day. Its usefulness was the primary reason for its importance, however. The strong wood was carved into weaver's shuttles, pulleys, and spoons and trowels. The early common name spoonwood indicates this usefulness for tools. The leaves also were valued for their supposed medicinal powers, especially when prepared as a wash for skin diseases.*
> *(Holmes 1956)*

Mark Catsby was in 1743 one of the first to report the poisonous properties of Mountain Laurel, *Kalmia latifolia*. He found that, when deprived of better forage, cattle and sheep died from eating the leaves of this species. Later, Peter Kalm wrote an extensive and interesting account of the appearance, habitat, and poisonous properties of both Mountain Laurel and Sheep Laurel, *K. angustifolia*. In this travel-log of 1770, he mentioned that young sheep were killed by eating only small portions of the leaves of Mountain Laurel, while older sheep became very sick and recovered with great difficulty. He also observed that after eating the foliage calves swelled, foamed at the mouth, and had difficulty standing. They could usually be cured by giving them gunpowder and other medicines. He reported that larger animals were also affected, but usually recovered.

It is now known that many members of the Ericaceae contain a toxic substance. This chemical, andromedotoxin, has been isolated from some members of the family and has produced similar symptoms in domestic animals. Most of the cases of andromedotoxin poisoning have occurred in the upland pastures of eastern North America and in the mountain ranges and coastal regions of the West, the areas where species of *Kalmia* are found. Since the species of this genus are extremely common, and grow in habitats readily accessible to livestock, some cases of poisoning have been attributed to them. Also, their evergreen habit makes them readily available during the winter and early spring when other food is scarce.

Cases of andromedotoxin poisoning occur most frequently among sheep; cattle poisoning is second. In the eastern United States poisoning is usually caused by Mountain or Sheep Laurel. The Eastern Bog Laurel, *K. polifolia*, is also poisonous but owing to its bog habitat is seldom encountered by livestock. Some experimental work has been done to determine the dosage, symptoms, and treatment for poisoning by these species. One of the first studies was made by Thomas Wood in 1883 who fed boiled extract of Sheep Laurel leaves to a sheep. He concluded that extremely small quantities would not harm animals but that large quantities caused sickness and death.

Recent studies confirm the poisonous properties of both Mountain Laurel and Sheep Laurel. In all experiments both species were found to be poisonous, producing almost identical symptoms. The major variable is the time from ingestion to the appearance of the first symptoms. Symptoms usually appear in 6 hours, depending on the amount of foliage consumed. In order of appearance, the symptoms are lack of appetite, repeated swallowing, copious salivation, dullness, depression, and nausea. As the poisoning progresses, the animal becomes weak, is unable to coordinate voluntary muscular movements, and falls to the ground. Vomiting and bloating are also common. In fatal cases death is preceded by coma and occurs from a few hours to a week after the first symptoms appear.

Observations suggest that Sheep Laurel is about twice as toxic as Mountain Laurel. The minimum toxic dose for Mountain Laurel fed to sheep is 0.35% of the animal's weight, while for Sheep Laurel the minimum toxic dose is only 0.15%. Similar results were found with other animal species tested. The minimum toxic dose of Mountain Laurel fed to cattle and goats is 0.4% of the animal's weight, while for Sheep Laurel the minimum toxic dose is 0.25% for goats and 0.2% for cattle.

At present no antidote to andromedotoxin poisoning is known. Lard or oil hinders absorption of the poison while also acting as a purgative. This practice, used since colonial times, still gives the best results. The recommended dosage is 4 fl oz (120 ml) of linseed oil administered every 2–3 hours. In a recent experiment 6 sheep were given lethal doses of Mountain Laurel foliage, and all recovered after being treated with linseed oil.

Like its eastern relatives, the Western Alpine Laurel, *K. microphylla*, is also poisonous. Because of its alpine habitat, this species native to the northwestern part of North America is rarely encountered by livestock. Moreover, livestock will rarely eat it, but instances of sickness and death among lambs have been reported when they were admitted to the high range too early in the spring. Experiments with Western Alpine Laurel revealed that both cattle and sheep could be poisoned; in fact, as little as 1 oz (30 ml) of fresh leaves made sheep sick. Studies by A. B. Clawson show that sheep are affected by eating as little as 0.3% of their weight of Alpine Laurel foliage, but they may consume as much as 2% without being fatally poisoned. In all studies the symptoms are similar to those reported for livestock poisoning with other *Kalmia* species.

While there is now no doubt that most species of Kalmia are poisonous, the number of domestic animals killed by these plants is fortunately very small, in spite of the fact that the species are extremely common and grow in areas where livestock graze. As pointed out earlier, losses are small because the Laurels are not very palatable and are therefore eaten only when other vegetation is scarce which occurs when pastures have been over-grazed and little vegetation is left, or in the spring after animals are turned into pastures in which grasses have not had time to grow (Figure 10-1).

Figure 10-1. Sheep Laurel, *K. angustifolia,* in a snow-covered pasture. If other food is not available, livestock may browse on it and be poisoned. (Jaynes)

Other cases of Laurel poisoning have resulted from the animals accidentally being fed the foliage or eating decorations made of Mountain Laurel leaves. For example, some cows were poisoned when they ate Laurel wreaths thrown into their pasture from a nearby cemetery. During Christmas week in 1894 6 trained goats on exhibit at the Philadelphia Dime Museum died after browsing on Laurel leaves that were being used for stage decorations. Angora goats were poisoned at the National Zoological Park in Washington, D.C., when they were fed Mountain Laurel leaves by a visitor. Later at the same park, a monkey died after eating a few flowers and leaves of Mountain Laurel offered by a visitor.

Reports from colonial times note that while Mountain Laurel is poisonous to most domestic livestock many wild animals, particularly deer, can eat the leaves with impunity. Recent studies confirm that Mountain Laurel and Rosebay, *Rhododendrom maximum,* are sometimes eaten by deer, particularly in times of food shortages. In experiments, confined deer rejected both Mountain Laurel and Rosebay and, provided alternatives, ate very little of either of the former. Furthermore, when restricted to a diet of these two species for 45 days the deer did not eat enough of either to maintain their weight. They all became thin and weak, suffered from the cold, and developed a mild case of rickets. None of the deer, however, showed the typical symptoms of andromedotoxin poisoning. In related experiments, deer exhibited the typical symptoms of andromedotoxin poisoning and died when force-fed 1.75% of their live weight of Laurel leaves. Clearly, the toxic principle of both Mountain Laurel and Rosebay is poisonous to deer, but they normally will not eat enough of either plant to exceed their tolerance for them.

Most species of *Kalmia* are probably poisonous to humans, but no deaths have been attributed directly to this genus. The first detailed study of human poisoning from Mountain Laurel was conducted by George C. Thomas in 1802. He found that, after eating very small quantities (0.4–1.0 grams) of dried leaves, unpleasant symptoms resulted: rapid pulse, headache, throbbing at the temples, nausea, vomiting, and dilation of the pupils. Other cases have been reported in which a strong decoction (boiled extract) of leaves caused vertigo, dimness of sight, reduction in heartbeat, and cold extremities. In each instance the decoction was being used in an experiment to determine its effect on humans, or it was being used as a medicine. It is unlikely that anyone would eat the leaves under normal conditions, because they are tough and bitter. There are reports, however, that the Delaware Indians used a decoction of the leaves of Mountain Laurel to commit suicide.

In addition to andromedotoxin, Gibbs in 1974 reported the presence of a cyanogenic glycoside in Sheep Laurel. Though the compound was not identified it was capable of liberating hydrogen cyanide when the leaves were crushed. Depending on the concentration, hydrogen cyanide may be poisonous to both humans and livestock. A recent study by the author (J. Ebinger) of more than 50 Sheep Laurel plants, indicates that cyanogenic glycosides are not commonly found in this species. However, Sheep Laurel may be polymorphic with respect to cyanogenic glycosides and the compound may occur in only a few members of a population. It is also possible that cyanide production only occurs under certain environmental conditions.

Occasionally humans and other animals have become sick from eating birds whose crops contained the leaves and buds of Mountain Laurel. As a result, the common belief during the last century was that the flesh of birds feeding on Mountain Laurel is poisonous. In all cases, however, the reported symptoms were identical to those associated with food poisoning so the probable cause of the discomfort was decompositon of the bird itself before it was cooked. There is no evidence that the flesh of any animal is itself inedible by virtue of eating any part of *Kalmia* species.

From colonial times until well into the last century, extracts from species of *Kalmia* have been used as medicine. The leaves of Mountain Laurel were occasionally found in drug stores and were principally used as a remedy for diarrhea. A decoction was made by softening 2 oz (60 ml) of dried leaves in a pint (0.5 l) of alcohol, letting it stand for a week, and then straining. The dosage customarily administered to an adult was 30 drops 4 times a day; stronger dosages caused vertigo. This preparation has also been used as a wash to relieve itching and skin infections and was recommended for use as a sedative, as well as a cure for syphilis and fever. Further, a powder of the dried leaves was popular as snuff.

Other species of *Kalmia* have also been used as medicine. The Sheep Laurel was used by the Cree Indians of the Hudson Bay region as a bitter tea both for the treatment of bowel complaints and as a tonic. The Sandhill Laurel has been used in the southeastern United States as a cure for itching and mange in dogs. Treatment consisted of applying a strong, warm decoction to the affected area. A single application was sufficient to effect a cure. There are no reports of the other species of the genus having been used as medicine, though most of them contain the drug andromedotoxin.

Andromedotoxin is not being used as a drug today, although experiments indicate that it has potent hypotensive action. These studies indicate that intravenous injections of small quantities of the drug into normal dogs caused blood-pressure reductions of 20–40%.

A great deal of evidence indicates that when honeybees work certain members of the Ericaceae family, they produce a honey poisonous to humans. Xenophon reported that his soldiers suffered from honey poisoning while they were camped at Trebizond on the shores of the Black Sea in 400 B.C. He noted that those who had eaten small amounts of honey were merely intoxicated, while those who had eaten a great deal became mad. It is believed that the honey was derived from *Rhododendron ponticum* which is now considered the chief source of poisonous honey in Asia.

In 1802, American botanist B. S. Barton observed that honey from Sheep Laurel is poisonous to humans. He reported that later in the 17th Century a group of young men moved their beehives to the savannas of New Jersey at the time of *Kalmia angustifolia* flowering. On eating the honey produced, the men became intoxicated. Since this early incident, a number of other cases of human poisoning have been reported in which species of *Kalmia* were thought to be the source of the honey. In all reported cases the honey acts as an extremely distressing narcotic, varying in its effect in proportion to the quantity eaten. The usual symptoms are nausea and vomiting and in extreme cases prostration and almost complete loss of the function of voluntary muscles. Since the honey produced is bitter and astringent, it is hard to imagine fatal amounts being eaten.

Some authors have expressed doubt that Mountain Laurel is responsible for poisonous honey. Since this species is common, contamination of honey might be expected much more often than is reported. On the other hand, honeybees are rarely found on Mountain Laurel. Possibly a unique set of environmental conditions are required to induce them to use Mountain Laurel flowers. In none of the reported cases of poisoned honey is the source of the flowers known for certain.

In addition to possible inclusion in honey and animal poisoning from foliage, Laurels may chemically limit growth of neighboring plants. Water-soluble extracts of Northern Sheep Laurel inhibit the growth of coniferous trees and in nature may thereby maintain open areas for extended periods of time. The extracts hinder primary root development of Black Spruce by destroying cell tissues and may be the reason for the abnormally poor growth of trees associated with Sheep Laurel on upland sites in the boreal region of eastern Canada (Peterson 1965).

Chemical studies of the poison principle (not necessarily the same as the substance hindering root growth) in genera of the Ericaceae other than *Kalmia* have recently been undertaken. The first detailed analysis was made by J. F. Eykman in 1882 using extracts from the Japanese Andromeda, *Pieris japonica*. The physiologically active substance was named asebotoxin after the Japanese name of the plant. At about the same time, the German chemist P. C. Plugge found the same substance in some species of *Andromeda*, *Pieris*, and *Rhododendron*, as well as the nongreen, herbaceous Indian Pipe, *Monotropa unifolia;* and Sheep Laurel, *Kalmia angustifolia*. The list has since been expanded to include Western Alpine Laurel, *K. microphylla;* Eastern Bog Laurel, *K. polifolia;* and Mountain Laurel, *K. latifolia;* and some members of the genera *Chamaedaphne*, *Leucothoe*, *Lyonia*, and *Pernettya*. Interestingly, some species of *Rhododendron*, *Lyonia*, and *Leucothoe* lack andromedotoxin, as does the Sandhill Laurel, *K. hirsuta*.

There is now general agreement on the structure and the properties of the poisonous substance found in many members of the Ericaceae. In addition to the names "andromedotoxin" and "asebotoxin", other designations of the substance include "rhodotoxin" (from *Rhododendron hymenanthes*); "acetylandromedol" (from *Rhododendrom maximum*); and "grayanotoxin I" (from *Leucothoe grayana*). This poisonous substance, now commonly referred to as grayanotoxin I, is a diterpene with an empirical formula (chemical composition) of $C_{22}H_{36}O_7$:

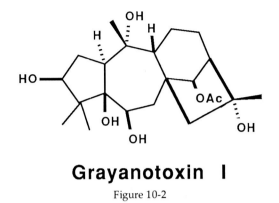

Grayanotoxin I

Figure 10-2

Related compounds, particulary grayanotoxin II and III, are known to exist in many species of the Ericaceae, and may also occur in members of the genus *Kalmia*. Several electrophysical studies suggest that the mechanism by which these toxins produce their effects in animals involves the opening of sodium channels of excitable cell membrances. Recent studies, which have shown that the physiologically active compounds extracted from many of the listed species have similar physical and chemical properties, do not preclude the presence of other compounds with characteristics similar to grayanotoxins.

Renewed interest in grayanotoxin I has led to the development of more exacting, although not technically difficult, methods of isolating the compound. In one study 198 lbs (90 kg) of fresh Rosebay, *Rhododendron maximum*, leaves were used to produce ¼ oz (7 g) of grayanotoxin I. Southern Sheep Laurel, *Kalmia angustifolia* var. *carolina*, is an even richer source of grayanotoxin I. Large-scale isolation experiments show that 100 lbs (45 kg) of leaves of this species yield 1 oz (28 g) of grayanotoxin. Thus, Southern Sheep Laurel yields 0.06–0.09% of the fresh weight or about 10 times the amount obtained from Rosebay. Small amounts of grayanotoxin can be extracted fairly simply with basic laboratory equipment.

Some of the other compounds in the sap of *Kalmia latifolia* are of special interest because of their therapeutic potential. S. D. Mancini and J. M. Edwards (1979) at the School of Pharmacy, University of Connecticut reported finding an active, anti-cancer compound in the sap which was not identified. A more recent letter from Professor Edwards states that the findings are reproducible and definite, but they were not able to identify the compound.

BREEDING BETTER LAUREL

Gardeners have developed many interesting and beautiful varieties of rhododendrons by breeding and grafting. It would seem as though there would be an equal field for this with the mountain laurel, yet it does not appear to have attracted their attention in this respect. (Buttrick 1924)

The breeding and selection of improved types of Laurel is of very recent vintage. Until my first paper was published in 1968 no literature on Laurel breeding existed. By contrast, the literature on breeding Azaleas and Rhododendrons was extensive. Fewer than 50 *Kalmia* cultivars have been named, but hybridizers and growers of Azaleas have named over 6,000 cultivars in 150 years, and that is to say nothing of the even more extensive hybridizing and selection done within the Rhododendron section of the same genus. While there are many fewer *Kalmia* than *Rhododendron* species, their variation is great, and therefore their potential for improvement by breeding is considerable.

Chapter 11 _____

PRINCIPLES OF PLANT BREEDING

In the beginning of June, when the days are long and warm and the daisies and clover in the tall grass are waving in the breeze, when the tulip-trees are in bloom and the roses and peonies fill the gardens with their perfume and color, then the flowers of the laurel may be found, rivalling in their delicacy of color and perfect symmetry of form any of the more showy blossoms of cultivation. It seems as if the climax of all that is dainty and lovely had been reached in this beautiful American wild flower. (Britton 1913)

Plants are propagated by either asexual or sexual means. As has already been discussed, cultivars are almost universally reproduced by such asexual propagation methods as cutting, grafting, layering, or tissue culture. New cultivars are, on the other hand, usually selected from large populations grown from seed; that is, they are a product of sexual reproduction. Each seed produces a completely unique individual, differing to a greater or lesser degree from all others. The frequency and kind of variations in a population of seedlings depends on the parents. The more similar the parents, the more uniform the progeny. The plant breeder controls the traits expressed in the offspring not only by selecting the seed parent but also by selecting the pollen parent.

POLLINATION AND FERTILIZATION

Each seed results from the union of a male gamete (contained in a pollen grain) with a female gamete, the egg (contained in the ovule of the pistil) (Figure 11-1). Pollination of Laurel is usually carried out by bumblebees which bring the two gametes together. The union of sperm and egg in the ovary is called fertilization. The male and female gametes contribute equally to the genetic content of the resulting seed and next generation. (It is recognized that the endosperm or storage tissue of the seed is triploid with a ⅔ contribution from the seed parent.) Thus, in a cross between any two plants it does not matter which one is used as the female parent as the reciprocal crosses are identical. (Reciprocal refers to reversing the parents or direction of the cross-pollination.) Exceptions to this rule occur only rarely. In Laurel only albino and yellow sectoring in the foliage are suspected of being dependent on maternal

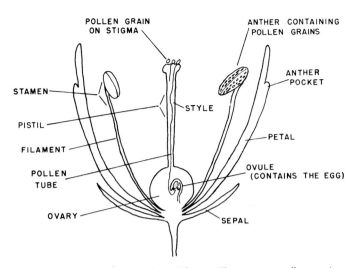

Figure 11-1. Stylized section through a Laurel flower. The ovary actually contains many ovules, which, after fertilization, develop into seeds. Typical of all Ericaceous plants, but not other flowering plants, the pollen grains are four-celled. Each is capable of producing 4 pollen tubes and fertilizing 4 eggs. (Jaynes)

inheritance. However, reciprocal crosses are sometimes not equally successful in producing seed, because pollen tube inhibition exists in the pistils of one plant. Some examples are cited in the next chapter.

SELF- AND CROSS-FERTILIZATION, INBREEDING AND OUTBREEDING

If the male gamete and the egg both come from the same plant or clone, the union is called self-fertilization or "inbreeding"; if from different clones cross-fertilization, or "outbreeding."

The Laurels, like many woody plants, are in nature predominantly out-breeders or "outcrossers". The mechanism limiting self-fertilization in Laurel has not been identified. It may result from inhibition of pollen tube growth in the style or, as my studies indicate, from inhibition at a later stage.

Inbreeding clearly causes a decrease in vigor. A 50% reduction in height growth of *Kalmia angustifolia, K. latifolia,* and *K. polifolia* after one generation was observed in in-bred as compared to out-bred plants. Self-pollination also often results in greatly reduced flowering and seed set in *K. angustifolia* and *K. latifolia.*

The reduced vigor associated with inbreeding is caused by the expression of recessive traits which are normally masked by outbreeding. True-breeding *Kalmia* lines resulting from selfing and which are completely uniform from generation to generatiion from selfing, are difficult to develop due both to inbreeding depression and reduction in seed set.

Inbreeding uncovers recessive traits that may or may not have ornamental value. In natural outbreeding populations of Laurel these recessive traits are normally hidden and are occasionally unmasked only by chance recombination. It should be noted however, inbreeding, particularly of Mountain Laurel, may result in compact growing forms of ornamental value (Figure 11-2). Such forms could be propagated vegetatively or by sibling crosses.

Figure 11-2. Comparison of a 4-year-old out-bred and in-bred Mountain Laurel, both unpruned. The seed parent was the same in both cases. The plant on the left is typical of those resulting from cross-pollination with another plant. The one on the right is characteristic of the more vigorous of those obtained from self-pollination. (Jaynes)

HYBRID VIGOR

A cross between two species or even between two plants within a species may produce offspring more vigorous than their parents. This phenonomen is called hybrid vigor. Crosses between Eastern Bog Laurel and Western Laurel (*K. polifolia* $\times$ *K. microphylla*) sometimes, for example, show hybrid vigor, usually expressed not as increased height growth but as a general thriftiness or well being.

CULTIVAR OR VARIETY SELECTION

Cultivars (cultivated varieties) of woody plants have usually been selected from wild populations or from seedlings grown in the garden. Such selected materials are commonly used to start breeding programs to develop improved cultivars. The plants judged to be the best garden forms are those named, propagated, and introduced into the nursery trade. Sometimes unusual plants are designated as botanical forms which may or may not have horticultural value. Feather-petaled (form *polypetala*) and Banded (form *fuscata*) Mountain Laurel and white flowering (form *candida*) Sheep Laurel are examples of botanical forms. Several banded selections have recently received cultivar names.

The gradual, controlled improvement and diversity of Mountain Laurel has resulted from selecting seeds from desirable plants. The deeply pigmented laurels (red-buds and pinks) originated in this way. C. O. Dexter of Sandwich, Massachusetts, started with one or more good pinks collected in the wild. He grew several generations of seedlings and from each generation gathered the seed of those plants with the deepest flower color. This method of selection in gardens and nurseries has been effective (notably at Weston Nurseries, Hopkinton, Massachusetts) but somewhat inefficient, because, while the seed parent is known, the pollen parent is not. With controlled crosses both seed and pollen parents are known so it is possible to determine how particular traits are inherited. This knowledge is valuable in planning the development of new cultivars and in reproducing desirable seed. Specific examples of gene inheritance are presented in the following chapters. Guidelines for naming plants appear in Chapter 3.

SPECIES HYBRIDIZATION

It is difficult to overemphasize the point that variation is the key to plant breeding and selection. The greater the variation between plants to be crossed, the greater the likelihood that diverse, improved cultivars will develop. When the characteristics desired occur in related species, the breeder can resort to species hybridization. For example, it would be wonderful if a Mountain Laurel hybrid could be developed possessing the general Mountain Laurel traits plus the solid, deep wine-colored flowers of Sheep Laurel and the easy rooting characteristic of Eastern Bog Laurel. Unfortunately, interspecific hybrids in Laurel are difficult to create and when successful are often sterile—a disappointment, but not a total surprise since genetic barriers, if not the rule, are normal between species. Crosses above the species level, i.e., between genera, are seldom successful. As one could predict, crosses of *Kalmia* with the genera *Rhododendron* and *Kalmiopsis* have all failed with one possible exception: *K. latifolia* × *R. williamsianum* (Chapter 11).

FIRST- AND SECOND-GENERATION CROSSES

The seedlings of a cross between two different plants or clones are referred to as first-generation, or F_1, hybrids. When two of these hybrids are then crossed, the offspring are called second-generation, or F_2, hybrids. To obtain the desired expression and recombination of characters, the breeder must usually select among offspring of the second or later generations (Figure 11–3). For example, red-budded and feather-petaled Mountain Laurel are known to be controlled by recessive traits; thus, in a cross of these two types, the F_1 would be expected to have normally colored and shaped flowers. A cross of two of these F_1 hybrids should then produce a small proportion of seedlings exhibiting the unique combination of flowers with red buds and petaled corollas. The actual proportion of such plants depends on the number of genes controlling these two traits.

Figure 11-3. Flower clusters from representative seedlings of a second generation cross of a red-budded and a banded Mountain Laurel. From a single seed capsule the parent types are recovered, as well as wild types and recombinants of red bud with banded. (Jaynes)

The odds of recovering the desired recombinant in the F_2 depend on the number of traits being selected for and on the number and nature of the genes involved; that is, whether the controlling genes are dominant, recessive, or additive. Additive genes are those whose expression are neither dominant or recessive but rather is dose dependent. (For details on segregation of genes and on selection, consult a basic genetic or breeding text, such as used in teaching general genetics. Some specific references are listed at the end of chapter.)

Since the effectiveness of selection decreases as the number of traits increases, we can express this relationship mathematically. If n traits are selected for, the effectiveness of selection for any one alone drops to $\sqrt[n]{v}$ where v is the size of the population from which one is selecting. Stated another way, the same degree of selection is exerted for one trait in a population of 10 as in a population of 10,000, if in the latter case four traits are selected for simultaneously.

If the desired recombinant characteristic does not appear in the F_2, and if it seems that a large number of plants will have to be grown to make it appear, then third- and fouth-generation seedlings must be grown. Thus, if the breeder is selecting for a Mountain Laurel recombinant which will be dwarf, red-bud, and feather-petaled, it may not be practical to grow enough F_2 seedlings to recombine all three traits in one plant. Therefore, among the F_2 seedlings, the breeder selects two plants that express separately all the desired traits, and these are crossed to produce an F_3: for example a dwarf/feather-petal crossed with a dwarf/red-bud. By going to the F_3 and successive generations the odds of recovering the long desired recombination of the original traits are dramatically increased, fewer plants need to be grown, but more time is needed to grow the successive generations.

BACKCROSS

The term backcross refers to the crossing an F_1 hybrid with one of the original parents. The backcross is used to maintain the identity of one parent (species) and to incorporate a particular trait from a second parent (species). The best strategy is to cross the F_1 hybrid back to the parent possessing the most desirable traits. Two or more generations of backcrossing may be necessary, but this is practical only if the characteristic sought is expressed in the F_1.

If a breeder wants to develop a cultivar possessing the small size and rooting ease of Sandhill Laurel but one which resembles Mountain Laurel, he/she will backcross small, well-statured plants of the F_1 hybrid to a good Mountain Laurel plant (possible, of course, only if the F_1 is fertile and practical only if cuttings of the selected F_1 plants root readily).

CHROMOSOMES

Strand-like structures called *chromosomes* are present in all living cells and contain within themselves the hereditary determinants called *genes*. Chromosomes are visible through a high-powered microscope and are most easily seen in properly stained dividing cells (Figure 11-4). The number of chromosomes in a plant cell is constant and usually the same for all plants in one species. Thus for any plant all the cells of the cambium, stems, roots, and leaves (somatic tissue) will have the same number of chromosomes. The chromosomes of each cell can be matched into pairs by size and shape, and if their origin could be traced, we would find that one chromosome pair was derived from the pollen parent and the other from the seed parent.

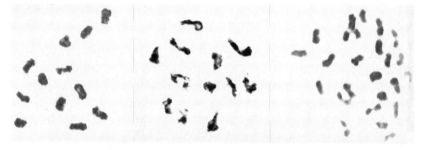

Figure 11-4. Chromosomes of 3 Laurel species, as seen under the microscope, at the time the pollen mother cells were undergoing reduction division. The cells were stained with acetocarmine. *Left to right, Kalmia hirsuta* (n = 12), *K. microphylla* (n = 12), and *K. polifolia* (n = 24). (Jaynes 1969)

The number of chromosomes in a gamete (sex cell of pollen or ovary) is half the somatic number. A single set of chromosomes is referred to as the haploid number. The normal somatic number of two sets is called diploid. If four sets of chromosomes are present it is called a tetraploid. The somatic chromosome numbers typical of the Laurel species are as follows:

Species	Chromosome number
K. microphylla	24
K. polifolia	48
K. latifolia	24
K. angustifolia	24
K. cuneata	24
K. hiruta	24
K. ericoides	unknown

I have introduced the matter of chromosome number and chromosome structure because this information is useful in planning and predicting the results of breeding experiments. In addition, unusual crossing results can sometimes be explained by investigating chromosome number and behavior. Unfortunately, gaining this knowledge is not easy; the chromosomes of most woody plants are small, about 1/10,000 in (1/2,500 mm) long. As a result, chromosome study of the laurels and their relatives has been insignificant as compared with that of the many herbaceous plants and even some insects, which have considerably larger chromosomes.

POLYPLOIDS

A polyploid is an individual with more than one set of chromosomes. The Eastern Bog Laurel with 48 rather than 24 chromosomes is a natural polyploid (Figure 11–5). Polyploid species result from a doubling of the chromosome number of an existing species, or from the hybridization of two species, followed by chromosome doubling.

Triploid and tetraploid plants (one and two extra chromosome sets, respectively) are valued for their large, heavy leaves and their flowers, which often have more body and are longer lasting. Their greatest value, however, may be as breeding stock.

Figure 11-5. An F. hybrid of the Eastern Bog Laurel and Western Alpine Laurel. This plant was a triploid and seed sterile. (Jaynes)

Artificial Production of Polyploids

The chromosome number of plants can be artificially doubled through the use of colchicine. This substance affects spindle formation in dividing cells so that the chromosomes, but not the cells, divide. Application of a 0.5–1% concentration of colchicine for 8–24 hours to the shoot of a germinating seed or a developing bud results in a doubling of the chromosomes and the production of a tetraploid.

In the numerous papers on the use of colchicine by plant breeders, Ericaceous plants have received little attention. However, August Kehr, formerly with the USDA successfully doubled chromosomes of Azalea. Others have used colchicine successfully on blueberries.

I have treated seedlings and buds of Mountain Laurel and Sheep Laurel to produce polyploids. The most successful technique uses newly germinated seedlings picked as soon as the cotyledons (seed leaves) spread and invert them on filter paper saturated with a 1.0% solution of colchicine in a small covered dish for 8–24 hours. This technique exposes only the developing shoot to the chemical and leaves the more sensitve roots unaffected.

Artificially produced tetrapoloids, if fertile, might conceivably be crossed with the naturally tetraploid Bog Laurel to produce new fertile species of hybrid origin. Attempts to double the chromosome number of developing buds on F_1 hybrids of Mountain and Sandhill Laurel to restore fertility have been unsuccessful. The attempt was made by immersing a growing shoot for 8 hours in a 1.0% solution of colchicine. Seedlings were not used in this case due to the difficulty in obtaining interspecific hybrid seedlings, and because they are often weak and would have difficulty surviving the treatment. When tetraploid plants of both species become available, the cross should be repeated. Seedlings from such a cross should be tetraploid and fertile. If fertile tetraploids of all the species were available, repeating all the interspecific crosses would be well worth the effort. However, manipulation of ploidy level in *Kalmia* is difficult and the few plants produced are slow to flower and/or sterile.

RADIATION AND OTHER MUTAGENS

The use of radiation and chemicals to cause the sudden genetic change known as mutation has caught the imagination of both amateur and professional plant breeders. Unfortunately, more than 99% of the mutations so induced are of no value. This is because a low rate of mutation occurs under natural conditions, and most of the beneficial mutations, such as those leading to increased vigor or seed production, have been selected for and incorporated into the native species. Mutation breeding has produced useful selections in grain crops, where millions of individuals can be screened in a single mutation experiment.

No doubt mutation breeding could play an important role in developing improved laurels. At present, however, breeders have so much variation available that there is little need to become deeply involved with a laborious technique to develop more variation.

OBJECTIVES

The plant breeder should have definite attainable objectives in mind before undertaking any breeding activity. It is a waste of effort to make unplanned crosses of whatever happens to be in bloom. Acquiring the knowledge to make intelligent planning possible is half the fun of plant breeding.

The amateur plant breeder should begin with a small-scale program lest he/she be overwhelmed and lose interest. The project can be expanded as interest, experience, and resources develop.

Improvements are usually sought in one or more of the following:

1. flowering characteristics—color, size, shape, abundance and pigment pattern.
2. seed capsule appearance and retentiion (fertility).
3. foliage characteristics—size, shape, color, and retention.
4. shrub form and size.
5. ease of rooting cuttings.
6. hardiness, including ability to withstand neglect and rough handling.
7. disease and insect resistance.
8. heat and draught tolerance.

In setting objectives, remember that the greater the number of traits being targeted at one time, the lower the chances are of recovering the desired recombination among the offspring.

The next two chapters review the crosses among and within species, to record what has been done, and, perhaps more importantly, suggest rewarding areas for additional work.

For more on the principles of plant breeding and genetics a booklet such as the handbook *Breeding Plants for Home and Garden*, published by the Brooklyn Botanic Garden, Brooklyn, New York, 1974, is suggested for beginners. If it is out of print it should at least be available in libraries.

Unfortunately, the ideal, contemporary guide to plant breeding for the amateur in the U.S. is yet to be written. One of the older, interesting and still relevant reviews is in the 1937 *Yearbook of Agriculture*, 1499p, published by the U.S. Department of Agriculture and widely available in libraries. A more contemporary book on plant breeding and genetics is *Flower and Vegetable Plant Breeding*, 1980, by L. Watts, Grower Books, 49 Doughty St. London, 182p. However, as the title indicates there are few examples or illustrations dealing with woody plants.

Regardless of approach or objectives the breeder has to be careful not to become too attached to his or her offspring. No more than a few plants should be kept from each cross. Mediocre material must be eliminated. What seems like ruthless culling is important, otherwise space, time and resources become limiting. Public institutions often find destruction of material to be most efficient in the long run (Figures 11-6, 11-7). Of course nurserymen and amateurs need not destroy good plants for they can be sold or given away.

Figure 11-6. A field of Mountain Laurel seedlings from controlled crosses of various color selections. (Jaynes)

Figure 11-7. The same field as Figure 11-6 above but a little later in the day. After the very best plants are removed, the plant breeder has to free him/herself of mediocre material and make space and time for new generations of plants. (Jaynes)

Chapter 12 _____

SPECIES HYBRIDS

So the hybridizer, the seedsman who's got his eye cocked toward the future, has got to take risks, to use his imagination to dream up something new, and then work his tail off trying to make it a reality. (Claude Hope in Farther Afield, *Lacy, 1986)*

One of the most fascinating aspects of breeding is the potential for making hybrids between species of the same genus. There are barriers to such crosses, but the occasional successes make the attempts well worth the effort and uncertainty. The variation within each of the seven *Kalmia* species is considerable but could be greatly increased through interspecific crosses. Appropriate crosses between Mountain Laurel and the other species could, in theory, produce Mountain Laurel-like plants with deeply colored flowers, compact growth, and stem cuttings that root readily, for all these traits are available in the other species.

I have crossed six of the Laurel species in all possible combinations, including reciprocals. For each species combination, at least two plants of each species and a minimum of 20 flowers were used. The average number of flowers pollinated for each of the 30 species combinations was 200. For one of the most difficult and yet occasionally successful combinations—*K. angustifolia* × *K. latifolia*—more than 1300 flowers were emasculated and pollinated, involving over 20 different plants of each species. In selecting the plants of each species, individuals were chosen that differed in flower color, growth habit, and geographic origin, so that failure or success would not be dependent on idiosyncrasies peculiar to a single plant.

Unfortunately, only a few of the crosses produced hybrid plants, and only the crosses between the two Bog Laurel species were easy to complete. The relative success of the F_1 crosses is summarized in Figure 12-1. The success rate from the crosses between species was extremely low. The amount of seed set and survival of seedlings averaged less than 1% of that obtained from crosses within species.

Following are some observations on the F_1 hybrids which survived more than 1 year. The female parent is listed first. Only three of these combinations have any ornamental or horticultural potential. The least valuable ones are discussed first:

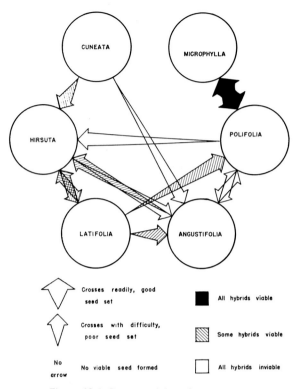

Figure 12-1. Crossing ability of 6 Laurel species in all possible F_1 combinations. (Jaynes 1968a)

K. hirsuta × K. angustifolia

Eight hundred hybrid seeds produced only 18 seedlings; all except 4 of which were weak, yellow-green plants which died within 1 year. *K. hirsuta* has alternately arranged leaves, while *K. angustifolia* has leaves in whorls of three. In the hybrids, whorled and alternate leaves sometimes occur on the same plant (Figure 12-2). The reciprocal cross produced no viable seedlings.

K. hirsuta × K. cuneata

Most of the seedlings produced from this cross were weak and produced at least sectors of albino or yellow-green tissue. One plant did flower but was leggy and had no particular merit as a garden plant.

K. polifolia × K. angustifolia

Only one of 17 combinations produced viable seedlings. They were weak, yellow-green, and all died within 3 years. In the reciprocal

Figure 12-2. F$_1$ hybrid of Sandhill Laurel × Sheep Laurel, with characters intermediate to those of the parental species. The open flowers are just over ½ inch (1.3 cm) in diameter. (Jaynes)

Figure 12-3. Pollen tubes growing down a style; stained with a fluorescing dye, pressed on a glass slide, and photographed through a microscope. *Left,* normal pollen tubes from a cross of Sheep Laurel × Sheep Laurel. *Right,* the same seed parent, but pollen from Eastern Bog Laurel, displaying inhibited, abnormal tube growth. Poor pollen tube growth is one cause of unsuccessful interspecific crosses. (Jaynes)

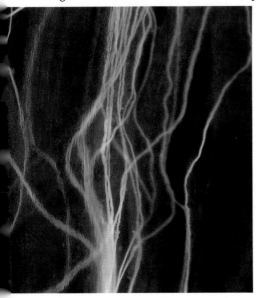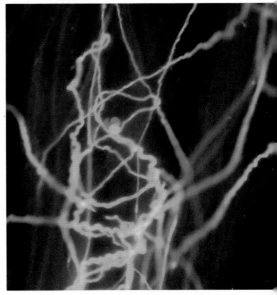

cross, pollen tube growth was abnormal in the style (Figure 12-3), resulting in little seed and no viable seedlings.

K. polifolia × K. latifolia

About 4% of the 3000 seeds from crosses of these two species germinated. The seedlings were extremely variable, ranging from weak and miniature to vigorous, large plants (Figure 12-4). The hybrids resembled the female more than the male parent. However, this was expected because Eastern Bog Laurel (*K. polifolia*) is a natural tetraploid with 48 chromosomes and it contributes two sets of chromosomes to the hybrid, while Mountain Laurel contributes but one. The hybrid should, therefore, be a triploid with 36 chromosomes. This was not confirmed, but the hybrids were pollen and seed sterile as one expects of a triploid. To obtain more vigorous and possibly fertile hybrids the cross should be repeated using a tetraploid Mountain Laurel. (Tetraploid *K. latifolia* plants have not been verified, but a few selections, such as 'Silver Dollar,' with heavy broad leaves are likely candidates.) The reciprocal cross, *K. latifolia* × *K. polifolia*, results in no seed set, apparently due to an inability of the pollen of *K. polifolia* to grow down the style of *K. latifolia*.

K. latifolia × K. hirsuta

Reciprocal crosses of this F_1 were the same except that the seed of *K. hirsuta* can be difficult to germinate; hence, it is more convenient to use *K. latifolia* as the seed parent. The more than 200 hybrid seedlings produced from this cross were highly variable in vigor, habit, leaf shape, and flower color (Figure 12-5, 12-6). Plants with leaves sectored green and white, or yellow (cholorphyll deficiencies), were common.

Sandhill Laurel is not reliably hardy in Connecticut, and the hybrids are not as hardy as Mountain Laurel but will survive in zone 6. Cuttings of the hybrid root more readily than those of Mountain Laurel. The more compact, multi-branched clones have horticultural promise but none has been released to date.

Fifty or more of the F_1 hybrids were flowered and none were ever fertile save for one of several plants grown from a stem cutting of one of the hybrids. The seeds harvested from this one fertile plant were grown. The offspring were apparently the product of a backcross to Mountain Laurel, which they resembled. Some of these plants have been intercrossed and some good Mountain Laurel-like plants with smaller leaves and stature are being selected from the offspring. Because of the single, fertile F_1, it has been possible to produce third and fourth generation hybrids of Mountain Laurel and Sandhill Laurel, something that has not been possible with any of the other interspecific crosses.

Tom Dodd, Semmes, Alabama, has grown second and third generation hybrids of *K. latifolia* × *K. hirsuta* and is enthusiastic about

Figure 12-4. F_1 hybrid of Eastern Bog Laurel × Mountain Laurel. The variable seedlings are generally slow-growing and resemble their Bog Laurel parent. Plant on the left is about 1 in (2.5 cm) high. (Jaynes)

Figure 12-5. Six-month-old seedling of the F_1 hybrid of Mountain Laurel × Sandhill Laurel, *middle;* Mountain Laurel, *left;* Sandhill Laurel, *right.* (Jaynes).

Figure 12-6. A second generation hybrid of Sandhill Laurel × Mountain Laurel selected at the Tom Dodd Nurseries, Semmes, Alabama. The painting is by Louise Estes, Mobile, Alabama.

Figure 12-7. The hybrid of Sheep Laurel ×
Mountain Laurel. New growth is pale yellow-
green, often tinged with pink. As the leaves
mature they turn green. (Jaynes)

Figure 12-8. Flowering Sheep Laurel ×Moun-
tain Laurel hybrid. The foliage and plant habit
display many intermediate characters; however, they are not strong growers and plants are
slow to come into flower. (Jaynes)

Figure 12-9. The F$_1$ hybrid of Eastern Bog
Laurel and Western Alpine Laurel. The hybrid
has many good attributes of both parents but,
like them, is difficult to keep growing well in
gardens in eastern U.S. (Jaynes)

Figure 12-10. A putative hybrid of *Kalmia latifolia* and *Rhododendron Williamsianum.* (Jaynes)

their resistance to foliage disease and root rot, as well as their ability to grow in full sun—problems that can be particularly serious in the South. It is almost certain that a few of these selections will be named and released soon.

K. angustifolia × K. latifolia

Of the more than 2,000 seedlings germinated from nearly 10,000 seeds sown of this cross, the vast majority were yellow-green, weak and eventually died. However, when the K. *angustifolia* parent was the pure white flowering form called *candida,* the cross produced more seeds per pollinated flower, and many of the seedlings survived. The hybrids are intermediate in appearance (Figure 12-7, 12-8); however, they are somewhat more tender than either parent and are slow to produce flowers. Foliage of new growth is white to yellow initially and then turns green. The flowers are a pale pink and they are pollen and seed sterile. Stem cuttings root more readily than K. *latifolia.* They have no special ornamental value in the garden. Interestingly, the reciprocal cross fails completely. Microscopic studies using fluorescent stain show that the tubes from pollen of K. *angustifolia* fail to grow down the styles of K. *latifolia.*

K. polifolia × K. microphylla and the Reciprocal

This is the only species cross which is easy to make and consistently gives healthy, green seedlings (Figure 12-9). Because the some chromosome numbers of the two are different (somatic numbers of 48 and 24, respectively) the hybrids are triploids and generally sterile. Some of these hybrids have horticultural merit; one released for test is named 'Rocky Top' (number ×356h). Their value lies in their greater tolerance of the hot summers and open (snowless) winters in the northeastern United States as compared to the western K. *microphylla* and, also, in their more compact habit relative to that of the eastern K. *polifolia.*

Unfortunately, rabbits find the hybrid shoots tasty, but they also enjoy the parental species. The rabbits' fondness for Bog Laurel is nothing new. In 1882, an anonymous writer (Alpha) reported in an English horticultural magazine that ". . . rabbits are very fond of it and will crop it close to the ground." The toxic effects on rabbits are not known. Another pest of the hybrid is red mites, but these are readily controlled by spraying. Yet, neither species nor the hybrids are long-lived in northeastern United States gardens.

The Cuban *Kalmia ericoides* is the only species that has not been crossed with other species. Morphologically it is closely related to the Sandhill Laurel. Hence it may cross with K. *hirsuta,* but I do not expect it to hybridize with K. *latifolia,* a species that does cross with K. *hirsuta.* There is, however, only one way to find out, and that requires live, flowering plants or at least pollen to make the cross-pollinations.

These attempts to hybridize the species show conclusively that genetic barriers to gene flow between *Kalmia* species are well developed. Natural hybrids among the species have not been reported and the results of experimental crosses suggest that such hybrids are unlikely ever to be found. The genetic barriers between species limit the prospects of fully utilizing the variation found among the species.

A few of the F_1 hybrids do have horticultural merit. Yet, all the hybrids that have flowered are pollen and seed sterile with two exceptions: 1) a few of the Western Laurel and Eastern Bog Laurel hybrids in which only partial seed and pollen fertility was observed on only a few plants and 2) one first generation hybrid of Mountain Laurel and Sandhill Laurel and the offspring of this one plant. However, this one exception may lead to some compact, disease and heat resistant plants. Fertility of other F_1 hybrids might be restored by doubling the chromosome number with colchicine (see page 175). To date our limited attempts with colchicine on the hybrids have not been successful. Because of sterility problems, development of improved Laurel cultivars must rely most heavily on variation within species rather than on variation between species.

INTERGENERIC CROSSES

Based on these observations with crosses between Laurel species, we assumed that crosses at the next level, between genera, would be impossible. Well, almost! My own attempts to cross *Rhododendron* species or *Kalmiopsis leachiana* with several of the Kalmias have been unsuccessful. Yet a plant does exist at the National Arboretum that may be a natural hybrid between *Rhododendron maximum* and Mountain Laurel. It is indeed an unusual plant but probably is only an aberrant form of *R. maximum*. A chromosome count would shed some light on the matter, because Mountain Laurel has 24 somatic chromosomes and Rosebay 26. An F_1 hybrid between the two would be expected to have 25. The chromosomes of this reputed hybrid have yet to be examined, because of the technical difficulty in preparing adequate slides for counting.

The late Halfdan Lem of Seattle, Washington, is attributed with a successful intergeneric cross between *Kalmia latifolia* (seed parent) and *Rhododendron williamsianum* (Figure 12-10). This cross came to the attention of horticulturists when a color photograph of the plant appeared in the January, 1974, *Quarterly Bulletin American Rhododendron Society*. The plant has informally been referred to as "No Suchianum" which may be prophetic. Although it was claimed that Mountain Laurel was the seed parent, the overall characteristics of the putative hybrid are that of a Rhododendron, e.g. stamens number more than 10, there is no evidence of pouches in the corolla, and the ovary shape is elongate rather than globose. Again, chromosome counts of the hybid would be helpful.

The science of genetics and plant systematics helps to predict the success or failure of a cross, but the science is not developed to the point where it can predict the exceptional, successful intergeneric cross such as that putatively performed by Lem. The usual failure of wide crosses is reason enough not to devote all one's effort to them, although the occasional and unexpected success may tempt even the conservative breeder to try a few.

Chapter 13

TECHNIQUES OF MAKING CONTROLLED CROSSES

> *The art of plant breeding has been practiced continually since primitive man gave up nomadic food gathering to settle in permanent settlements around dependable sources of food. . . . Plant breeding continued to be largely based on empirical knowledge until the "discovery" of Gregor Mendel's great 1865 paper on inheritance which gave rise to the science we know today as genetics. (Moore and Janick 1975)*

Crosses between individual plants of Mountain Laurel are not difficult to make because the flowers are relatively large; however, dexterity is needed in handling the small flowers of Sheep Laurel. Controlled crosses are pointless unless there is the intention of planting the seed and nurturing the seedlings until they flower. Occasionally, desired characteristics can be determined in the seedling stage, and then only such selected seedlings need be grown. The advantage of selecting both the seed and the pollen parents lies in the tremendous increase in odds of recovering desired types in the offspring and in the ability to repeat the cross exactly.

The principles of the crossing technique are simple. Before the flowers open, remove the male parts. When the stigma becomes receptive, apply pollen from the selected male parent. Prevent contamination with pollen from other laurel plants. If the cross is successful, the resulting seed will produce hybrid seedlings. Crosses can be made in a greenhouse, outdoors, or even between distant plants. Geographically distant plants, as well as plants which flower at different times, can be cross-bred by the techniques of storing and shipping pollen.

ISOLATION BY EMASCULATION

Flowers to be used as females should be selected before they have opened. Otherwise there is no way to tell if they have already been pollinated. Use the largest tight buds. Small buds fail to develop after emasculation. To emasculate use tweezers (forceps) to remove the corolla and the 10 anthers (Figure 13-1). In this way, not only are the

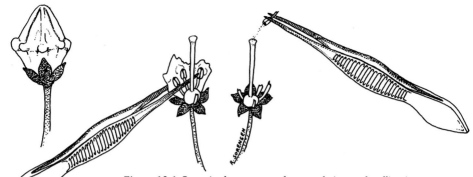

Figure 13-1. Steps in the process of emasculation and pollination. *Left,* flower bud at emasculation and pollination. *Left,* flower bud at proper stage for emasculation. *Center,* removal of the anthers and corolla. *Right,* pollination, usually carried out a day after emasculation. (Sorensen-Leonard)

anther sacs and pollen removed to prevent self-pollination, but by removing the corolla, the visual attractant and landing platform for insects are absent. Remove all flower buds within 1 ft (30 cm) of the emasculated buds to eliminate insect activity in the area and thereby reduce chances for contamination of the emasculated flowers.

As described in Chapter 2 Laurels are insect-pollinated. Because of the spring-loaded anthers, and the powdery pollen of some of the species, we were curious about airborne pollen distribution. So we placed glass slides greased with petroleum jelly on stakes 1 ft (30 cm) high and 1 ft apart in a line from east to west among flowering Sheep Laurel and in another test line among flowering Mountain Laurel. The results are shown in Figure 13-2. Pollen blew downwind, but most of it fell within 2 ft (60 cm) of the plant. These experiments demonstrated that pollen can in fact be airborne for short distances but that it is not widely distributed in air. The hybridizer should take heed. When using large plants for crosses, and when it is impractical to remove all the flowers, use flowers near the top to reduce the chance of pollen contamination from above. These simple precautions make bagging unnecessary, and accidental outcrossing is rare.

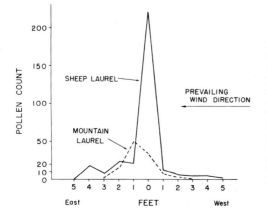

Figure 13-2. Distribution of airborne pollen from Mountain and Sheep Laurel, caught on petroleum-jelly-coated slides and counted after 24 hours of exposure. The results support other evidence that the pollen is not primarily airborne. Of the two species used here, one, Sheep Laurel, has pollen which is loose and free as it comes from the anther, whereas pollen of Mountain Laurel clings together. (Jaynes)

POLLINATION

Although some of the stigmas may be receptive at the time of emasculation, wait and apply the pollen the next day. During very cool or rainy weather it may be necessary to wait 2–3 days. The stigma is receptive if it is viscid and moist. The pollen of Mountain Laurel and Sandhill Laurel clump together. With these species the whole anther can be transferred to the stigma. There it can be gently tapped or teased with the forceps to release pollen onto the stigmatic surface. If the pore end of the anther is placed against the stigma, the sticky surface will catch a mass of pollen from the anther. This method works with Sheep Laurel and White Wicky, but their pollen readily scatters. To avoid this difficulty, collect anthers from about-to-open or newly opened flowers where the anthers are still held in the anther pockets. To remove the anthers without losing the pollen, pinch the filament with tweezers just below the anther sacs and place the anther along with others in a vial. The pollen will collect at the bottom of the vial and can be picked up on a slightly moistened artist's brush and applied to the stigmas.

POLLEN STORAGE

Pollen will remain viable for at least a week when stored at normal room temperature and humidity and out of direct sunlight. To ship pollen, place the anthers removed from the flowers in gelatin capsules (available from druggists). To guard against high humidity and mold during shipment, put the capsules in a larger container with a drying agent such as silica gel or calcium chloride.

Long-term storage is possible by drying and refrigerating the pollen. Do this by placing the pollen in a small open vial or in a gelatin capsule which is placed inside a larger closed vial containing a drying agent (Figure 13-3). Label the container clearly with the pollen source

Figure 13-3. A means for keeping pollen in good condition for up to a year. Pollen is placed in a vial or a gelatin capsule, labeled, sealed in a larger container with a drying agent in the bottom, and stored in a freezer. (Jaynes)

and date collected. In 4–8 hours when the pollen has dried, place the closed vial in a freezer at 0 to −20°F (−18 to −30°C). Laurel pollen stored in this manner has been used successfully in crosses a year later. Pollen storage is invaluable when the flowering times of the parent plants are different.

CAGING (A LAZY MAN'S WAY TO PRODUCE HYBRID SEED)

Emasculation and pollination of individual flowers are tedious tasks, especially if large quantities of seed are desired from the crosses. Comparative hand-pollination tests have shown that seed from cross-pollination of Mountain and Sheep Laurel is 85% more successful than seed set from self-pollination. This led me to experiment with two plants of the same species placed in a cage with bumblebees. The scheme has worked, selfing is minimal, and hybrid seed is produced in quantity.

The cages were made of cube-shaped wooden frames covered on four sides and the top with aluminum screening (Figure 13-4). The plants were planted next to each other in the spring, and, just before the flowers opened, the cage was placed over them and sealed around the lower edge with two inches of soil. When the flowers began to open on both plants, a bumblebee was released under one edge of the cage by temporarily removing some soil with a trowel.

Figure 13-4. Controlled cross-pollination with bees. Parent plants are set closely together and covered with a screened cage prior to flowering. The cage excludes pollinating insects. One or two bees are introduced at onset of flowering to carry out cross-pollination. (Jaynes)

Catching the bees was a challenge. Our first attempts with nets were hazardous at best. To reach Black Locust flowers, where bees were plentiful, we would drive under a tree and, standing on the van's roof, operate a long-handled insect net. Securing a bee in the net was only half the problem; getting it into a jar proved fully as risky! Difficulty, however, soon led to devising a better technique. The net was discarded and the bees were collected directly in quart jars from a variety of flowers. They were easiest to catch from shrubs with deep-throated flowers, like Weigelia, where our approach could be made while the bee remained busy within the flower.

In the first caging experiments we even washed the bees in luke-warm water to remove pollen on the chance that they might be carrying some Laurel pollen. Bathing a bee sounds tricky but was accomplished simply by placing two jars together, the lower with the water and the upper with the bee. A flat cardboard lid on the jar with the bee was slid from between the two jars and the bee landed in the water. After a quick rinse, the water was drained and the wet and befuddled bee taken to the caged plants. In subsequent experiments we decided that the washing was unnecessary as long as the bees were collected several hundred feet from flowering Laurel.

The cages were checked every day or two. If the bee had died, a fresh one was put in. After all the flowers had faded the cages were removed.

The amount of seed obtained depends on the number of flowers, the cross involved, and weather. For example, the 1972 flowering season in Connecticut was so wet that many flowers collapsed (molded) without setting any seed. A few of the plants, including some of the highly selected red-buds, have shown partial pollen sterility and low seed set. To maximize seed set from controlled crosses, avoid such infertile plants, and, if possible, cage several plants together to increase cross-fertilization and seed set.

Be careful with insecticides when bees are used. If you must combat leaf rollers or other insects on the caged Laurel, spray them several days before the plants flower with a short residual spray (like pyrethrin), or delay the spraying until after flowering.

Honey bees are neither effective pollinators of Laurel flowers nor do they survive for more than a day away from the hive. Bumblebees can, however, survive in the cages, if enough flowers are open to provide nectar and pollen for the entire flowering period of 2 weeks.

I have used cages successfully to obtain seeds for red-budded and white-flowered Mountain Laurel and for white-flowered Sheep Laurel. A cage of six flowering miniature plants (f. *myrtifolia*) in 1976 produced enough seed to distribute to seed exchanges and individuals over a period of 11 years. And better yet, 'Elf' was selected from this cross. In the 11th year the seed was still good and producing 99+% Miniature Mountain Laurel. True-breeding seed of other types of Laurel can also be produced by the same method (see next chapter).

The bee cages worked even with the interspecific cross of Sheep Laurel by Mountain Laurel. I estimate that one cage over a Sheep Laurel and a Mountain Laurel plant saved 2–3 man-days which would have been needed to emasculate the more than 1500 flowers by hand. In addition, the rate of seed set was probably higher from the bees than we could have achieved with hand emasculation and pollination. Bumblebees are more successful because of their light touch and because they visit each flower many times.

There is no reason why bumblebees could not be used advantageously in making controlled crosses of other ornamentals, such as azaleas and rhododendrons, especially where large quantities of hybid seed are desired. Bee cages can be used to obtain large quantities of seed of known parentage. It allows certain color or foliage forms to be reproduced in quantity from seed and is an alternative to stem cuttings or tissue culture started plants.

ISOLATION OF PLANTS FOR INTERCROSSING

Another nonintensive means to produce large quantities of seed from crosses between selected plants is to isolate those plants several hundred feet from other flowering Laurels of the same species. I planted clusters of 3–8 plants each of white, deep pink, and red-budded Mountain Laurel. Each group was isolated from each other and other flowering Mountain Laurel by at least 350 ft (100 m). Seed collected from these plants produced seedlings that were virtually as true-to-type for flower color as would be expected from hand-pollination or bee-caging. This then is another means of obtaining "hybrid" seed without having to emasculate and hand-pollinate. Since the method works with color forms of Mountain Laurel, it surely also will be successful with other traits like miniature that we know will breed true.

The reason such isolated clusters of plants get intercrossed among themselves has to do with the habits of the pollinating bumblees. They tend to work plants within small areas rather than moving back and forth over long distances. Some "outcrossing" with plants beyond a cluster is likely to occur but it is small compared to intercrossing among neighboring plants.

_____

Chapter 14

INHERITANCE OF FLOWER COLOR
AND OTHER SELECTED TRAITS

> *Nevertheless, selection is a major part of horticultural plant breeding,*
> *even when the most sophisticated modern techniques and knowledge*
> *are used. To be able to carry out effective selection it is essential for the*
> *breeder to know and to have a 'feeling' for the crop being worked. The*
> *person who knows plants may 'pick a winner' without having a*
> *scientific background, but the scientist who has no feeling for plants*
> *has little hope of becoming a successful plant breeder. Genetics are not*
> *synonymous with plant breeding but a knowledge of genetics is*
> *essential if a breeder is to achieve his or her full potential. (North*
> *1979)*

It takes a long time to accumulate data on the inheritance of specific traits when the plant has a generation time (the period from seed to flower) of five years. The following information is based largely on more than 1400 controlled crosses I have made since 1961. Not all the crosses were successful. Many of the crosses between species produced no seed and even crosses among Mountain Laurel plants occasionally failed in a given year. Reliable inheritance data has been obtained for several striking foliage and flower traits but much remains to be learned.

At least 40 dissimilar flower, foliage, and physiological Mountain Laurel traits have been identified (Table 14-1). Of these, inheritance data are available for about 12. The extent of natural variation is less well known in the other species, and, of course, there is a corresponding lack of information on the inheritance of specific traits in these other species.

Table 14-1   Variations of Mountain Laurel and representative named cultivars. The reader must understand that these groupings are not definitive and that other variations and intermediates exist.

Flower types
    Bud color
        white ('Stillwood')
        pink ('Clementine Churchill', 'Pink Surprise')
        red ('Olympic Fire', 'Ostbo Red')
    Corolla, inside ground color

      white ('Stillwood')
      pink ('Pink Charm', 'Sarah')
      candy stripe
   Pigment distributiion on inside of corolla
      A) no spots at anther pockets
           spots at anther pockets ('Splendens')
           interrupted band (*fuscata* forms, 'Freckles')
           continuous narrow band (*fuscata* forms, 'Fresca', 'Star Cluster')
           broad, continuous band virtually filling corolla (*fuscata* forms,
           'Bullseye', 'Carousel')
      B) no pigmented circle at base of corolla
           heavily pigmented circle at base of corolla ('Sarah')
           heavily pigmented circle with five radiating points (star-ring
           types)
   Corolla shape
      normal with 5 rounded to pointed lobes
      multilobed, up to 9 lobes instead of 5 (expression often variable)
      five deeply cut lobes that reflex ('Shooting Star')
      lobes completely cut, 5 petals usually strap-like (*polypetala* forms)
      corolla fails to open ('Tightwad')
      reduced corolla ('Bettina')
      no corolla (apetala)
   Flower size
      normal (most)
      large ('Silver Dollar')
   Flower distribution
      loose inflorescences
      tight, ball-shaped inflorescense ('Hearts Desire')
   Time of flowering
      normal (most)
      early
      late ('Shooting Star', 'Tightwad')
Foliage and plant habit
   Growth habit
      normal
      compact (*obtusata*) ('Carol' is semi-compact)
      miniature (*myrtifolia* forms, 'Elf', 'Minuet')
   Leaf shape
      normal
      willow-leaved (*angustata* forms, 'Willowcrest')
      ovate or obtuse (*obtusata*)
      large ('Silver Dollar')
   Leaf color
      all green
      sectored, white and green, and sometimes yellow-green
   New shoots
      yellow-green
      reddish bronze ('Bullseye', 'Raspberry Glow', 'Sarah')
Rooting ability
   Difficult (most)

Can be rooted ('Carousel', 'Nipmuck', 'Pink Charm', 'Pink Surprise')
Hardiness or tolerance of:
Cold
Heat (*latifolia* × *hirsuta* hybrids)
Drought
Heavy soils/elevated pH ('Star Cluster')
Disease Resistance
Leaf spot resistance
Phytophthora resistance

MOUNTAIN LAUREL

Little plant selection or breeding to date has been designed to extend the length of the flowering season. Variations occur in the species, but the normal flowering season lasts about three weeks. Having some plants that flower a week earlier and others two weeks later could effectively double the length of the blooming season.

The age at which seedlings flower varies from plant to plant as does the number of flowers. Such variation occurs among different Mountain Laurel crosses and sister seedlings as well. The most precocious seedlings are often those that continue to produce flowers in successive years. Thus, breeding plants that flower at a young age and flower profusely each year should not be difficult.

White Bud and Corolla Color

Pure white flowered plants are rare. Several have been reported but at the time of the first edition of this book I still had not seen a pure white (anthocyaninless) Mountain Laurel. However, in 1977, Tony Dove, Horticulturist with London Town Publik House and Gardens, Edgewater, Maryland, sent material of a pure white-flowered plant; in 1980 Clarence Towe sent cuttings from a pure white-flowered plant found earlier by Henry Wright in the Carolina mountains; and, more recently, Walter Sutcliff discovered a landscape plant on Long Island (Figure 14-1). I grafted cuttings of the Wright and Dove plants and, when both selections flowered a few years later, crossed them. Virtually all the seedlings lacked red pigment (anthocyanin) in the foliage and are pure white in flower. New growth on these plants is yellow-green, but the color deepens to the normal dark green as the foliage matures. Thus pure white flowered plants appear to breed true, or nearly so, when intercrossed. The few plants, less than 5%, with pigment may have resulted from outcrossing (contamination).

Crosses between plants with nearly pure white flowers produce all light-colored or white-flowered plants. A plant like 'Stillwood', for instance, is white flowered but when grown in full sun produces an

Figure 14-1. A pure white selection found by W. Sutcliff on Long Island. After further testing it may be named. (Jaynes)

occasional fleck of light pink in the corolla and a faint pinkish ring near the corolla base (Figure 3-35). Crosses of deep pink and white result in seedlings with a variable, intermediate pink color. The purer the white parent, the less likely is pink to be strongly expressed in the offspring. Seedlings of 'Stillwood', a good white, seldom have much pink color even when the other parent is a stong pink, because white is usually dominant.

Pink Bud and Corolla Color

Numerous shades and patterns of pink exist, and crosses of pink parents generally produce a range of pink types (Figure 14-2). The results of crosses between the deepest pinks suggest that a true-breeding line can be developed. Apparently several major and modifying genes affect the expression of pink flower color. One of my best crosses between two deep pink flowered plants produced 35 seedlings, all with richly colored flowers: 30 flowered in the fourth growing season, fully a year earlier than the seedlings of many other crosses.

Among the crosses of deep pink and red-budded plants, a low frequency of dwarf seedlings with purplish foliage may appear.

Figure 14-2. Flowers from 20 seedlings of a controlled cross of two pink-flowered plants. A flower of one of the parents is in the bottom row, center. All the offspring had good, rich color. (Jaynes)

Figure 14-3. Flowers from 13 representative seedlings of a controlled cross of two red-budded plants. Flowers of the parents are in the center. An example of true breeding from seed for the red-budded trait. (Jaynes)

Figure 14-4. A new selection having a particularly waxy and bright red-bud color. Further observation will determine if it is better than existing cultivars. (Jaynes)

Although the seedlings are fairly vigorous at first, they grow slowly and are difficult to raise to maturity.

Red Bud Color

Although no Mountain Laurel with a solid red corolla is known, plants with brilliant red buds can be bred true from seed (Figure 14-3, 14-4). These red-buds are often almost iridescent and some so intensely pigmented that they have a purplish black hue. However, only plants grown in some sunlight fully express this trait. Red is recessive relative to both white and the normal light pink flower bud color, but pigmentation on the inside of the corolla is under separate genetic control and may be white or pink in color. Because the red-bud character is recessive, such plants breed true when intercrossed and can be mass-produced from seed using caged bees as described in Chapter 13. Lack of vigor noted in some of these red-bud crosses may be due to inbreeding which inadvertently resulted from the intense selection pressure exerted in developing these vibrantly colored plants.

As indicated, red-bud seedlings are distinctive as a class, yet variable among themselves. Plants with lighter colored red buds may be difficult to distinguish from those with deep pink buds. 'Ostbo Red' selected in cultivation on the West Coast was the first red-bud clone named and vegetatively propagated. Several have since been named for their ease of propagation and improved habit, including 'Sarah' and 'Olympic Fire', the latter an offspring of 'Ostbo Red'.

Banded (*fuscata*)

The Banded Laurels form a distinct class, but considerable variation exists in the width, continuity, and hue of the band. Presence of the band itself is controlled by a single dominant gene (*B*) (Table 14-2) while other genes control size and color modifications (Figure 14-5). One unusual plant was discovered in our plantings in 1973. All the flowers on the plant were characterized by a narrow band except for one cluster on one branch which had flowers with an intense broad band. I have not observed this kind of a chimera before or since.

The genetic basis for the tremendous variation in band width has not been determined but it appears that there are different forms of the gene (alleles) for banding which control interrupted, narrow, and broad bands as well as other modifying genes. Plants with the double dominant (*BB*) are rare. I had one plant that, whether used as pollen or seed parent, always yielded offspring with banded flowers. Unfortunately, by the time the offspring had flowered the parent plant had been lost. Such a double dominant, banded plant is quite valuable since all the offspring would have banded flowers no matter what other plants were crossed with it. But even the common heterozygous, banded plants yield seedlings that are 50% banded when out-crossed to normal natives, and as high as 75% banded when crossed with another banded.

Several newly named cultivars resulting from controlled crosses combine the banding character with other traits, e.g. 'Minuet' (banded/miniature), 'Kaleidoscope' and 'Yankee Doodle' (banded/red bud) (Figure 14-6).

Table 14-2 *Kalmia* traits under single gene control: capital letter = dominant, lower case = recessive.

Trait	Gene symbol
Kalmia latifolia	
fuscata (banded)	B
star ring	Sr
angustata (willow leaved)	w
apetala	p
bettina (reduced corolla)	be
compact	c
myrtifolia (miniature)	m
obtusata	b
polypetala	p
shooting star	s
K. angustifolia	
anthocyanin	A

Figure 14-5. Banded Mountain Laurel, form *fuscata*, with a fairly typical band. The trait is variable in expression and under the control of a single dominant gene. (Jaynes)

Figure 14-6. A striking flower on an unnamed selection; note the red-bud color, banded pigmentation, white edge, and star-shape. (Jaynes)

Star-Ring

This flower characteristic was first observed by the late Edmund Mezitt in one of his plants at Weston Nurseries in Massachusetts and pointed out to me in 1968. Star-ring is distinguished from the normal type by the greater prominence of the inner pigmented ring and especially by the five radiating points which travel up the creases of the corolla to the margin of the flower (Figure 14-7). Such plants are rare in the wild. Star-ring was crossed with three other plants having prominent but not starred, inner rings. Of 45 flowering seedlings, just over 50% had the star-ring trait. Thus the star-ring appears to be under the control of a single dominant gene (*Sr*). Subsequent crosses confirmed this outcome.

If the pigmentation and width of this star pattern could be enhanced it would make a striking ornamental selection. I have intercrossed star-ring plants to obtain the homozygous dominant, but of those plants that have flowered none are notably better than the original selection. However, crosses of star-ring plants with selections like 'Freckles', having an interrupted band, have yielded selections with "busy" and attractive flowers (Figure 14-8), one of which may be worthy of naming and propagation.

Figure 14-7. A plant with the star-ring pattern of pigmentation on the inside of the corolla. (Jaynes)

Figure 14-8. A selection from a cross combining the star-ring pattern with an interrupted band to give an interesting and "busy" flower. (Jaynes)

Stem and Foliage Color

As previously noted, pure white-flowered plants can produce no red pigment, hence the stems and leaves are green, indeed new flushes of growth on such plants are yellow-green but they darken as they mature. Deep pink and red flowered plants often, but not always, have purplish red stems and reddish bronze new foliage (Figure 14-9). Plants in the normal flower color range may have either red or green stems, although the red stemmed plants are generally found on plants bearing darker colored flowers.

Figure 14-9. Reddish bronze foliage of the cultivar 'Sarah' that is also characteristic of some of the other cultivars having deeply pigmented flowers. (Jaynes)

Feather-Petal (*polypetala*) and other corolla modifications

This form with strap-like petals was first described in 1871 in Massachusetts (Figure 14-10). Analysis of several first- and second-generation crosses indicates that this character is controlled by a single recessive gene (p). A great deal of variation exists in expression of the trait from partially to fully cut corollas. Most feather-petal type plants have narrow, strap-shaped petals. I have grown numerous feather-petal seedlings, but none yet have had an apple-blossom type flower, with good vigor and plant habit. The corolla types of 'Shooting Star' (partially cut) and 'Bettina' (reduced) are under control of different genes than feather-petal (full cut), so each should be considered a different botanical form. The gene for the 'Shooting Star' type flower (s)

and the 'Bettina' type flower (*be*) are both recessive and apparently not linked (Figure 14-11, 14-12). All three variant types have a tendency to lack vigor and overall thriftiness. Offspring of 'Shooting Star' with that flower type have also proved to be somewhat weak growers, but additional seedlings are being grown to get a superior, thriftier growing plant.

Figure 14-10. A collection of unusual Mountain Laurel flowers from different plants. *Left column*, three different expressions of the feather-petal (*polypetala*) trait. The lowest cluster is derived from a banded/feather-petal cross and expresses the banded pigmentation on the strap-like petals. *Center column, top*, 'Bettina' having a reduced corolla; *middle*, an unnamed seedling; *bottom*, apetala. *Right column, top*, a larger than normal flower with six lobes instead of the normal five; *middle*, normal flower; *bottom*, an abnormal type occasionally obtained from crosses of deep-pink-colored plants. (Jaynes)

Figure 14-11. Flowers of the 'Bettina'-type, *left*, and 'Shooting Star'-type' *right*. The plant in the middle, from a second generation cross, combines the two traits in a plant with mini-star flowers. (Jaynes)

Figure 14-12. One of several second and third generation seedlings from 'Shooting Star' being testing for vigor and hardiness. (Jaynes)

Apetala

Plants of this botanical curiosity lack a corolla, but they have functional anthers and pistils and can be quite attractive in full "bloom" (Figure 14-10, 14-13). Like the *polypetala* types, apetala is apparently under the control of a single recessive gene. When crossed with normal Mountain Laurel, all the offspring are normal; but when these F_1s are backcrossed to the apetala parent the seedlings segregate, with 50% being apetalous.

Figure 14-13. Even the apetala form is attractive when in full "flower". (Jaynes)

Miniature (*myrtifolia*)

The terms used to designate plants reduced in size can be misleading and so it is with Miniature Mountain Laurel. These plants generally have leaves and internodes reduced one-third to one-half normal size, although the flowers are often somewhat less reduced in size. "Miniature" as used here does not mean "midget". Under nursery conditions miniature plants can easily produce two flushes of growth in one growing season and have an increase in height of 5+ in (12+ cm). My oldest and largest plant is about 5 ft (1.5 m) tall after 20 years for an average height increase of 3 in (7.5 cm) per year. The Royal Horticultural Society Garden, Wisley, England has a much older plant that is at least 6 ft (1.8 m) tall. A plant found by the late Henry Wright and planted in his garden in North Carolina is 8 ft (2.4 m) tall.

Although the Miniature Laurel has been·in cultivation since 1840 it has been largely unknown and unavailable. It is extremely rare in the wild. The most recent find was a plant discovered in 1984 by Glenn Dreyer of Connecticut College growing near the Connecticut River in New London, Connectict (Figure 14-14). This plant is very dwarf and slow growing. If propagated and released it will be called 'Connecticut College Miniature'.

Plants grown from seed obtained from open-pollinated *myrtifolia* specimens are usually normal in appearance, unless they happen to self-pollinate. If the normal looking seedlings of *myrtifolia* parentage are intercrossed, 25% of the seedlings will be miniature. The form is under the control of a single recessive gene (m); therefore, miniature crossed with miniature breed true for this character.

I have crossed plants of the miniature form with banded, deep pink, and red-budded plants of normal growth habit. Some second and third generation crosses have bloomed and the results are exciting. For the first time we are seeing miniature plants with banded, deep pink, or red-budded flowers (Figure 14-15). Heretofore miniature plants bore only normal flower color: light pink in bud and white open, e.g. 'Elf' (Figure 3-8). Now a range of types are becoming available. The first to be named is 'Minuet', a banded-miniature (Figure 3-15). As always, the

Figure 14-14. A recent and rare find of a native miniature Mountain Laurel. This was found by Glenn Dreyer in 1984 near the Connecticut River, New London, Connecticut. It has not yet flowered. (Jaynes)

task of identifying the best selections is not simple for there are numerous striking, as well as subtle, variations from which to choose. There are vast opportunities to produce an assortment of "new" plants well suited for today's landscapes from the miniatures.

Figure 14-15. A young miniature Mountain Laurel with pink flowers. Miniature cultivars in a range of flower types will become available soon. (Jaynes)

Willow-leaved (*angustata*)

This form with strap-shaped leaves is also rare in the wild. As with miniatures, Henry Wright collected one a half century ago in the southern Appalachians. There are only two other reports of it ever being found in the wild. The flowers are sometimes sterile; the styles may be mis-shapened (fasciated) so seed set does not occur. But this is not always the case, for I have successfully crossed 'Willowcrest,' a named selection of the form. The trait is inherited as a single recessive gene (*w*).

One of the more interesting crosses is miniature by willow-leaved. All the first generation seedlings had normal growth habit; however, four types of plants segregated in the second generation (Figure 14-16): (1) normal foliage and habit, (2) miniature, (3) willow-leaved, and (4) miniature/willow-leaved. They segregated in the ratio expected for two independant recessive genes (9:3:3:1). The double recessive, miniature/willow-leaved, that only appears in approximately 1 of every 16 plants in the second generation is of potential value for rock garden use. The plants are handsome and slow growing, but difficult to propagate. The densely packed leaves and glandular stem and leaf surface have so far resulted in contamination in all attempts to isolate and multiply them in tissue culture.

Figure 14-16. Six-month-old seedlings from the second generation cross of miniature ✕ willow-leaved Mountain Laurel: miniature on the *left,* normal on the *right,* willow-leaved on the *center left,* and the recombinant miniature/willow-leaved on the *center right.* (Jaynes)

Compact and *obtusata*

The compact form is distinguished by shortened internodes and closely packed leaves. Although a sparse bloomer, it makes an attractive compact plant (Figure 14-17). When it does bloom, the flowers are buried in the foliage. Like *myrtifolia,* the compact trait is apparently under the conrol of a single recessive gene (*c*).

The form *obtusata* can be distinguished from compact by the large thick and bluntly tipped leaves and thicker stems. It is also under the control of a single recessive gene (*ob*).

Figure 14-17. A compact Mountain Laurel, characterized by slow growth and very close spacing of leaves along the branches. This plant is at least 20-years old, 2 feet high and 3 feet across. It is sparse flowering and the few flowers produced are usually buried in the foliage. Sheep Laurel can be seen in the background. (Jaynes)

Variegated Foliage

These plants have leaves and whole shoots that are sectored green and white or yellow. Several reciprocal crosses indicate that this trait is not transmitted through the pollen (male parent) but only through the egg (female parent). A factor in the cytoplasm (extra-chromosomal material) may be responsible. Other types of sectoring and chlorophyll mottling have been observed, and certainly the different kinds may be under different sorts of genetic control. The attractive and unusual foliage color pattern give these forms good ornamental potential (Figure 14-18), but to date an attractive, stable and strongly growing plant has not been found.

Figure 14-18. A superb, sectored Mountain Laurel was collected in New York state several years ago by Ralph Smith but it subsequently died, probably due to a root infection of phytophthora. Some of the seedlings from that plant were sectored but none were worth propagating. Sectors on a plant may be white, yellow, or yellow-green and in various patterns as in A. The sectoring on the branch in B is atypical in that it is marginal rather than radiating from the midvein. Bassett described a similar laurel, with a white marginal variegation, in 1893, but the border was so narrow as to be judged not worth propagating. Sectored seedlings of sheep laurel are not uncommon but seldom maintain the character to maturity. (Jaynes)

Albino Seedlings

Commonly about 1% albino seedlings occur among newly germinated seedlings. Lacking chlorophyll and the ability to manufacture food, they soon die. A much higher proportion of albino seedlings occurs among crosses of some of the banded plants. The percentage varies widely from 14–65% but is generally about 25%, suggesting that the cause may be a single recessive gene. The reason for the wide variation in frequency of albinos from the different crosses is not understood.

Other Traits

There are many other traits of which we know little about their genetic control. Among these are plants with a weeping or prostrate habit; those with ovate leaves or leaves with a notch rather than a point at the apex; remontant plants (i.e. reblooming late in the season); or plants blooming very early in the year. Additional foliage and habit types can be identified, including one exhibiting slow growth, thick stems and heavy textured, wavy leaves. Their genetic control is also unknown. Inheritance patterns of physiological traits such as cold, heat, and drought tolerance are also not known. Similarly we know little about the inheritance of ease-of-rooting or disease and insect resistance. Thus, there are an abundance of tasks for the stout hearted to undertake.

SHEEP LAUREL

White Flowers

Sheep Laurel plants bearing white flowers lack the red pigment anthocyanin. As young seedlings they can be recognized by the lack of red pigment in the stems and leaves. White-flowering Sheep Laurel plants are rare in the wild, but are not difficult to reproduce from seed. The presence of color is governed by a single dominant gene (A); hence, white plants are homozygous recessives (aa). When two white-flowered forms are intercrossed, all the seedlings are white-flowered. I have demonstrated that the bee-caging techique described in Chapter 13 can readily be used to mass produce seed of white-flowering Sheep Laurel.

One of the interesting findings in studies of the white-flowered forms is that, although white-flowered plants are seldom found in nature, the recessive gene is present in a high frequency in some populations. Among 300 flowering, colored plants in Madison, Connecticut, it was estimated that 24% carried a single recessive gene for white. While no white-flowered plants were found in the wild they did occur among seedlings grown from seed collected from the native plants.

COLLECTIONS AND SOURCES OF LAUREL

A Short List of Gardens and Nurseries

Arnold Arboretum, Jamaica Plain, MA
Bartlett Arboretum of the University of Connecticut, Stamford, CT
Briggs Nursery, Olympia, WA 98502 (wholesale only)
Broken Arrow Nursery, Hamden, CT 06518
Calloway Gardens, Pine Mountain, GA
Connecticut Arboretum at Connecticut College, New London, CT
Cultivart, 144 Lovejoy Rd, Andover MA 01810
Tom Dodd Nurseries, Semmes, AL 36575 (wholesale only)
Garden-in-the-Woods, Sudbury, MA
Greer Gardens Nursery, Eugene, OR 97401 (mail order)
Henry Foundation, Gladwyne, PA
Holden Arboretum, Mentor, OH
Kalmthout Arboretum, Kalmthout, Belgium
Kinsey Gardens, Knoxville, TN 37914
North Carolina Botanical Garden, University of North Carolina, Chapel
    Hill, NC
Planting Fields Arboretum, Oster Bay, Long Island, NY
Royal Botanic Gardens, Edinburgh, Scotland
Royal Horticultural Gardens (Wisley), Ripley, Surrey, England
Sheffield Park, Uckfield, England
Skylands of Ringwood State Park, Ringwood, NJ
Summer Hill Nursery, Madison, CT 06443 (wholesale only)
Susie Harwood Garden, University of North Carolina, Charlotte, NC
United States National Arboretum, Washington, DC
Vermeulen & Son Nursery, Neshanic Station, NJ 08853 (wholesale
    only)
Wayside Gardens, Hodges, SC 29695 (mail order)
Weston Nurseries, Hopinkton, MA 01748
White Flower Farm, Litchfield, CT 06759

LABORATORIES DOING MICROPROPAGATION OF LAUREL

(Some labs do not have material for sale)

B&B Laboratories, Inc. 206-424-5647
    1600 D. Dunbar Rd., Mount Vernon, WA 98273
Bolton Plant Technologies, Charles Addison 203-643-8068
    502 Hop River Road, Bolton, CT 06040
Briggs Nursery, Bruce Briggs, Steven McCulloch 206-352-5405
    4407 Henderson Blvd., Olympia, WA 98502
Clay's Nurseries & Laboratories, Les Clay 604-530-5188
    Box 3040, Langley, British Columbia, Canada V3A 4R3
Eggs-Plants Products, Pat Chavez 203-446-1984
    77 Valley Rd., Groton, CT 06340
Elliotts Wholesale Nursery, J. W. Elliott 584-210
    234 Whithells Rd., Christchurch 4, New Zealand
Evergreen Cloning Nurseries, Dr. Keith Jensen 203-443-0374
    30 Trumbull Road, Waterford, CT 06385
Herman Losely & Son Nursery, Edward H. Losely
    3410 Shepard Road, Perry, OH 44081
Knight Hollow Nursery, Dr. Deborah McCown 608-233-4322 (off.)
    2433 University Ave., Madison, WI 53705 608-231-3990 (lab.)
Micro Plants, Ashok P. Ranchod 029-883-550
    Longnor, Derbyshire, England SK17 ONZ
Micro Propagation Specialists, Robert Alexander
    12150 Tech Road, Silver Spring, MD 20904
Phyton Technologies, 7327 Oak Ridge Highway, Knoxville, TN 37931
Plane View Nursery, Michael Medeiros 401-849-2464
    770 Wapping Rd., Portsmouth, RI 02871
Pride's Corner Farms, Mary Chapman 203-642-7535
    Waterman Rd., Lebanon, CT 06249
Verkade's Nursery, Gerald Verkade 203-443-4406
    PO Box 289 (office 2 Dimmock Rd.), Waterford, CT 06385
Weston Nurseries, Sylvia Pidacks, Wayne Mezitt 617-435-3414
    East Main St. (Rt 135), Hopkinton, MA 01748

BIBLIOGRAPHY

Alpha. 1882. Garden Flora. *The Garden* 52:6–7.

American Forest Association. 1986. National Register of Big Trees. *American Forests* 92 (4):21–52.

Anderson, W. C. 1975. Propagation of Rhododendrons by Tissue Culture: Part 1. Development of a Culture Medium for Multiplication of Shoots. *Int. Plant Prop. Soc. Proc.* 5:129–135.

Barton, B. S. 1802. Some Accounts of the Poisonous and Injurious Honey of North America. *Trans. Amer. Philos. Soc.* 5:51–70.

Bassett, W. F. 1893. A Variegated-leaved *Kalmia. Gardening* 1:222.

Beal, W. J. 1867. Agency of Insects in Fertilizing Plants. *Amer. Nat.* 1:254–260.

Bean, W. J. 1897. Trees and Shrubs. *Gardens* 52:77–78.

Benson, A. B. 1937. *Peter Kalm's Travels in North America.* Wilson-Erickson, New York.

Brickell, C. D. (ed.) 1980. International Code of Nomenclature for Cultivated Plants—1980. *Regnum Vegetabile* vol. 104.

Britton, E. G. 1913. Wild Plants Needing Protection. *Jour. New York Bot. Garden* 14:121–123.

Buttrick, P. L. 1924. Connecticut's State Flower, the Mountain Laurel, a Forest Plant. Yale Univ., New Haven, Conn., *Marsh Bot. Garden Publ.* 1:1–28.

Clayberg, C. D. and R. A. Jaynes (eds.). 1974. *Handbook on Breeding Plants for Home and Garden.* Plants and Gardens, Brooklyn Botanic Garden, New York 30:1–76.

Clawson, A. B. 1933. Alpine Kalmia (*Kalmia microphylla*) as a Stock-poisoning Plant. *U.S. Dept. Agr. Tech. Bull.* 391:1–9.

Copeland, H. F. 1943. A Study, Anatomical and Taxonomic, of the Genera of Rhododendroideae. *Amer. Midl. Nat.* 30:533–625.

Coyier, D. L. and M. K. Roane (eds.) 1986. *Compendium of Rhododendron and Azalea Diseases.* APS Press, St. Paul, MN. 65 pp.

Crane, M. B., and W. J. C. Lawrence, 1938. *The Genetics of Garden Plants.* 2nd ed. Macmillan, London. 287 pp.

Crawford, A. C. 1908. Mountain Laurel, a Poisonous Plant. *U.S. Dept. Agr. Bur. Pl. Ind. Bull.* 121:21–35.

Davis, L. D. 1957. Flowering and Alternate Bearing. *Proc. Amer. Soc. Hort. Sci.* 70:545–556.

Dudley, T. R. 1967. Ornamental Mountain Laurel and a New Cultivar: *Kalmia latifolia* 'Bettina', *Amer. Hort. Mag.* 46:245–248.

Ebinger, J. E. 1974. A Systematic Study of the Genus *Kalmia (Ericaceae). Rhodora* 76:315–398.

Flemer, W., III. 1949. The Propagation of *Kalmia latifolia* from Seed. *Bull. Torrey Bot. Club* 76:12–16.

Forbes, E. B., and S. I. Bechdel. 1930. Mountain Laurel and *Rhododendron* as Food for the White-tailed Deer. *Ecology* 12:323–333.

Fordham, A. J. 1979. *Kalmia latifolia* Selections and Their Propagation. *Jour. Amer. Rhododendron Society* 33:30–33.

Galle, F. C. 1985. *Azaleas*. Timber Press, Portland, Oregon 486 pp.

Gibbs, R. D. 1974. *Chemotaxonomy of Flowering Plants*. McGill Queen's University Press, Montreal.

Grant, J. A. and C. L. 1983. *Garden Design Illustrated*. Timber Press, Portland, Ore.

Gray, A. 1877. Large Trunks of *Kalmia latifolia*. *Amer. Nat.* 11:175.

Hardin, J. W., and J. M. Arena. 1969. *Human Poisoning from Native and Cultivated Plants*. Duke Univ. Press, Durham, N.C.

Heichel, G. H., and R. A. Jaynes. 1974. Stimulating Emergence and Growth of *Kalmia* Genotypes with CO_2. *HortScience* 9:60–62.

Holmes, E. M. 1884. Medical Plants Used by the Cree Indians, Hudson's Bay Territory. *Amer. Jour. Pharm.* 56:617–621.

Holmes, M. L. 1956. *Kalmia*, the American Laurels. *Baileya* 4:89–94.

Hope, C. 1986. In *Farther Afield* by Allen Lacy. Farrar Straus Giroux, New York. 286 pp.

Howes, F. N. 1949. Sources of Poisonous Honey. *Kew Bull.* 167–171.

Huse, R. D. and K. L. Kelly. 1984. *A Contribution Toward Standarization of Color Names in Horticulture*. Amer. Rhododendron Society Publications Comm. 43 pp.

Jaynes, R. A. 1968a. Interspecific Crosses in *Kalmia*. *Amer. Jour. Bot.* 55:1120–1125.

————. 1968b. Self Incompatibility and Inbreeding Depression in Three Laurel (*Kalmia*) Species. *Proc. Amer. Soc. Hort. Sci.* 93:618–622.

————. 1968c. Breaking Seed Dormancy of *Kalmia hirsuta* with High Temperatures. *Ecology* 49:1196–1198.

————. 1969. Chromosome Counts of *Kalmia* Species and Revaluation of *K. polifolia* var. *microphylla*. *Rhodora* 71:280–284.

————. 1971a. Laurel Selections from Seed: True-breeding Red-budded Mountain Laurel. *Conn. Agr. Exp. Sta. Cir.* 240, 10 pp.

————. 1971b. A Gene Controlling Pigmentation in Sheep Laurel. *Jour. Hered.* 62:201–203.

————. 1971c. Seed Germination of Six *Kalmia* Species. *Jour. Amer. Soc. Hort. Soc.* 96:668–672.

————. 1971d. The Kalmias and Their Hybrids. *Quart. Bull. Amer. Rhododendron Soc.* 25:160–164.

————. 1971e. The Selection and Propagation of Improved *Kalmia latifolia* Cultivars. *Int. Plant Prop. Soc. Proc.* 21:366–374.

————. 1974. Inheritance of Flower and Foliage Characteristics in Mountain Laurel (*Kalmia latifolia* L.). *Jour. Amer. Soc. Hort. Sci.* 99:209–211.

_____. 1975. *The Laurel Book—Rediscovery of the North American Laurels.* Hafner Press, New York. 180 pp.

_____. 1976. Mountain Laurel Selections and Methods of Propagating Them. *Proc. Int. Plant Prop. Soc.* 26:233–236.

_____. 1981. Inheritance of Ornamental Traits in Mountain Laurel, *Kalmia latifolia* L. *Jour. Heredity* 72:245–248 (plus color cover).

_____. 1982a. Germination of *Kalmia* Seed after Storage of up to 20 Years. *HortScience* 17:203.

_____. 1982b. New Mountain Laurel Selections and Their Propagation. *Int. Plant Prop. Soc. Proc.* 32:431–434.

_____. 1983. Checklist of Cultivated Laurel, *Kalmia* spp. *Amer. Assoc. Botanic Gardens and Arboreta* 17:99–106.

Johnson, E. A., and J. L. Kovner. 1956. Effects on Stream Flow of Cutting a Forest Understory. *Forest Sci.* 2:82–91.

Kinsey, J. 1985. Propagating and Producing *Kalmia latifolia* Conventionally. *Proc. Int. Plant Prop. Soc.* 35:626–629.

Kingsbury, J. M. 1964. *Poisonous plants of the United States and Canada.* Prentice-Hall, Englewood Cliffs, New Jersey.

Kurmes, E. A. 1961. *The Ecology of Mountain Laurel in Southern New England,* Ph.D. dissertation, Yale Univ., New Haven, Conn. 85 pp.

Kyte, L. 1983. *Plants From Test Tubes: An Introduction to Micropropagation.* Timber Press, Portland, Ore.

Leach, D. G. 1961. *Rhododendrons of the World and How to Grow Them.* Scribner, New York. 544 pp.

Lipp, L. F. 1973. Propagating Broad-leafed Evergreens. *Handbook on Broad Leaved Evergreens.* Plants and Gardens, Brooklyn Botanic Garden, New York. 29:78–80.

Lloyd, G. and B. McCown. 1980. Commercially-feasible Micropropagation of Mountain Laurel, *Kalmia latifolia,* by Use of Shoot Tip Culture. *Proc. Int. Plant Prop. Soc.* 30:421–427.

Lovell, J. H., and H. B. Lovell. 1934. The Pollination of *Kalmia angustifolia. Rhodora* 36:25–28.

Mancini, S. D. and J. M. Edwards. 1979. Cytotoxic Principles from the Sap of *Kalmia latifolia. Jour. Natural Products* 42: 483–488.

Marsh, C. D., and A. B. Clawson. 1930. Mountain Laurel (*Kalmia latifolia*) and Sheep Laurel (*Kalmia angustifolia*) as Stock-poisoning Plants. *U.S. Dept. Agr. Tech. Bull.* 219:1–22.

Mastalerz, J. W. 1968. CO_2 Enrichment for a Small Greenhouse. *Flower and Garden.* Nov. pp. 27, 28, 47.

Moore, J. N., and J. Janick (eds.). 1975. *Advances in Fruit Breeding.* Purdue Univ. Press, Indiana. 623 pp.

Muensche, W. C. 1957. *Poisonous plants of the United States.* Rev. ed. Macmillan, New York.

Murashige, T. and F. Skoog. 1962. A Revised Medium for Rapid Growth and Bioassays with Tobacco Tissue Cultures. *Physiol. Plant.* 15:473–497.

Nichols, L. P. 1955. Diseases of Ornamental Shrubs and Vines. *Penn. State Univ. Coll. Agr. Ext. Serv. Cir.* 429, 26 pp.

North, C. 1979. *Plant Breeding and Genetics in Horticulture.* J. Wiley and Sons, New York. 150 pp.

Pierce, L. J. 1974. An Unusual Intergeneric Cross. *Quart. Bull. Amer. Rhododendron Soc.* 28 (1):45, plus color plate.

Peterson, E. B. 1965. Inhibition of Black Spruce Primary Roots by a Water-soluble Substance in *Kalmia angustifolia. Forest Sci.* 11:473–479.

Pirone, P. P. 1970. *Diseases and Pests of Ornamental Plants.* 4th ed. Ronald, New York. 546 pp.

Pritchard, W. R. 1956. Laurel (*Kalmia angustifolia*) Poisoning of Sheep. *N. Amer. Veterinarian* 37:461–462.

Rehder, A. 1910. Notes on the Forms of *Kalmia latifolia.* Rhodora 12:1–3.

Southall, R. M., and J. W. Hardin. 1974. A Taxonomic Revision of *Kalmia* (Ericaceae) *Jour. Elisha Mitchell Sci. Soc.* 90:1–23.

Sprague, E. 1871. *The Rhododendron and American Plants.* Little Brown, Boston.

Tallent, W. H., M. L. Riethof, and E. C. Horning. 1957. Studies on the Occurrence and Structure of Acetylandromedol (Andromedotoxin). *Jour. Amer. Chem. Soc.* 79:4548–4554.

Ticknor, R. L. 1987. Weed Control Around Rhododendrons. *Jour. Amer. Rhododendron Soc.* 41:10–14.

Towe, L. C. 1985. The Garden of Henry Wright. *Jour. Amer. Rhododendron Soc.* 39:125.

Trumpy, J. R. 1893. Propagating Kalmias. *Gardening* 1:222.

Viehmeyer, G. 1974. In *Handbook on Breeding Plants for Home and Garden.* Plants and Gardens, Brooklyn Botanic Garden, New York. 30:1–76.

Wahlenberg, W. G., and W. T. Doolittle. 1950. Reclaiming Appalachian Brush Lands for Economic Forest Production. *Jour. Forestry* 48:170–174.

Waud, R. A. 1940. The Action of *Kalmia angustifolia* (Lambkill). *Jour. Pharm. Exp. Ther.* 69:103–111.

Williams, R. F., and T. E. Bilderback. 1980. Factors Affecting Rooting of *Rhododendron maximum* and *Kalmia latifolia* Stem Cuttings. *HortScience* 15:827–828.

———. 1981. Comparison of Intermittent Mist and Polyethylene Tent Propagation of *Kalmia latifolia* L. Stem Cuttings. *The Plant Propagator* 27:4–6.

Wood, C. E., Jr. 1961. The Genera of Ericaceae in the Southeastern United States. *Jour. Arnold Arb.* 42:10–80.

Wood, H. B., V. L. Stromberg, J. C. Keresztesy, and E. C. Horning. 1954. Andromedotoxin. A Potent Hypotensive Agent from *Rhododendron maximum. Jour. Amer. Chem. Soc.* 76:5689–5692.

Index